BEYOND IDEALISM

BEYOND IDEALISM

A Way Ahead for Ecumenical Social Ethics

Julio de Santa Ana

with

Joanildo Burity, Bob Goudzwaard, Robin Gurney, Heidi Hadsell,
Ninan Koshy, Lewis Mudge, and Leopoldo Niilus

Edited by

Robin Gurney, Heidi Hadsell, and Lewis Mudge

WILLIAM B. EERDMANS PUBLISHING COMPANY
GRAND RAPIDS, MICHIGAN / CAMBRIDGE, U.K.

Wm. B. Eerdmans Publishing Co.
255 Jefferson Ave. S.E., Grand Rapids, Michigan 49503 /
P.O. Box 163, Cambridge CB3 9PU U.K.

Printed in the United States of America

10 09 08 07 06   7 6 5 4 3 2 1

Library of Congress Cataloging-in-Publication Data

Santa Ana, Julio de.
   Beyond idealism: a way ahead for ecumenical social ethics /
   Julio de Santa Ana with Joanildo Burity . . . [et al.];
   edited by Robin Gurney, Heidi Hadsell, and Lewis Mudge.
     p.   cm.
   Includes index.
     ISBN-10: 0-8028-3187-7   ISBN-13: 978-0-8028-3187-3 (pbk.: alk. paper)
     1. Interdenominational cooperation. 2. Social ethics. 3. Church
and social problems.   I. Gurney, Robin. II. Hadsell, Heidi.
III. Mudge, Lewis Seymour. IV. Title.

BV625.S26   2006
241 — dc22

                                         2005037996

www.eerdmans.com

Contents

ACKNOWLEDGMENTS   vii

INTRODUCTION   ix

I. Contemporary Challenges to Ecumenism:
Testing Our Resources and Charting Our Course   1

1. Stating the Problem   3
Julio de Santa Ana with *Bob Goudzwaard*

2. Ecumenical Social Ethics Now   17
Heidi Hadsell

3. On the Meaning of "Ecumenical"   30
Ninan Koshy with *Julio de Santa Ana*

4. Forming Frameworks That Uphold Life:
An Historical and Social-Ethical Approach   56
Julio de Santa Ana

v

II. Globalization and Its Discontents:
   Examining the Spheres of Economic,
   Political, and Civic Life   89

   5. The Modern Roots of Economic Globalization   91
      Bob Goudzwaard with *Julio de Santa Ana*

   6. Tensions and Dilemmas in Today's Global Politics   125
      Robin Gurney with *Leopoldo Niilus* and *Ninan Koshy*

   7. The Framework(s) of Society Revisited   138
      Joanildo Burity

III. Broadening the Ecumenical Covenant:
    Following Paths of Hopeful Realism   161

   8. Covenanting for a Renewing of Our Minds:
      A Way Together for the Abrahamic Faiths   163
      Lewis S. Mudge

   9. Following the Way through the Paths of the World   209
      Julio de Santa Ana

   CONTRIBUTORS AND PARTICIPANTS   221

Acknowledgments

This book is the product of an interdisciplinary research group studying accelerated globalization phenomena launched in 1999 under the leadership of Julio de Santa Ana by the Board of Directors of the World Council of Churches Ecumenical Institute at Bossey, Switzerland. This work was finally completed in the spring of 2005. The names of the persons involved, all of them long committed to the cause of ecumenism, are indicated at the end of the volume. Here we want to mention especially the generous and committed contribution of Dr. Faitala Talapusi, Professor at the Ecumenical Institute, who died, much too soon, early in our final year of work together.

The members of the group met regularly two or three times each year in order to share the findings of their personal investigations and to be exposed to the views and thoughts of their colleagues. By 2003 it was decided that some of the results of this work deserved to be shared with others interested in ecumenical social ethics and religious studies. The chapters that follow represent a selection from the much larger number of papers presented during the group's five years of existence. Several papers chosen, as will be clear, are the products of collaborative efforts.

We are happy to acknowledge the continued support, encouragement, and direction that this enterprise received from the members of the Executive Board of the Ecumenical Institute. We mention especially the Moderator of the Board, the Rev. Dr. Robert Welsh, as well as Professor Heidi Hadsell, Director of Bossey from 1997 to 2001, and Father Ioan Sauca who succeeded Dr. Hadsell as Director.

Our work benefited from financial support provided by the Council of World Mission in London, the Inter-Church Committee for Development Cooperation of the Churches in the Netherlands (ICCO), the Multi-Cultural Study Centre of the Churches in the Netherlands (MCKS), and the Nathan Söderblom Foundation of Stockholm, Sweden. We are deeply grateful to these organizations and to those individuals who were responsible for their work during the time that our studies were in progress.

We also acknowledge here the special contributions that the group received from advisors recognized internationally for their competence and knowledge on matters of social ethics. We are especially grateful to Rob van Drimmelen, of APRODEV, Brussels; Pedro Morazán, of Südwind, Köln, Germany; and Prof. Cees Hamelink, of the University of Amsterdam and the Free University of Amsterdam. These persons contributed substantially to our understanding of the impact of finances on economic globalization and communications at this particular moment of the social and cultural evolution of the *oikoumene*.

We express our gratitude as well to the members of the staff of the World Council of Churches who shared with us their knowledge and insights: Martin Robra, Rogate Mshana, and Kersten Storch. We add the names of colleagues at the Lutheran World Federation and the World Alliance of Reformed Churches who participated in different meetings of the group: Karen Bloomquist and Professor Seoan Wong Park, respectively.

We offer a special word of thanks also to the whole staff of the Ecumenical Institute of Bossey, who assisted our work with kindness and care. Among all the Bossey colleagues we have in mind particularly Mrs. Gisèle Bourrel, who unfailingly facilitated our task with commitment and grace.

And last, but far from least, we are indebted to two other persons. The first is Norman Hjelm, former Director and Senior Editor of Fortress Press and himself a distinguished ecumenist of long standing, who, in the midst of multiple and pressing personal demands, took on major editorial tasks in the final stages of preparation of this work. Without his experience and expertise, it is hard to imagine that this project could have come to fruition. And the second is William Eerdmans, President of the William B. Eerdmans Publishing Company, who demonstrated his own ecumenical commitment by agreeing to be publisher of this book.

Introduction

Historic crises occur when society-sustaining beliefs and ideals begin to lose their perceived validity or motivating power. At such moments (*kairos* moments), the way forward is not always clear. In such situations, cynicism and despair can sometimes prevail, opening the gates to violence and cultural regression. Such conditions invite charlatans and freebooters to impose their views on humankind. Nevertheless, the word "crisis" means, simultaneously, both judgement and opportunity. Crises in history call for new social and political constructs that foster new ways of affirming life.

Scholars and writers on ecumenical social ethics — by which we mean the shared reflection on social questions carried on by ecumenically committed churches that are themselves part of the societies in question — have repeatedly tried critically to respond to such crises, producing a rich literature fostering various sorts of shared witness and action.[1] Today, however, this ecumenical ethical enterprise is itself in a crisis of self-understanding. Ideals that once seemed compelling now fail to address the human condition. This book asks what can be done about this. How should ecumenical social ethics be understood in order better to address the crises of meaning and purpose besetting humankind in today's "globalized" world?

Attempting to answer this question, we have chosen the title *Beyond*

---

1. See the chapters on this subject in the three volumes of the *History of the Ecumenical Movement* (Geneva: WCC Publications, 1986, 2005).

Idealism. By this we mean not only that certain idealistic assumptions once definitive for our lives have failed us, but also that we must renounce our hyper-dependence on high-minded moral generalizations. We must name and embrace the condition of being "beyond" this sort of "idealism." It is not that we think we can live without ideals. If we had none, we would not be writing this book. But today we perceive the insufficiency of much that has until recently passed as the language of "ecumenical correctness." We feel that today we should exchange self-satisfied slogans and formulas for a hopeful realism about this world born not of theory but of walking a certain way together with fellow disciples and worldly companions. We need to move at a pace that permits us to feel, in each place, the actual ground beneath our feet as well as to see, close-up, what is actually going on around us.

This Introduction looks first at the fate of idealism in the public world of our time, then at the state of affairs in ecumenical social thinking carried on in, but hopefully not entirely of, that world, and finally at scriptural images of the Way along which we need to walk together.

Beyond Idealism in the Worlds of Human Thinking, Action, and Social Imagination

By speaking of our being "beyond idealism," and by affirming our being in that condition, we can connect what we are going through in ecumenical social ethics with certain broader contemporary phenomena of the human mind and heart. The word "idealism," and therefore also the notion of being "beyond" it, has many possible meanings. Obviously, the one we have in mind depends on the context in which we are speaking. Dictionaries divide the likely usages into two large categories: philosophical, and of common human experience. We add a third: one that identifies the politically and economically distorted idealisms of the present day.

The Collapse of Metaphysical Idealisms

In philosophy, "idealism" refers to a kind of metaphysics in which reality, the "really real," is thought to be knowable only through the organizing and synthesizing powers of ideas in our minds. From such beginnings, elaborate metaphysical systems, some of them enormously influential in human affairs, have been constructed over the centuries. But such idealistic notions of reality, including those underlying notions of properly constructed social orders, have been eroding since Immanuel Kant (1724-1804) built a roof over them with his critical philosophy and Auguste Comte (1798-1857) undermined them with his mathematical positivism. But the effects of this erosion have become more salient as a result of various twentieth-century attacks on the very possibility of metaphysical certainty about reality, whether in the realm of science or the realm of society. To some extent, these attacks on idealistic metaphysics, or on views that imply such metaphysical groundings, have begun to have consequences in what, ironically in this context, we call the "real world." Hence the "crisis" of previously held certainties with which we began this Introduction.

Lecturing in Madrid in the 1930s, José Ortega y Gasset (1883-1955), already the author of *The Revolt of the Masses* (1932), introduced the notion of historic crisis itself. He recalled that a crisis of previously held ideas in Western European consciousness emerged just as Galileo (1564-1642) and René Descartes (1596-1650) perceived a new dimension in the workings of human reason leading to the birth and expansion of modern science. Former frames of reference began to collapse in the face of new constructs of the real. Likewise in the 1930s, Edmund Husserl (1859-1938) began to see that scientific understandings — greatly expanded from the seventeenth to the twentieth century — were entering an epistemological crisis of their own. In *The Crisis of the European Sciences and Transcendental Phenomenology* (1936), Husserl argued that the basic presuppositions of scientific research, grounded on certain understandings of the use of reason characteristic of the Western Enlightenment, had lost their persuasiveness. He sought to "bracket," that is, set aside, prevailing frames of reference — essentialist idealisms of every kind — to make way for a phenomenological effort to reach and describe "the things themselves." Hannah Arendt (1906-75), writing after World War II and influenced by Husserl's pupil Martin Heidegger (1889-1976), abandoned idealized notions of humanity's essence to describe our actual situation in *The Human Condition* (1958) and also took up the theme of historic crisis in *Between Past and Future* (1961). And in the early 1990s Eric Hobsbawm, the Austro-British historian, was writing his *Age of Extremes: A Short History of the 20th Century* (1994), describing the permanent feeling of crisis that prevailed among many protagonists of that period.

More recently Jacques Derrida (1930-2004) has spoken about "a new enlightenment to come [that] would show the world what it meant to base politics on something more sophisticated than simplistic binary positions." Here Derrida challenged the old human habit of demanding — for reasons either of logic or of politics — that we choose between competing and necessarily selective idealizations of reality, recognizing the way "language thinks us" and thereby undermining our confidence in the capacity of thought-processes as such, fundamental to our different idealisms, to grasp an objective reality of the world. Instead, Derrida sought to "deconstruct," with some exceptions named late in his life,[2] nearly all metaphysically maintained and justified frames of reference. He recognized, as did Emmanuel Lévinas (1906-95), the link between such ideal constructs and the power alignments that make them, sustain them, and often profit hugely from them. Lévinas in particular argued that ethics, not metaphysics, is "first philosophy." He found the basis for ethics not in idealized principles but in the immediate demand made upon us by the Other, the neighbor, the companion we meet along the pathway of life.

The Collapse of Moral Idealisms in Common Human Experience

What the philosophers were thinking, people in the streets were also feeling. By the early twentieth century, the sense that there could be an ethic connected with some comprehensive ideal of the human began to break down under the pressures of common human experience. With the dawn of the twenty-first century, people across the globe began to sense that they live in a new historic situation. What is this new situation? We are no doubt too much immersed in it to be able to define it. There are certainly elements of cynicism involved. But once again the root issue seems to be a collapse of ideals: an undermining of the forms of idealism — about religious teachings, moral traditions, institutions — that have shaped our behavior in the past.

2. Derrida, toward the end of his career, exempted at least two general terms (and perhaps others) from his work of deconstruction: "justice," and "forgiveness." Asked what he would then call such exempted ideas, he often replied that was not for him but for the questioner to say! Do we have here a revival of transcendental ideas, or of something also "beyond idealism"?

In spite of the attention these norms still deserve, at one moment or another, people increasingly find themselves faced with situations in which consecrated principles, even the most idealistic ones, do not tell them how to make decisions and carry those decisions into action. What seemed unquestionable according to older norms may now seem ethically vulnerable. There are cases when to choose an option, and to follow the line that emerges from that option, means that people have to act in ways not considered by their neighbors to be morally correct in any traditional sense. Men and women sometimes are caught in paradoxical situations. They face dilemmas not easy to manage. Experiences of this kind, seemingly bypassing traditional moral idealisms, can lead to dramatic situations of ethical conflict. Such personal dilemmas, we think, are related to the larger forms of human crisis identified by the philosophers.

One widespread response to this seeming breakdown in the broad applicability of conventional ideals is to say that the broad ethical questions we used to ask are too comprehensive to be answered in today's climate of highly specialized forms of knowledge. These questions used to be about what it means to be human as such. Bereft of our former, broadly applicable idealisms, we are not sure how to approach such issues, let alone resolve them. We tend today to flee from such large questions toward interest in the rules of behavior (not really rising to the level of "ethics") appropriate to different discrete sectors of life. People are asking not about what it means to be human beings, but only about how to act correctly in specialized fields: business, medicine, law, journalism, and the like. For example, what is the duty of journalists to protect confidential sources? Or what norms should rule the behavior of women and men who practice medicine or do research in the life sciences? Or what about business ethics where there is money to be made, yet also where there are questions about whether it is right to make it in a certain way? Or what about the behavior of academics like those writing this book? There is, in short, a tendency to reduce what used to be generalized ethical reflection to a series of codes of behavior for specific occupations and situations.

Such reduction to convenient contextualizations of what used to be the larger field of ethics, this tendency only to write professional rule books, ironically enough can lead to the development of miniature idealities in which we may speak loftily of the standards or ideals of our profession and even ceremonially ritualize these. Such tendencies may even help explain the fragmented multiplicity of specifically focused causes pursued

INTRODUCTION

by "non-governmental organizations" of every type. Each NGO seems to
have its own particular form of idealism gathered around its own particular frame of reference. It appears to be easier for many contemporary human beings to be idealistic about very specific (and obviously worthwhile)
things — combating AIDS in southern Africa, saving the whales, promoting the next Middle Eastern peace agreement — than to entertain visions
for the human race as such. In several ways, of course, this is sheer gain, for
it focuses attention on myriad particular situations about which something may indeed be done, rather than on well-meant but vacuous generalizations. Yet there is a curious lack of ideational linkage among these different moral enterprises: an absence of coherence that appears to be part
of the crisis of our time.

Manufactured Idealisms for Economic and Political Purposes

But lo and behold, into the vacuum left by the collapse of our formerly
overarching idealisms — those concerning human meaning and destiny as
such — have come a host of meretricious slogan-peddlers anxious to
profit by filling the moral void so many people feel. These are the "charlatans and freebooters" mentioned earlier. Unhappily today they include
certain heads of state with their staffs skilled in "spinning" every event for
public consumption, as well as other ideological (and sometimes religious) leaders who represent their particular visions as keys to life's purpose. Some of these offerings are honest and well-meant, but others seek
deliberately to mislead people for economic or political gain.

In some cases of this sort we find an egregious misuse of idealistic
expressions that once had profound meaning (and in some contexts still
do): justice, peace, freedom, democracy, and so on. In the hands of powerful interests such terms are now being used to cover up realities that are
nearly opposite in meaning to the original sense of the words. Ordinary
people are being persuaded by clever manipulation to vote against their
own self-interests and deepest convictions. Christians are being told from
pulpits that the market forces fuelling economic aggrandizement really
represent the world-wide spread of the gospel, or that the destruction of
welfare policies and programs represents the triumph of "moral values."

Christian churches and religious communities around the world that
wish to resist being taken in by all this now seem baffled about what to do.

xiv

The pollution of idealistic language has accompanied the rise of economic and other forms of globalization. How do we respond appropriately to the often tense relations between church groups advocating the global integration of financial and other markets following the neo-liberal paradigm, and others who defend the view that the state has a moral role to play in confronting these economic actors in the interest of ordinary citizens? Here Derrida's vision of a new sort of social logic not bound to ontologized binary oppositions, if it can take root among people and policy-makers, may help us see more clearly "the things themselves."

But there are also countervailing trends. Ironically, traditional moral ideals have been taken out of the hands of many by another quite different sort of ideal, what the globalized world of exchange relationships calls "money." The circulation of money as the modern substitute for Hegel's *Geist* or spirit has been described as the truly foundational reality unfolding itself throughout the historical process. Money, after all, is an idea or ideal substance that manages today to shape our perceptions of "reality" itself. Nothing could be more idea-like than impulses traveling through space that transfer financial power from one center to another. If one wants to verify the evanescent idea-character of money one need only imagine what happens when confidence in markets collapses. "Money" simply disappears into thin air, just as *Geist* or spirit does when we encounter a crisis of confidence in what, a moment previously, seemed so real. The reduction of traditionally rooted human relationships to a shallow global culture of never-ending negotiations within financial markets — while it certainly works to "get things done" — generates an ersatz sort of ideality that crowds out all other values.

Beyond Idealism in the World of Ecumenical Social Ethics

We who practice ecumenical social ethics are much less confident today than we were two generations ago that we are able to offer the churches any single, shared perspective on global social issues, let alone those of the sort set out above. Gone is the confidence (some would say arrogance) with which we once proclaimed "the responsible society." Gone is the confidence, even, that we can agree on what we meant a half-generation ago by speaking of "justice, peace, and the integrity of creation." Just when coherent Christian thinking-together about the life of the world is more needed than ever, we find this effort, in its comprehensive sense, stalled in favor of radical concentration on myriad particular contexts. We seem to have lost the assurance we once had that we can agree on fundamental approaches to the large questions of our time.

Our Own Use of Idealistic Expressions

One reason for this loss of confidence, we believe, lies, ironically enough, in *our own* overconfidence in the use of certain idealistic expressions — human rights, justice, responsibility, solidarity, sustainability, democracy, peace. It is not merely that our ideals are being polluted beyond theological usefulness by the powerful interests that exploit the words for other purposes, although that is bad enough. It is also that we are being blinded by our own use of idealistic terminology to the nature of the actual social realities around us. "Ecumenically correct" language is too often being substituted for rigorous inquiry into the way things are. Our current preference for local, situational analyses is in its own way a defense against such naive idealistic tendencies.

This is partly a question of the adequate correspondence of language to actual social reality. We too easily speak of "justice," "peace," "democracy," and the like, even as we know that, with words like these, the complexity of references to actual situations and events is often overlooked. We have just seen that such terms, used by political propagandists, often function as a cover for the absence of the very thing to which they are supposed to refer. But our own idealistic language, sometimes taking the form of slogan-like formulas, has in many cases degenerated into expressions of "ecumenical correctness," the sort of thing we must say if we want to be accepted in circles important to us. One might almost say that, behind our "correct" language, a kind of holy cynicism has begun to infect the thinking even of the most idealistic among us.

Put this in a slightly different way. Idealism means picturing something in its ideal, or idealized, form. In those afflicted by too much of it, the ability to hear and internalize criticism is undercut. Idealists mean well, but often "think of themselves more highly than they ought to think." Idealism about themselves and their ideas may afflict *both* the traditional upholders of frameworks, who will not hear of any fault in these frameworks, *and* the ethical critics of these frameworks, who will not hear of any inadequacy in the ideas used to criticize them. Both priests and prophets may be idealists, if in different ways, and bloody battles may be fought between "-isms" thought by their holders to have metaphysical warrants. Dangerous idealisms may be generated in the defense of our illusions. Rheims cathedral in France, shimmering in golden light as in Monet's impressionist painting, is not a good guide to repairs needed to that rather gray stonework. Closer to the mark was Oliver Cromwell, who wanted to be painted "warts and all."

Indeed the ecumenical "idea" itself, the *grand récit* (in Fernand Braudel's terms) of post–World War II ecumenists that had churches visibly and somehow inevitably coming together "that the world might believe" has suffered a series of real-world setbacks that make one wonder whether this idealism, in its original form, is still functional. To say such a thing at the moment is certainly very "incorrect," if not ecumenically inconvenient and inopportune. Yet this inspiration, as originally conceived, has certainly lost some of its cachet for the new generation of Christian believers and leaders. One wonders whether its fulfillment — for fulfilled it will be — will not come to pass in surprising ways. The point here is that clinging to a particular idealistic vision of what unity ought to look like *could* blind us to other ways in which that promise is coming to be kept, ways both less "grand" than those we had imagined, yet more remarkable in a manner yet to be revealed. We now realize, for example, that Christianity cannot continue to impose its own forms of ecclesiastical ideals, implying that there is in these matters a universal law for all. We gain the same insight as we look to peoples' diverse cultures and religions.

Realism versus Idealism in Ecumenical Social-Ethical History

A brief look at the history of ecumenical social thinking may provide a "thickness" in ways that help show the complexity of such thinking in practice. When the Life and Work Movement was launched at Stockholm (1925),[3] many delegates wanted to put the "Great War" of 1914-1918 behind

3. A stunning array of theological talent was present in Stockholm for the 1925 Life and Work meeting, among them Karl Barth, Paul Tillich, Friedrich Gogarten, and Reinhold Niebuhr. With their arguments they made evident that the optimism and illusions of the theology of the "social gospel" had become anachronistic. They quickly became the core of the group called "crisis theologians."

them. They insisted, with the idealism of a continuing faith in human progress, that it had been a very regrettable accident, an interruption in the onward march of the human species. Other theologians of that time saw this attitude as a form of uncritical idealism, criticizing it as blind to the fundamental and continuing crisis in humanity's self-understanding, of which the War had been a sign. These critics claimed that it was necessary to hear God's rebuke to all human pretensions, even the most morally idealistic of them, and to follow the commandments revealed in Holy Scripture, rather than adjust Christian social ethics to the guidelines of the Western Enlightenment. This evolving "theology of crisis" saw the collapse of Western civilization as a real possibility, and led to the dialectical theology of Karl Barth (1886-1968) and the "Christian realism" of Reinhold Niebuhr (1893-1971).

The debate between moral idealism and ethical realism erupted again at the Second World Conference on Life and Work at Oxford in 1937. The context then was dominated — at least in Europe — by the rise of totalitarian and authoritarian regimes, and the mobilization of social forces that tried to resist such growing reactionary tendencies. World War II confirmed the views of those who had foreseen a collapse of civilized values. When the War ended, a new historic situation, dominated by the victorious powers, came into existence across Europe. It was necessary to reconstruct societies that had been damaged in the conflict and to establish new political structures. The vision of a "responsible society," adopted by the founding assembly of the World Council of Churches (WCC) at Amsterdam in 1948, became an anchor that gave firmness to ecumenical social ethics in the post-war period. This vision furnished a guideline for ecumenical social thought and action that functioned well until the end of the 1950s and the beginning of the 1960s when it, too, began to be seen as a form of uncritical idealism by those who saw other forces at work in the world. By then, de-colonization processes in the southern hemisphere were well under way. Revolutionary movements were beginning to challenge European and North American political and economic domination of the "third world." Solidarity on the part of Christians with such processes and movements became the order of the day. Ecumenism abandoned its lofty principle of "a responsible society" for a determination to walk side by side with the poor.

A practical enactment of such solidarity could be seen in the Program to Combat Racism, launched by the WCC in 1969. The decision to take up this work was a recognition that even "solidarity with the oppressed" or "a preferential option for the poor," could be little but expressions of uncritical idealism — mere "ecumenically correct" posturing — if not accompanied by concrete involvement in struggles for justice and peace. The decision actively to combat racism was taken in a period of new historical tensions — social, racial, political, economic, cultural, and more — that the churches of the WCC needed to recognize. For some, the WCC's decision to take this on at all contradicted the basic vocation of the Council. How could the WCC implement such a program in view of ongoing disagreement and debate on this subject among Christian bodies? For others, the decision was absolutely necessary, indeed unavoidable, especially in contexts where peoples were struggling to be free of oppression. Those who supported the WCC's decision realized that they should actively and concretely express their solidarity with those who suffered injustice, oppression, and discrimination.

With the changes that were experienced in different parts of the planet during the 1970s, notions of people's participation, sustainable society, and people's liberation flowed into new formulas expressed in well-meant, admirably crafted, ecumenically correct, and highly idealistic language. The "just, participatory, and sustainable society" was one of these formulas. And in the 1980s the notion of "integrity of creation" was linked to the traditional calls for justice and peace to produce the program called "JPIC." One could see this mantra-like combination of ideas both as a justifiable way of bringing things together that belonged together and as a dangerous move to yet another level of abstraction for purposes of conceptual convenience. One could easily see here a sort of crypto-metaphysical overview designed to make complex reality graspable, at the cost of direct experience of the wide range of the circumstances in question.

The sequence of events from the Seoul Convocation of 1990 to the present continued this process of searching out ever-new formulas in which to grasp (compare the German word for "concept," *Begriff*) the complexity of circumstances and events. The "ten affirmations" of the Seoul meeting — surely in themselves a series of idealistic visions for humanity — when projected hopefully into the reality of people's lives around the world through the WCC's subsequent "Theology of Life" program, produced responses seemingly so varied and conceptually unassimilable as to defy any attempt to reduce them to a globally articulated principle. For at least a decade this program has been an object lesson for living in an ecumenical age beyond beguiling forms of idealism, even as we hold on to our ideals.

The Danger of Institutional Solipsism

The authors of this book are far from dismissing what those who fashioned these instances of idealistic shorthand were trying to do. We do regret the extent to which many, ourselves included, were induced to think that each new slogan at last captured the heart of the social witness required of Christian believers. Programmatic expressions like these came to be idealized in ways that obscured the detail, the complexity, and the paradoxes to be found in the midst of struggles by people for a better life. The problem with each slogan, ecumenically correct for a few years between WCC assemblies or in certain cases for a "decade" of concerted effort, often lay in the fact that thought about the implications of the words themselves inhibited the task of grappling with the realities to which the words were supposed to point. In short, ecumenical idealism has, at times, threatened to induce an institutional solipsism of in-house correctness in which ethical discourse took on well-meant but overly formulaic characteristics and limitations, too far away from the realities concerned.

Searching for a Way Forward Together

Where does this sort of critique leave us? Are we left stranded with a purely situational, purely contextual ethics? Certainly not, if by that we mean an ethical occasionalism where every situation is approached *de novo*. Or, should we, in despair at our own floundering, seek the wisdom of Roman Catholic thinkers who pursue the notion of "the common good"? We view that tradition with respect and appreciation, but yet suspect that it, too, deals in idealisms vulnerable to deconstruction by the realities we encounter in actual human societies. We approach our problem, rather, without *any* conceptual or formulaic answer, but with the biblical image of "being together on the way" with fellow believers and fellow human beings.[4] The

---

4. The difference is a little like that between Max Weber's "ideal type" approach and that of Michael Walzer's book *The Revolution of the Saints* (1982). Weber asked himself how to account for the shift in attitudes and self-understandings that produced, in seventeenth-century English Puritans, the self-disciplined, goal-oriented behavior that allegedly led to early-modern capitalism and its consequences down to the present day. Weber found his answer in an idea he thought endemic to Calvinism, that of salvation-anxiety. He thought that he could understand a complex historical shift, not by examining evidence for it on the

gospel for us is embodied in the lived intentionality of this walk itself: on the way to Jerusalem, the way to Emmaus, the way to Damascus, the way to the ends of the earth.

Biblical Perspectives on the Way

In the Bible, the way toward critical ethical awareness moves forward in the context of lived-out tensions with pre-given moral frameworks. Religiously established ways of life, considered good by the majority, are attacked on ethical grounds by prophets driven by their faith convictions. These prophets evince a personal piety that they believe to be coherent with the very sources of their faith. They believe they should follow their convictions rather than the religious and social traditions around them. For them, the contrast between religious traditions and the ethical demands of faith is stark. Those today who read the Bible to orient themselves ethically in times of crisis should remember that the tensions they feel are not new. The legislators and prophets of the old Israel felt them too.

Martin Buber (1878-1965) approached this phenomenon with much wisdom and clarity in his book *The Prophetic Faith* (1938). He showed how the convictions of the prophets were translated into actions exposing the contradictions between the sacred character of the Law and the changes that were taking place in history, challenging Israel to reach for new understandings of JHVH's revelation. Look, for example, at the case of the prophet Jeremiah. He lived in agony between his need to speak the word of God and his desire to support and comfort those who were suffering in Babylon because they had been uprooted from their former dwellings. For Jeremiah, God's word of judgment was not in agreement with the illusions of the Israelites who idealized their memories of home.

Jesus of Nazareth clearly expressed this sort of tension at different

---

ground, but by spinning a scholarly hypothesis about how actual people did their thinking. Michael Walzer decided to test Weber's hypothesis by moving beyond the latter's "ideal typical" method to examine the actual words and actions of the Puritans in question. Walzer looked at what actually happened, and how people actually understood, on the basis of letters and other writings, what was going on in their lives. He also consulted more than two hundred Puritan sermons of the many preserved from the period. He found that Weber's salvation-anxiety formula, however enticing it may have been to the German scholar, was hardly to be seen in the actual Puritan material.

moments of his public ministry: "You have heard what was said to those in ancient times . . . but I say to you . . ." (Matt. 5:21–47). He also warned those who decided to follow him about the tensions that they would face along the way:

> As they were going along the road, someone said to him, "I will follow you wherever you go." And Jesus said to him, "Foxes have holes, and birds of the air have nests; but the Son of Man has nowhere to lay his head." To another he said, "Follow me." But he said, "Lord, first let me go and bury my father." But Jesus said to him, "Let the dead bury their own dead; but as for you, go and proclaim the kingdom of God." Another said, "I will follow you, Lord; but let me first say farewell to those at my home." Jesus said to him, "No one who puts a hand to the plow and looks back is fit for the kingdom of God." (Luke 9:57–62)

And this was true not only for Jesus of Nazareth. Similar tensions are found in the scriptures of other world religions. One thinks of Muhammad, the founder of Islam. Much earlier Prince Siddhartha, Gautama Buddha, was motivated to look for a "way" of life different from that in which he had been brought up. Siddhartha saw that the Vedas, once living rules for human existence, had evolved into the Upanishads, thereby becoming rigid and tied to the caste of Brahmans, who claimed to be the only ones who could and might fulfill the appropriate sacrificial rites for the gods. Experiencing the agonic tensions between consecrated correctness and necessary renewal, Prince Siddhartha proposed new ways to live a meaningful human existence.

These were, and continue to be, instances of tension between consecrated teaching and faith renewal; between principles and norms that have the weight of tradition behind them and a concern that seeks to give a relevant witness that motivates people to act with a living faith; between established moral codes and prophetic discernment of what is really happening; between what we high-mindedly idealize and the ethical crises provoked by confrontation with reality; between long-consecrated correctness and the pressure of actual circumstances that generate ethical critiques; between the self-congratulatory idealism of high principles and the more difficult grappling with actual events.

Ethics for Here and Now

In the light of this insight, this book attempts to root social ethics in the *now* of history, which is experienced differently in the many different *heres* where Christian communities try to give witness to their commitment to the gospel. For Christians, the biblical faith tells us that God came to participate in human history, that God became incarnate in the person of Jesus Christ and that the Holy Spirit moves freely through the changing trends of history. This book is about the *oikoumene,* the whole inhabited world that cannot be reduced to the picture that economic and cultural globalization gives to it. The uncritical idealism that reduces human beings to economic units as well as the idealism of well-meant competing conceptual abstractions are both dangers to avoid when social thought and action attempt to be relevant for people who have needs and often suffer pain under the burden of existing global powers.

What may following a "way" mean in practical terms when informed by such insights? "The way" is a dynamic, moving, gospel metaphor, yet one that constantly confronts us with reality. Following it, we recognize several things. What is "good" in a given context, can lose touch with reality in a changing world. It may not be good everywhere. The determination of what is good is not a matter of dogma. Unquestionable dogmas about justice, freedom, peace, care for life on earth — good words all of them — are in some moments of human history put in question by concrete evolving historic situations that require new determinations of what good requires.

Furthermore, we also recognize that changes and innovations are not always appropriate. Seeking change for the sake of change may be an indication of a certain disposition to avoid confrontation with hard facts of history. It may be what in French is called *une fuite en avant,* an escape forward, to run ahead, again without taking reality into account. The option for change, if that is necessary, must be chosen following careful analysis of facts and discernment of viable possibilities for action.

We are encouraged by our knowledge that many ecumenical partners along our common way now resist and protest — with us — what seems to be the generalized "social contract" in the world today, as it is imposed by the financial, industrial, and military complex. This is not experienced by all in the same manner. But the challenge it puts to the ecumenical movement is clear. We need to search for alternatives. We join our voices with those who meet annually at the World Social Forum and proclaim "another world is possible." There are, after all, certain decisions like this one that in certain contexts are almost elementary. It is basic for followers of the way to resist the violence and war carried on by those who want to impose their own conceptions on peoples who have different values and ways of life, especially when these peoples did not ask for the intervention of the powerful in their situations.

At every moment along this way we must pay the most careful attention to the meanings and concrete references of the words we use. If there is any handle on the complexity of our human situation it may lie in our awareness that we are content frequently to substitute concepts or labels for reality. In short, we often practice a kind of shorthand both for things we like and for things we do not like. Where things we like are concerned, this shorthand becomes what is called in this book "idealism." In the midst of our perplexities we use expressions like "human rights" as if the mere utterance of them could dispel the clouds of darkness. But some generalizing expressions are inevitable along the way, so long as we remember that "globalization" is not only about "integration of markets"; it also has to do with multi-cultural relationships and religious pluralisms in our societies. Again, followers of the way who try to describe what the powers that be are doing use words like "neo-liberalism," "empire," "terror," and "terrorism," once more holding such terms as close as possible to reality. There are other words that call the attention of other dimensions of peoples' lives; these are especially related to those threatening aspects of human social existence that bring about the deterioration of the vital conditions in which people live: "sustainable development," "the plight of the poor," "gender," "climate change," "violence," "the hypnotizing power of the media," as well as discriminations and exclusions of various kinds.

Finding Our Way

The ways we must follow, even where such terms helpfully apply, are not shown on any map we can consult or to which we can refer as we try faithfully to place our steps each day. To chance a contemporary metaphor, there is no "global positioning system" anonymously marking our progress on electronic charts from geosynchronous satellites a thousand miles up. Nor are we always peering through clouds at the earth, courtesy of

Boeing or Airbus, from twelve thousand meters. We move, not according to a-historical abstractions, generalized principles, or traditionalized pieties, but we rather trust that our steps are guided at each turn by a call to integrity in the gospel. The gospel-shaped intentionality of the way only unfolds as we make decisions at every turn, seeking with our companions to walk in the company of Jesus. The advantage we have in discerning the way to go in each case lies in the fact that we can feel the ground under our feet and see plainly through the doorways of human dwelling places as we pass by or stop to give assistance.

The Christian message, we believe, has within it a kind of immanent covenantal impulse that bids us reach out to others as not merely fellow citizens, but as neighbors to be served. This is a logic of love as applied to the person who happens to be before our eyes at any given moment. But does this mean that Christian ethics applies only in person-to-person relationships? No, it also applies to social structures. We acknowledge that we need just institutions to live as the gospel bids us live. If we perceive that institutions are unjust, but yet idealize themselves so that fine words cover up their actual reality, or if we indulge in "if only" (i.e., "terminally wistful") kinds of arguments, we are being diverted from judgment of the ways such institutions as the economy, politics, and civil society do or do not function as frameworks for the well-being of ourselves and our neighbors. Walking the way together above all means walking without illusions about these things, putting our faith in Jesus Christ.

The following chapters seek, above all, to avoid such illusions. They offer no new ecumenical formulae or detailed programmatic proposals. They aim to help those concerned people, within the church and in all other faiths, who are seeking to discern a way to be followed in constructing a more just world where life can be abundant for all. The persons involved in the studies that produced this book are convinced that ecumenical social ethics needs to be articulated in a wider context than that of the ecumenical movement as we now know it. *Beyond Idealism* does not mean passively to accept reality as it is. It calls, rather, for people of different faiths to work together on the basis of hopeful realism. The important thing is to converge on "the way," to not lose the direction that leads us to meet with "the others." The writers of this book think that this is possible and, above all, that this search for a common way expresses a strong historical imperative that to be implemented calls for decisive courage.

PART I

Contemporary Challenges to Ecumenism:
Testing Our Resources and Charting Our Course

This book opens with four chapters that together help define our situation, test our resources, and discern a frame of reference for the work now needed in ecumenical social ethics. We do indeed live at a moment of history when much that ecumenism itself has previously taken for granted is now being called into question by the march of events. The phenomena of economic and other forms of globalization confront us with what in some ways can be seen as an alternate *oikoumene,* a rival way of conceiving and organizing the life of all the world's peoples — a way ultimately oppressive to life on earth. The chapters in Part I unpack and explore these observations in several closely interrelated arenas of concern.

Chapter 1, by Julio de Santa Ana with Bob Goudzwaard, lifts up ethical challenges in the spheres of environment, technology and modernization, labor, media, and violence. Taken together, these challenges, shaped as they are by the many different contexts in which they arise, both reflect and contribute to the phenomenon widely called "globalization." Some see this phenomenon as a kind of secular ecumenical movement. Others see it as a Babel-like campaign for power by ruling elites. Practitioners of ecumenical social ethics must look carefully at these globalizing developments as they continue to unfold, avoiding generalizing judgments that can raise passions but also obscure the nature of what is actually going on.

Chapter 2, by Heidi Hadsell, focuses on the difficulties ecumenical social ethics has faced in recent years: from the confident affirmation in the West of the principle of "responsible society" and the analysis of "mid-

1

dle axioms" by an ecclesiastical and social establishment, to a time of uncertainty and fragmentation, our own time. This chapter affirms that ethics — and especially ecumenical Christian social ethics — is always a
contextual discipline. This makes the use of generalizations and ideal categories in most cases inappropriate. Decisions about how to act must take
into consideration the concrete conditions under which people live.

Chapter 3, by Ninan Koshy with Julio de Santa Ana, looks at the
power, or potential power, of the ecumenical idea as such for an age such
as this. Caught between its own tradition and the possibilities of innovation, today's ecumenism is called to propose new orientations for social
thought and action. The search for the unity of the church cannot be isolated from the reconciliation among the different families of humankind.
Ecumenical social ethics is a movement of faith that affirms a hopeful realism. It is about how to find "the way" through the difficult situations
that challenge human beings to struggle for a better — more peaceful and
just — life together.

Chapter 4, by Julio de Santa Ana, argues that through the history of
Christian theology there has been an ongoing process aiming at the construction of frames of reference that seek to make life more abundant for
each person and for all peoples. This process can be observed in the work
of such figures as Paul, Augustine, Chrysostom, Aquinas, Luther, Calvin,
Bonhoeffer, and others. We are called today to join forces (not only among
Christian believers, but also with other faithful persons of Judaism, Islam,
Buddhism, and other religious families) to aim at the construction of new
frames of reference for life today. These efforts can be risky. Some frameworks of the past have done more harm than good, and ours could as well.
Tensions can arise in such a reframing process between "convictions" and
"responsibility," between "ethics" and "morality," between "regulations"
and "legitimacy." Such tensions need to be resolved: not through idealistic
principles but through the application of practical wisdom (i.e., Aristotle's
phronesis, Ricoeur's *sagesse pratique*) to these concrete dilemmas of common human experience.

CHAPTER 1

Stating the Problem

Julio de Santa Ana with *Bob Goudzwaard*

The Rise of Ecumenical Social Ethics

The history of the modern ecumenical movement demonstrates that social ethics is one of the most important realms of reflection for those churches and communities involved and committed to the unity of the people of God. After the "Great War" of 1914–18, World War I, persons involved in the movement for Christian unity launched a world conference on issues related to the "Life and Work" of the churches. Nathan Söderblom, Archbishop of Uppsala, Sweden, played a major role in the meeting that took place in Stockholm in 1925. It was seven years after the end of the war. The Bolshevik revolution had begun at the end of 1917. The League of Nations had been established in 1920. Fascism under Benito Mussolini had taken hold in Italy. The factors that brought about the economic depression of 1929 were already at work.

In such circumstances, nevertheless, there was in 1925 a widespread climate of optimism. The church leaders in Stockholm underlined that "the Christian way of life" was the world's greatest need. They created the ecumenical Life and Work movement aiming to "formulate programmes and devise means . . . whereby the fatherhood of God and the brotherhood of all peoples will become more completely realized through the work of Christ."[1] Pre-

---

1. Paul Abrecht, "Life and Work," in Nicholas Lossky et al., eds., *Dictionary of the Ecumenical Movement,* 2nd ed. (Geneva: WCC Publications, 2002), 691.

sciently, perhaps, noted theologians severely criticized that first Life and Work Conference because it did not perceive the harsh realities of the world. Karl Barth, Paul Tillich, Reinhold Niebuhr, Emil Brunner, and others made clear that the kind of idealism that prevailed at Stockholm should be avoided at any price.

Since the beginning of the World Council of Churches (WCC) in Amsterdam in 1948 the Life and Work Movement has continued under the broad rubric of "Church and Society." Its work of reflection and action has tried to be attentive to the realities of the contexts in which the churches witness to the Christian gospel. Through its history it has become clear that there is not a once and for all time-defined ecumenical social ethics. Changing contexts in the world challenge ecumenical communities to respond to problems faced in their particular situations. So, after World War II (1939-1945) and the foundation of the WCC, an important guideline for ecumenical social ethics came to be found in the phrase "the responsible society." Later, seeing the impact of rapid social change on the life of the churches, other criteria were proposed, e.g., churches were seen as being in the world as agents of "humanization." When "development" became a major world issue, from the 1950s to the 1970s, ecumenical social thought and action used the phrase "a just, participatory, and sustainable society." Following this, younger churches of the South proposed "liberation" as the guiding criterion. By the late 1980s, ecumenical social ethics sought to uncover the substance of "justice, peace, and the integrity of creation." Today, what matters is to understand that changing contexts demand a renewal of social thought and action.

Globalization

Since the end of the 1970s, leaders of some Western governments — Margaret Thatcher in the UK, Ronald Reagan in the USA — underlined the need to "deregulate" markets and transform economic institutions. This has since been followed by those who support the "neo-liberal ideology." The word "globalization" has became one of the notions that media, academia, and politicians, followed by much public opinion, use to describe today's major historic trends. As often happens with these kinds of words — words which, for some, help in understanding the prevailing historic forces, while for others they hide and hinder what is really happening in society — there is not only a semantic problem, but also issues reflected on by social scientists under the rubric "sociology of knowledge." Ecumenically minded churches, as well as many ecumenical associations active in civil society, do not share a common appreciation of "globalization." Some traditional churches celebrate the benefits brought about by globalization, while others — especially those of the South — affirm that the prevailing globalizing process is detrimental for many, above all for the poor. These latter churches and the ecumenical organizations related to them denounce the forces of neo-liberal globalization because of the number of people excluded.

For those who support neo-liberal views, globalization is understood as "the integration of markets." A major contribution to such integration is the impressive development of science and technology at such points as information and communication. None can deny the progress of human efficiency in economic matters that has resulted from such developments. Nevertheless, the majority of the world's population still cannot enjoy the products of this progress. Globalization excludes many people who cannot afford access to the new technologies. Perhaps even more important, and linked to the paradigm of the process of globalization and technological advancement, is a cultural phenomenon taking place at the global level. This is the imposition of a kind of uniformity and conformity, a single frame of thought that affirms that the market resolves what neither political institutions nor political agents or social actors in civil society are able to do. French thinkers call this *la pensée unique*. As Margaret Thatcher, who was, perhaps, the government leader who affirmed most convincingly that this kind of globalization should be accepted everywhere, said, "There is no alternative."[2]

The French sociologist Pierre Bourdieu (d. 1998) was critical of neo-liberal globalization. He denounced what he called "the neo-liberal utopia of a pure and perfect market" imposed by the politics of financial deregulation. There is what amounts to a market imperative for competition.

---

2. Three elements are often seen as constitutive of globalization: the integration of markets in line with the paradigm established by the current integration of world financial markets; the advance of new scientific developments and communication technologies which have made possible the global integration of financial markets; and the gradual imposition and — for many — the fascination provided by the single frame of thought *(la pensée unique)*. Cf. Julio de Santa Ana, ed., *Sustainability and Globalization* (Geneva: WCC Publications, 1998), 7-8.

This affects the life of workers who in consequence abandon the practice of solidarity and suffer the impact of a strong trend for flexibility. Bourdieu stated: "In this way, a Darwinian world emerges — it is the struggle of all against all at all levels of the hierarchy, which finds support through everyone clinging to their job and organization under conditions of insecurity, suffering, and stress."[3] This is a situation characterized by structural violence.

However, it should also be said that many thinkers, Pierre Bourdieu included, have stated, either explicitly or implicitly, that globalization can create better opportunities of life for all. For example, an independent and globally representative commission of the International Labor Organization (ILO) of the United Nations, chaired by the President of Finland, Tarja Halonen, and the President of Tanzania, William Mpaka, reflected on "The Social Dimension of Globalization." This commission diagnosed some of the dimensions of human existence affected by globalization, offering suggestions for appropriate political action. The title of its report, *A Fair Globalization: Creating Opportunities for All,*[4] points the way. The report affirms that the prevailing trend of globalization is not a just one; it creates unevenness and requires serious reorientation. The commission, however, also stated its conviction that the process of globalization can be converted into a strong force that could contribute both to the growth of freedom and well-being for all women and men, and to the consolidation of democracy and community development. It is important to underline that the majority of the members of this ILO commission held that globalization is an irreversible phenomenon. Nonetheless, the current political application of the imperatives of neo-liberal globalization continue to create clashes that bring people to act violently. Globalization processes are not all following the same pattern throughout the world; a careful study of how globalization happens in concrete situations proves it to be a process in permanent change.

Having said this, there are several valid points that clearly need to be taken into consideration in social thought and action: (1) Although globalization is perceived as a world process, it is not experienced in the same

3. Pierre Bourdieu, "L'essence du néo-liberalisme," in *Le Monde Diplomatique* (December 1998).

4. World Commission on the Social Dimensions of Globalization, *A Fair Globalization: Creating Opportunities for All* (Geneva: International Labor Organization Office, 2004).

way by all. (2) The roots of globalization are provided by modern culture and the processes of modernization. The social class that leads this process, the Western European bourgeoisie, continues to lead, although other types of bourgeoisie have emerged in other parts of the world. (3) Globalization is a process, but it is also a project oriented to and dominated by neo-liberal ideology. As a process, it is intimately linked to the development of the world capitalist system, which at present is oriented to international financial capital. This means that the process, the project, as imposed today affirms the priority of money and financial markets and is thus highly de-personalized, introducing dramatic changes in the international division of labor. (4) As enhanced by the bourgeoisie, globalization in some ways cannot evolve without freedom, but this freedom is mainly that of the market rather than that of human beings. (5) This supremacy of the market influences the life of the state and, although potentially interesting, this threatens to transform functions and organization.

Perhaps even more important is the tendency of the prevailing neo-liberal project of globalization to establish *growing domination*. Such a tendency is shown clearly at a number of levels: First, in the *financial realm*. This can be seen clearly in the growing influence of global financial markets over the real economies of nations, even to some extent controlling national governments. Second, in the *political realm* imperial domination is facilitated by neo-liberal globalization. This affirmation is proven by the dominant role played by the Federal Reserve Bank and the Treasury of the United States over certain decisions of the International Monetary Fund (IMF) and the World Bank, including the political nomination of their authorities. The power of the G-8 and the Club of Paris over the political life of many nation-states of the South is also a sign of the growing dominion of certain major powers, notably the USA, in today's world. Third, in the *military realm*, the notion that preemptive wars can solve tense situations in favor of the powerful in order to meet their own "vital interests," indicates that the dominion of the powerful is growing. This is accompanied by the frightening development of new sophisticated military technologies that the powerful can apply when it is convenient to them. Fourth, *at the level of international business and trade,* the growing assertiveness of the oligopolies and even monopolies of large transnational corporations in almost all markets, is another manifestation of domination — even though this is actually against the ideology of the free market and free competition. Fifth, but not least, the growing domination of very powerful *centers of media* is also part

7

of the concentration of might today; it is turning real life into a spectacle of entertainment and the manipulation of instinctive emotions.

This drive towards domination is to be seen as an overall tendency of the current project of globalization. However, over and against this tendency toward growing domination there is also growing vulnerability in our world. There are increasing signs of threats to national societies, to national and international institutions, and even to peoples' cultures. For example, the growing annihilation or erosion of cultures and traditional cultural values, caused mainly by the present global, Western oriented dynamics of production and consumption, is leading to the rapid growth of monetarism in some African, Asian, and Middle Eastern societies (Latin American societies fell earlier in this process). Such a cultural impact can bring about aggressive and sometimes sharp and violent reactions. (Al-Qaeda terrorism can be said to be part of these reactions, although this group does not possess an exclusive hold on such types of action.)

Other examples of rising world-wide vulnerability are:

- *An alarming increase in the critical situation of the natural environment.* This is related to population growth as well as to uninterrupted and rising consumption, especially in the richest countries. It threatens the life-sustaining capacity of the earth: ice-caps are melting, animal habitats are shrinking, bio-diversity is being lost.
- *Growing threats to human health.* With the prevailing trends of globalization, some epidemic diseases are expanding rapidly, among them most notably HIV/AIDS.
- *The growing number of harmful risks* emanating from the developments of science and technology, often ironically related to possible errors and misuse of human knowledge.[5]
- Alongside all this is *the growing vulnerability of some national economies,* especially vis-à-vis the ebbs and flows of global capital. This has led to deep concern in a number of national governments, e.g., the Asian and Argentinian financial crises of recent years.

These global examples show that more instances of social, economic, and natural vulnerability have come to the fore in recent years than perhaps

5. Cf. Martin Rees, *Our Final Century: Will the Human Race Survive the 21st Century?* (London and Portsmouth, NH: Heinemann, 2003).

ever before in human history. They harm the vital interests of everyone. The human situation is becoming one of risk. An ecumenical social ethics is strongly challenged by the growing domination and increasing vulnerability that the peoples of the world experience today.

Some Crucial Issues

The will to dominate and the need to offer protection to what is vulnerable create tension. On occasion a dialectical element appears: for while growing domination leads to a higher vulnerability, so a threatened vulnerability can sometimes result in a higher degree of domination. Here appears an unavoidable challenge to ecumenical social ethics. Some observations illustrate how vulnerable life has become, at a personal and social level as well as at the level of the natural environment, as life is increasingly threatened by the powers, named and unnamed.

Violence

René Girard, the French philosopher and anthropologist, has carefully analyzed the nature and implications of violence. The will of the powerful to dominate imposes sacrifice on the dominated. Further, violence always tries to legitimate its application. The mechanism of the scapegoat, known from long ago, implicitly affirms that violence is not only necessary but also has a legal status.[6] Human beings use violence to resolve difficult situations of human life. There is an irrational violence; there is also an uncontrollable violence. Unfortunately there is also a religious violence that is not exclusive to any particular religious family. And, what is worse, there is structural violence.[7]

For example, there is direct military violence, not only as applied by the different forces involved, as in Iraq, but also as a result of the prolifera-

6. René Girard, *Violence and the Sacred,* trans. Patrick Gregory (Baltimore: Johns Hopkins University Press, 1977); idem, *The Scapegoat,* trans. Y. Freccero (Baltimore: Johns Hopkins University Press, 1986).

7. In 2001 the WCC launched "A Decade to Overcome Violence." This was an action of the WCC Central Committee whose members had listened carefully to the voices of churches experiencing the precarious character of life in today's world.

tion in local and regional situations of small destructive, personal weapons offered by the world arms trade. Next to such military action there are the violent acts caused by the fear of a possible future, preemptive use of arms not only against nations which are considered to be undemocratic or not democratic enough. There is horrifying violence against children and women, a gender violence that creates new forms of discrimination grounded in the socio-psychological levels of life.

In addition, forms of economic-structural violence are evident everywhere; these break the idea that globalization is a process that aims primarily at peace. This is particularly apparent where and when private market interests, as instigated by transnational corporations and other agents of global capital, use force to secure full entry into the national economies of developing and less-developed nations, including at the level of legal property and patent rights. Such violence reveals the misuse of liberty, which is used to bring down or end protective barriers.

Technology and Science

Technology and science do not by nature play a dominating role in human life. But alongside their possible misuse by groups and countries striving after domination — as shown, for instance, by the use of existing weapons — there is what Sir Martin Rees has recently called the "dark side" or the "downside" of 21st century technology, which, although often not intended, increases the degree of human or natural vulnerability. "Science is advancing faster than ever, and on a broader front: bio-, cyber-, and nanotechnology all offer exhilarating prospects; so does the exploration of space. But there is a dark side: new science can have unintended consequences; it empowers individuals to perpetuate acts of mega-terror; even innocent errors could be catastrophic. The 'downside' for the 21st century could be graver and more intractable than the threat of nuclear devastation that we have faced for decades."[8] These warnings from a world-renowned scientist call for precautionary measures, procedures for careful testing, and kinds of legislation to protect the vulnerable dimensions both of human life and of the earth itself. Already the modern food industry adds taste additives and chemical and biological ingredients to its prod-

8. Rees, op. cit.

ucts, ingredients which in the long run might do great harm to human health. Such measures are usually implemented more easily on the national than on the world-wide level, and they will surely not be effective if subjected to one-sided interpretations of a "freedom of competition" directing and orienting the patterns of globalization between chemical, bio-engineering, and pharmaceutical industries.

The Crisis of Labor

One of the main causes of the growing worldwide crisis of labor is the rise of so-called structural or technological unemployment. Labor-productivity is still increasing relatively rapidly, especially in wealthy countries, mainly as a result of the implementation of new technologies of organization, information, and communication. But the peril is that average productivity can easily become equal to or even rise above the speed of economic growth itself, thus failing to create more jobs, even diminishing their number in what is called "jobless growth." This is especially the case in those segments of the so-called labor market where unskilled labor is used. This is often defended as simply unavoidable in the present competitive global setting. On the contrary, it should more correctly be seen to be a form of the domination of prevailing economic systems over vulnerable human lives. Nearly fifty years ago Hannah Arendt predicted in her book *The Human Condition* that Western society could become a society of laborers without labor.[9] Additionally, the present crisis of labor has more aspects. It is a crisis of inhuman working conditions, including child labor, especially in the new industrial zones in the South where labor unions are generally weak or absent. This creates a situation that can induce an even stronger economic domination on the side of employers. And it is a crisis directly related to the pressure of labor-migration. Hundreds of millions of young people and deprived families in despair continue to try to migrate to the rich countries, often failing to find gainful employment.

Finally, there has been an internal shift in labor conditions. It cannot and should not be denied, of course, that there have been positive improvements in the conditions of many workers as a result of changing

9. Hannah Arendt, *The Human Condition* (Chicago: The University of Chicago Press, 1958).

11

technologies, for instance reductions in the senseless repetition of one or two actions in conveyor-belt jobs. This does not, however, contradict the empirical fact that too many modern-day workers are in stressful situations and show features of "burn-out" brought about by an overburdening of their mental and physical capacities. This is happening in the South as well as in the North.

The Environment

The phenomenon of economic globalization is closely linked to patterns of production and consumption that are often wasteful and surely not sustainable. When these patterns are combined with a rapid growth of the population and of the economy as a whole, an unbearable stress on the environment and its available resources often results. A recent UN study, *Ecosystems and Human Well-Being,*[10] underlines this with empirical facts and detailed investigations. Written with the cooperation of more than 1300 scientists from more than 100 countries over the last four years, the report comes to the conclusion that the world is now near "a fatal collapse" of several of its vital ecosystems. Due to an exaggerated and abusive use of natural resources we are, so the report states, on the brink of irreversible harm being done to the environment. The decline of plant and animal species is now so rapid that one third of such species is threatened by extinction. Twenty percent of the coral colonies is already lost forever, and the same is true for one-third of the mangrove woods. *These are signs of sharply increasing environmental vulnerability.*

Churches, like those in the South Pacific, have warned for years about the far-reaching consequences of a style of world-wide economic expansion which leads to global warming and accelerates climate change. The resulting rise of the sea level will flood most of the Pacific islands. What is remarkable is that most of the churches of the South attribute these harmful effects to forms of economic domination made possible by the neo-liberal forces that are shaping the current process of globalization. The churches of the Pacific use the metaphor of "mine-birds," which were often used in the past to check if mines were polluted with poisonous

10. Millennium Ecosystem Assessment, *Ecosystems and Human Well-Being,* 5 vols. (Washington, DC: Island Press, 2005).

gases; if the birds died the mines were declared unsafe. Are not the inhabitants of the low Pacific islands now like the mine-birds of the past in the eyes of today's wealthy nations?

The Media

The role of the media in today's society goes well beyond that of communicating news or diffusing information. "The media" today covers far more than the communications industry. It includes advertising, entertainment, education, visual programming, virtual reality, and software and hardware as used everywhere — from culture, to politics, to medicine. The media, defined as such, is now an instrument that gives many people access to reality and awareness of social, cultural, political, and economic issues.

Globalization has both benefited from and magnified the role of the media. Media standards and content have spread to the remotest corners of the globe. Much of what is now seen, discussed, and consumed, bears the imprint of Western culture and lifestyle and this creates tension within more traditional communities, spreading patterns of aspiration and habits of consumption beyond the reach of average citizens. What people read, listen to, or see in the media are often Trojan horses that awake our curiosity: we open our minds to such messages only unconsciously to experience ideological colonization. Thus, a great part of the public audience is ready to accept violence and competitive habits that make human beings consider "the other" to be an adversary that must be neutralized in public life. This especially influences children, for whose attention commercials are increasingly adapted in order to gear them to consume. Children are also induced by widespread violent computer games to accept violence in their own lives.

The media is, moreover, affected by globalization through the expansion of the industry's profit-seeking and controlling companies. Worldwide, there is a tendency toward concentration of ownership by means of huge mergers. For instance, in 2001 the global market for entertainment was dominated by just six companies. Without even mentioning the overlap of media conglomerates, similar figures could be offered for the music and international news markets.

It is through media that patterns of global consumption spread, sustaining the circulation of products and messages across boundaries and interacting with local markets. Goods tailored for various groups' preferences and lifestyles, particularly those of youth, are spread through advertising, merchandising, and the construction of pop culture icons who are portrayed as models to be followed. Various social groups and organizations have systematically resorted to media exposure in order to gain public prominence; fight cultural, economic, or political competitors; or simply secure the loyalty of their own constituencies. The attainment of social cohesion and political effectiveness has to a large extent become a function of access to the media, even for disadvantaged groups and resistance movements.

Of singular importance in contemporary life is the relentlessness of the "mediazation" of social life. This contributes to blurring the boundaries between reality and fiction. Facts are manipulated and edited for public consumption. All areas of life are subject to this pattern, thereby altering much of our understanding of what constitutes experience. The role of media — in everyday life, in the economy, in politics, and in culture — has led to a markedly different understanding of reality than that of decades ago. Technological innovation has created a prosthesis of nature and material culture which captivates us and gives us our visions of "life as it is" in the most distant places with no need for cultural translation or critique. There is also a double connection between media and religion: there has been a substantial investment by religious organizations in the media, and a religious dimension has been given to the media in everyday life (e.g., its awesome feasts, and its power to frame our vision of what is real, possible, and desirable).

These developments raise issues regarding the social control of the media and the holding of media companies and their practices accountable to citizens and governments. There is an urgent need to open a sustained dialogue with media professionals in regard to social responsibility and public accountability. To provide access for ordinary people to media literacy so that they can appropriate knowledge and monitor the effects of media activity globally should also be on this agenda.

A Call to Renew Our Minds

The crucial issues reviewed here obviously indicate that globalization is now developing in such a way that, on the one hand, it is sharpening itself in forms of increasing domination and, on the other hand, it is deepening itself by creating new forms of vulnerability. This contradictory nature of globalization challenges ecumenical awareness. However, the situation that we experience is not easy to approach. First of all, because globalization, a product of a long-term historical process, cannot *a priori* be denied or disqualified. We may criticize the prevailing neo-liberal ideological trends that characterize the current process, and reject how the powerful are dominating the vulnerable lives and minds of the people of the world. But at the same time it is not possible to ignore the value and significance of the life-enriching processes of cultural and social integration that men and women experience nowadays. This paradoxical situation brings into clarity the dilemmas that churches and ecumenical communities face when they are called to decide how to orient their actions. Such dilemmas require us to make choices and assume responsibilities as we consciously decide to follow difficult guidelines for social thought and action.

Something similar can also be stated about the crucial issues mentioned above. The problems raised by violence, science and technology, labor, the environment, and the mass media must be perceived in their concreteness and the traps of idealism and undue generalization must be avoided. Ecumenical social ethics has learned the lesson that optimism is not an obligation, and that false optimism is just a lie. The real experience of churches and ecumenical communities must be approached carefully, with respect. We need to discern what is going on, discerning both the roots and the evolution of current realities. The experiences of many of the peoples being served by churches throughout the world make clear that there are great doses of idealism in current talks about globalization — for example, in the circles where the powerful meet and deliberate, it is common to hear that "globalization does this or that," or that "globalization demands that we adopt this or that position." Such arguments reveal that there are many who give a "soul" to globalization without perceiving that globalization is the result of human efforts developed within certain historical conditions. They don't see that the process of globalization, and above all the neo-liberal ideology that orients the process, is part and parcel of the whole world situation. It is the evolving situation of the *oikoumene,* the whole inhabited world. In this, historical processes are manifested differently in different parts of the world. When globalization becomes a theme isolated from history, those who support the prevailing neo-liberal project fall into idealism. It is an idealism nourished by power

15

and domination that does not take into account the pains, sufferings, and frustrations of those upon whom neo-liberalism is imposed.

We are now called to discern the truth in what is happening — not only because the insights of simplistic solutions will not work, but because it is in the real world where we meet God and experience the strength of the Holy Spirit. It is in the world as it is and not in the spaces of strange galaxies that we are called to follow the way that is proposed to us. It is a way which can be followed when we open ourselves to the world, keeping the ecumenical spirit, and at the same time becoming aware of the complexities that we face, the challenges put to us, the opportunities that God offers to us, to all of which we must respond.

With the intention of following this way, aiming to be faithful to the truth in the different contexts of our complex world, trying to respect "the other" as well as to be enriched by the wonderful diversity of the peoples of the whole inhabited earth, searching for a better life with increased justice and peace, the chapters that follow present an ecumenical social ethics for these times of historic transition.

CHAPTER 2

Ecumenical Social Ethics Now

Heidi Hadsell

Ethics is the study of morality, of right and wrong, good and bad. It asks the question of what should be, what one ought to do, what the good is. It is the distance between the "is" and the "ought" which makes ethics possible and necessary. If human life, human hopes, human social organization are reduced to simply what is, what exists, and we no longer dream about what ought to be, normative ethics no longer makes sense. In order for normative ethics to exist with any real meaning there must be some measure of human intellectual freedom and imagination.

Enrique Dussel captures something of this distinction by drawing a line between an ethics which simply serves the function of helping people adapt themselves and their behavior to a given system, and one that has an open horizon, a utopian element to it. He calls the first "relative morality," the second "absolute ethics." He says: "Morality is relative to the system itself, ethics is valid in any system at any time . . . the ethical critique of a moral system de facto generates a new morality, a new moral world."[1]

One can talk meaningfully about a variety of kinds of ethics. In the United States one talks of philosophical ethics, religious ethics, humanist ethics, and the like. Within religious ethics one can distinguish as an area of study Social Ethics, which refers to ethical thought oriented toward the social world and has to do with ethics related to groups, institutions and structures, and to social, political, and economic questions. Social ethics

1. Enrique Dussel, *Ethics and Community* (New York: Orbis Books, 1988), p. 103.

does not focus primarily on the individual nor primarily on the intimate relationships between individuals. If it looks at intimate relationships at all it is likely to ask such questions as how the larger social world and its dynamics structure and help shape intimate relationships between individuals.

Because social ethics exists in the dynamic tension between what is and what ought to be, it has one foot in the world that we describe and understand sociologically, politically, and economically. But it has its other more normative foot in the world of religious ethical thought and theology, which are the primary sources for the core values of religious social ethics. What we do as research is theologically shaped in that our values and our ethical vision are related to each one's understanding of the Christian faith. Our ethical vision is also shaped by our experiences, our cultures, our countries, our denominations, and our assumptions about the social world.

These non-theological influences find their way into what we think of as a Christian ethic in many different ways. How much this happens is always debatable, and there is always someone — Stanley Hauerwas in the United States, Jacques Ellul in France — who insists that Christian ethics must purify itself from all other influences and be separate, distinct, and rigorous. This, in one form or another, is a perennial question in Christian ethics. It appears in ecumenical social ethics as we ask ourselves if an ecumenical ethic should be intended for the wide sweep of Christianity across the globe, or more oriented towards those comparatively few who are willing and able to follow a clearly defined, rigorous, and demanding ethic.

So in what sense is our thinking together *ecumenical* social ethics? In the descriptive sense what an ecumenical, international group thinking about ethics together does, is ecumenical ethics. So, the way we think together is inevitably, even if unintentionally ecumenical. But, what else is ecumenical about the way we do ecumenical social ethics? One way some people think about ecumenical social ethics is that it is simply what studies, consultations, conferences and meetings of representatives of the ecumenical movement have produced about, for example, the environment, or racism or whatever other topic or subject. I don't think we mean simply that when we use the term "ecumenical social ethics." Rather, we mean our common commitment to think together about these social issues starting from our own perspectives — denominational, national, and so on. I think also that we mean to express a common intuition, that our thinking to-

gether will be richer, more perceptive, and less tied to any particular interests or set of interests in the social world. In that sense, it will be more
likely to challenge all of us in equal measure. In addition I think we also
mean that our thought will build on much of the ethical thought and values developed through the ecumenical movement.

It is the case, as I have argued elsewhere, that today much of the
Christian ethical thought taught at least in liberal seminaries in the United
States is de facto ecumenical social ethics. Thus, when I teach a course on
environmental ethics I use material from the Roman Catholic Bishops or
the Lutheran Church or the Presbyterians and so on. There is a religious
conversation defined by the ethical area — environment, economic justice,
racism, imperialism — that is ecumenical and one cannot teach that issue
well without tapping into the full range of sources.

Having said this, it is necessary to remind ourselves that Christian
church denominations do have traditions in terms of doing ethics and
have characteristic ways of going about thinking ethically. They also have
their own chosen authors and authorities that they appeal to. In some
sense there may even be differences among us in what our denominations
choose as the most pressing or fundamental ethical issues. It's not just
what they think, or whether they cite Luther, or Calvin, or Wesley, or
whomever else as primary authorities, but how they go about their
thought that is ethically relevant, along with what building blocks are used
and how they are used to put together an ethical argument. Thus while for
instance one can affirm clearly a common Christian understanding of human nature, traditions nuance this in different ways. The ways they do so
end up being relevant for social ethics.

Another element important in thinking ethically and in understanding the work of one's own tradition or that of another tradition is not so
much what we think but how we think it; how we think methodologically,
when we think in a disciplined methodological way. Karl Barth for instance was usually a clear deontologist. By that I mean that his primary
manner of proceeding was thinking through and acting on what is right,
good, what God demands, apparently independently of consequences and
results.

For many deontologists, ethics is primarily a matter of rules and
principles, and decisions regarding those rules and principles. One applies
each rule to each new situation in which one finds oneself. So that for instance if the rule is "never lie" or "always tell the truth" one must in new

situations discover what lying might mean in that context. The reference is to the rule and its application, more than to the effect that the rule might provoke. Many people for instance have a deontological position on the death penalty — they think it is morally wrong. It would continue to be wrong even if it could be proven that the death penalty is a direct and efficient deterrent to crime.

In contrast, if one thinks not about rules and principles so much as the end one wants to achieve, one is thinking teleologically. Liberation theologians of all denominations are characterized by their teleological ethics in which the ethical nature of the act is assessed according to the ends that it hopes to achieve. Methodologically, utilitarians are also teleologists. Utility, or the greatest good for the greatest number, being the end they wish to achieve, and the measure by which ethical acts and decisions are judged.

As we have noted previously, the ecumenical movement has tried a number of ethical methodologies. For instance, J. H. Oldham developed middle axioms for use in the ecumenical movement. Although not always appearing so, middle axioms function like rules; they signal an attempt to create agreed-upon general principles, which are to be applied appropriately in each context. This is a deductive way of proceeding. That is, one deduces ethical obligation in specific situations and contexts through reasoning from the more general principles already spelled out.

The recent work on the "theology of life" of the Justice, Peace and Creation team of the World Council of Churches provides a contrast to this middle axiom approach. Here has been an attempt to work somewhat inductively. It has brought together people from many places and traditions and attempted through their conversations, ranges of experiences, and stories, to arrive at common ethical themes and areas of interest. The theology of life has had the advantage of being decentralized, and rich with the details of particularity and the drama of the human story. In the end, however, I'm not sure that what it has produced sheds new light on how to proceed in thinking together ethically.

One of the tasks of the Bossey Research Group's work has been to follow and try to understand the ever-changing and multi-faceted nature of globalization, in order to help Christians think and act in relation to it. This task is well served by thinking together about what difference it makes to think together — internationally and ecumenically. What do our traditions have to offer, what do our differing perspectives bring to our understanding? Part of this conversation is how much we want to and need to think about method. Method for me is not an end in itself. But it does help us to think more profoundly and carefully together.

One of the criticisms leveled against ecumenical ethical thought is that it is often shallow. That especially in recent years, it tends to settle on the lowest common denominator of what everyone or most everyone can agree upon. Therefore it is not demanding or helpful, and sometimes not even very relevant in terms of guiding behavior in meaningful ways.

I understand this criticism. But I also remember that ecumenical ethics opened up for me and many others the power of thinking internationally and ecumenically about ethical issues. I realized that such thought went beyond what my own tradition could offer at that particular point and it opened up the field of ethics for me in many new ways. That was thirty years ago. Since then the world has grown smaller, the stakes are much higher, and we need a genuine ecumenical, international ethics like never before.

A lot depends, as Julio de Santa Ana often says, on whether we are thinking about an ethic for the few — a demanding ethic that only a few can observe, or whether we are thinking about an ethic for an institutionalized movement. In the first case, the ethic is a demanding one that is ecumenical and international, but one that only a few around the world can commit themselves to. This is the kind of ethic that acts as leaven in the loaf, challenging all our churches and denominations. The second is an ethic of compromise, containment of disagreement, the resolution of differences, in order to serve the common end, not of an exemplary and rigorous ecumenical ethic, but the end of greater visible and institutional Christian unity.

Some years ago, Charles West described the ethical methodology of the ecumenical movement, contrasting what he calls the "traditional method" with the method used by the Commission of the Churches' Participation in Development (CCPD).

> Ethical method in the ecumenical movement has been dialogical, sometimes confrontational, in the context of a common commitment to Christ and the church. Persons are brought into this dialogue from radically different, sometimes opposing, positions and convictions, churches and social backgrounds; issues are defined and new truth is sought in the encounter. This truth is then offered as guidance for the

churches, but questioned and tested anew in the lives and actions of Christians and churches themselves.[2]

He contrasts this method with that of the CCPD, which he calls an activist ethic which is "committed to a concept of justice through participation in political and social conflict."[3]

Each side of this polarity carries its own danger: that of having a conversation structured to include everyone but because it includes everyone, activists and theorists, it cannot go very far, very fast, or very deep, versus a conversation that has clear principles and assumptions and thus can explore issues more profoundly and systematically but which may not include fully all the actors in the ecumenical movement.

While considering the possibilities for a contemporary ecumenical social ethic it is instructive to look at the ethically oriented thought of the early ecumenical movement. Doing so one notes that the founders (mostly fathers) of the ecumenical movement were themselves convinced not only of an ecumenical social ethic, but that they had already articulated such an ethic, if not in detail, at least in broad brush strokes. Indeed the certainty of the early ecumenists about an ecumenical ethic stands in sharp contrast to those of us today who raise the question of the new possibility of an ecumenical social ethic. To trace the history of what started as an idealistic, self-confident, and universalist ecumenical ethic through the decades to today is in some ways to trace the history of the ecumenical movement itself. Inquiry into the possibility of an ecumenical social ethic today is tantamount to examining the possibility of an ecumenical movement today.

I will not delve deeply into historical documents. A few short quotations suffice to catch the spirit of early ecumenical ethical thought and at the same time demonstrate some of its more salient characteristics.

(a) Early ecumenical thought has a broad scope, and a wide reach. This is ethical thought that considers itself widely valid, even universal. It is thought that is intended for all situations, thought that sees itself as equally distant from, and equally critical of all human political

2. James F. Childress and John Macquarrie, eds., *The Westminster Dictionary of Christian Ethics* (Philadelphia: The Westminster Press, 1986), p. 181.
3. Ibid., p. 182.

and economic systems, which it views as equally tainted by human limitations and sin. This ethical thought is focused on the big picture — societies, countries, the international order are the subjects of ethical reflection. More intimate subjects such as family, women, children are NOT in the first instance the primary subjects of this ethical reflection, which remains focused on the classically public and political, and which stresses commonalities, not differences:

> We have also set forth the guiding principles of a Christian inter-
> nationalism equally opposed to a national bigotry and a weak
> cosmopolitanism.[4]

(b) Early ecumenical ethics viewed the discipline of ethics as a matter of careful formulation of rules and principles that then can be applied to life — to specific groups and situations, by those in those situations. The methodological bias was that of ethics as a deductive enterprise, that is, thought which goes from the general to the specific, from the rules to their application. Ethics is viewed as a rule oriented guide to common moral life, but it is not explicitly seen as itself a product of human life together.

> We have not attempted to offer precise solutions — the mission
> of the church is above all to state principles, and to assert the
> ideal, while leaving to individual consciences, and to communi-
> ties the duty of applying them with charity, wisdom and cour-
> age.[5]

(c) Early ecumenical ethical thought was remarkably unself-conscious. It is thought that is critical of the evident human limitations found in all groups and societies. But it remained largely uncritical of the limitations of its own thought, or of the bases of its own thought. It was unaware that its ethical thought was itself a social product of the societies from which it emerged. This is thought that while sharply

---

4. Michael Kinnamon and Brian E. Cope, eds., *The Ecumenical Movement: An Anthology of Key Texts and Voices* (Geneva: WCC Publications and Grand Rapids: Wm. B. Eerdmans, 1997), p. 266.
5. Ibid.

aware of the historical moment, saw differences in culture, language, experience, but was confident that the ethical rules could be fruitfully applied to all.

> Responsible Society is not an alternative social or political system, but a criterion by which we judge all existing social orders and at the same time a standard to guide us in the specific choices we have to make.[6]

(d) Early ecumenical thought is self-confident and optimistic. It not only expects that Christians around the world will form an attentive audience, but it also expects to be seated at the secular political and economic tables of power and decision. Early ecumenists were sure that ecumenism provided added value to the Christian voice in political debates and deliberations.

> e.g.: The ecumenical church . . . by virtue of its ecumenicity brings a special perspective to the international order. . . . The church is already international in its ecumenicity. . . . It therefore has something to offer.[7]

In short, like a lot of other social thought of its time, ecumenical thought was shaped by enlightenment hopes for reason and its ability to be universally applied. Indeed, such enlightenment assumptions were central to the founding of the ecumenical movement as a whole and they continue to be carried by the movement. However, while it is possible to find ethical thought today which shares the characteristics sketched above, much contemporary ethical thought is in sharp contrast to these characteristics. In fact in some ways contemporary Christian ethical thought has been shaped in reaction to the certainty, the scope, the rules and method sketched above. Where early ecumenical thought is broad in scope, contemporary ethicists tend towards the well-defined social group or issue. Where early ecumenical thought is aimed at the formation of rules and principles, contemporary ethical thought focuses on the specific, the contextual, the unique. While early ecumenical ethical thought views ethics

6. Ibid., p. 283.
7. Ibid., p. 274.

primarily as deductive, contemporary ethical thought tends toward the inductive, the fragmented. Where early ecumenical ethical thought ignored itself as an object of its investigation, and evidenced confidence in its own premises and conclusions, contemporary ethical thought is often focused excessively on itself and the investigation into the biographical and social factors which shape it in one way or other. Where early ecumenical ethical thought is self-confident and proud, contemporary ethical thought views self-doubt as a moral and an epistemological obligation.

Where early ecumenical thought aimed at the eventual overcoming of differences between Christians, contemporary ethical thought takes the narrow construction of identity as a given and seeks ways to encounter the other without the expectation that the other will cease to be other. Much of ethics therefore, even Christian ethics, has changed its focus dramatically and moved away from the enlightenment-informed hopes of an ultimate unity of Christians. This has involved a post-modern re-reading of the meaning of the biblical texts, with Jesus now often seen as the model of one who encounters the other as other, without the attempt to convert or transform.[8]

Still, most contemporary ecumenical thought maintains the form and many of the assumptions of earlier days. But the good conscience of those decades is greatly diminished. With this loss has gone much of the clarity of thought and voice addressed both to other Christians and to the world at large. Contemporary ecumenical ethical thought often seems to have lost its creativity and vision. It has, like other ethical thought, lost much of its self-confidence as it has acquired the self-critical post-enlightenment spirit. At the same time it has not fully embraced the quest for new ethical grounding, methodologies, and conversation partners upon which post-modern ethics has embarked. It has a neither here nor there quality to it. Moreover, the ear of contemporary ecumenical ethical thought tends to be so attentive to the conflicts inside the ecumenical movement that it seems to have given up its attempt to hear or speak to the wider world.

In the 1960s the moral voice of the ecumenical movement began to change. The voice became no longer primarily men with classical theological education from Europe and North America. Instead it increasingly included voices from around the world that were different from the domi-

---

8. See for example the work of Emmanuel Levinas.

nant voice. This was the voice of people who came from the margins of the international world or even their own societies, or people who had learned to identify with the margins; people who were learning to think autonomously about theology, ethics, the church, and the world.

The voices were new not merely because of their social and geographical location. The World Council of Churches had long included voices from the margins, although perhaps not in great number. The power of these new voices was great because many of them came armed with a new way to think. These were voices that, while taking themselves seriously, began with themselves, their own social locations in terms of class, nation, language, experience, and so forth. These were voices which tested the more universal sounding perspectives and truths against their own experience.

Today these voices are well-known. In fact, today the WCC is well known for the inclusion of voices from the underside, the poor and oppressed, women, the downtrodden and under-represented. The inclusion of these voices in itself was a change. An even greater change was methodological as these voices in their specificity looked outside of the traditional European oriented theological thought to new sources for guidance.

Richard Shaull, in a speech before the World Conference on Church and Society in Geneva in 1966,[9] went right to the heart of the matter:

> What I take it to mean is that ethical orientation can be provided only as values are translated into specific goals, specific human needs, and specific technical possibilities and priorities. No set of abstract principles, or ideas like the responsible society, will be of much help unless we succeed at this job of translation, which will have to be done again and again in changing situations.[10]

Taking social science as a conversation partner, particularly the interests and methodologies of Marxist social science instead of primarily the patterned thought of traditions and denominations, the object of ethical reflection also changed. This shifted from national governments, the wealthy and powerful, to social movements and the poor and dispossessed. Meth-

9. Harold E. Fey, ed., *A History of the Ecumenical Movement, Volume 2, 1948-1968*, 3rd ed. (Philadelphia: The Westminster Press, 1993), p. 254.
10. Kinnamon and Cope, eds., *The Ecumenical Movement*, p. 302.

odologically this began to move inductively from the concrete to the more general. Thus it moved away from the rules and formulas worked out by an earlier generation, which were intended to be valid for all. The call was for justice, for change, Jesus not so much as unifier but as liberator, and the burden of proof was on all those who did not go along.

Currently, we are in an era in which certainties are being stripped away, including those of the liberationist perspective. We no longer always trust our own motives in relation to the other. We no longer believe, as early ecumenical thought seemed to, that difference is something to be overcome through reason and intelligence and progress over time. Today the encounter with the other is one that is not expected to persuade, convert, or destroy. Rather it is to know the other in his or her otherness. The self-importance and optimism of early ecumenical thought has faded. So too has the self-righteousness of some liberationist thought as the "other" proves to be much more complex and perhaps more subtle than the economically powerful and imperial other of liberation thought, and the relation with the other is accordingly much more ambiguous.

So the question persists: What is the hope for ecumenical ethics now? With the post-modern critique Humpty Dumpty has fallen off the wall. Can we put Humpty Dumpty back together again?

From my North America liberal Protestant perspective, which views ethics as constructed not given, a social product informed by biblical faith but not fully determined by it, ethics is in the end the product of human life together. Fragmentation and conflict in ethical thought are the inevitable result of fragmented communities that cannot agree to live together easily. New communities and new relations will in the end give birth to new ethical thought. Thus the possibility of an ecumenical social ethic has more to do with how we live together than how we think together, although the two are intimately related and affect each other.

Our different Christian communities have not in fifty years come together. There is no ecumenical ethical hegemony either in how we live or how we think. As we have seen, the early unity of ecumenical social thought — built around a rule-oriented, deductive methodology devised by ethical elites distributed in traditions which still seemed to make sense — gave way to a liberationist-inspired inductive methodology done by ethical challengers of the given order, able to silence for some time the defenders of a traditional order. One cannot credibly return to former methods and the dominance of former voices. But neither have the challenging methodologies and voices prevailed. In addition post-modernism has enabled us to see limits in method and intent of much ethical thought, but it has not enabled clearly the constructive task.

It is interesting that, in effect, much of Christian ethical thought today is already ecumenical since the divisions between traditions are increasingly porous and the theological or ethical work in one tradition increasingly informs other traditions. Still, as noted above, today there seems to be two ethical currents inside one ecumenical movement: one committed to issues closely tied to tradition and to denominational history and authority and one more fluid, shaped by and attentive to context and a multiplicity of voices. The first, although found in denominations and traditions that are a part of the ecumenical movement, is itself not necessarily ecumenical in spirit. It is often more interested in spreading its own truth than in having ecumenical conversation or dialogue with others and being challenged and changed by it. The second is a more open system, interested in dialogue and valuing virtues such as openness to the other and to context. The potential for a truly ecumenical ethic resides, it seems clear, with this second ethical current or perspective although hopefully enriched by tradition and history.

Today there are many ethical concerns which in an increasingly globalized world cross all kinds of national, social, religious, and cultural boundaries. Such common ethical concerns include, for example, a broad range of environmental, human rights, and economic justice issues. These are issues that one can enter from one's own experiences or the experiences of one's community in a specific time and place, and that at the same time are broadly based. I think, for example, of small, rural communities in the Amazon basin in the early 1990s who learned about the concept of and the shared importance of sustainable development through their own concrete experiences of protecting their fishing grounds from commercial fishing fleets. They made this connection in part through the work of the Catholic CPT (Commisao Pastoral da Terra), which helped the rural communities connect their more specific experience with the more general concept of sustainable development, linking it also with the Christian idea of stewardship.

Today it seems clear that ecumenical ethics, in order to be faithful to its calling that values a common concern for and commitment to the world, and that insists on openness to the other, needs once again to push against boundaries. It seems that this indicates going outside Christianity to extend a welcoming hand to other religions, and to people who have passion for similar ethical concerns, although perhaps not from a religious conviction. The experience in thinking ethically together inside the ecumenical movement will be invaluable for learning how to construct a new, more broadly conceived ecumenical social ethic. Such an ethic will be, for a long time to come, experimental and tentative in terms of moral content, and unstable in terms of conversation partners. It will be an open, not a closed system, and one that will have to learn as it goes along. As such, it is probably an ethics to be lived in small circles, not yet ready for mass consumption. Rather it will be an ethic that can and should act as leaven, informing the wider circles in which it participates.

CHAPTER 3

On the Meaning of "Ecumenical"

Ninan Koshy with *Julio de Santa Ana*

The Rise of the Ecumenical Movement

The modern ecumenical movement began to take shape as early as the 18th century. It developed among groups of lay Christians during the early part of the 19th century, and began to influence the Christian missionary movement during the latter part of that century. The World Missionary Conference held in Edinburgh in 1910 is widely regarded as the initiating event of the movement as now known. Following several centuries in which divisions and conflicts prevailed in church relationships, ecumenism has emerged in the 20th century as one of Christianity's most important characteristics; the movement for unity and renewal has become a powerful trend. To a large extent, 20th century ecumenism is to be seen as a response by many church bodies to a period of human history marked by the horror and despair of two world wars and many other confrontations that have brought death and pain to the planet.

To be sure, the ecumenical movement was not the only major development in Christianity during the 20th century. Other tendencies, such as the growth of evangelical fundamentalism, were also present and perhaps the most important development — because it affected the life of the largest Christian communion — was the decision of the Roman Catholic Church to begin a process of modernization, opening itself to contemporary society and culture. The decision to convene the Second Vatican Council (1962-1965) resulted, among many other things, in the participation of the Church of Rome in the ecumenical movement. This launched the Roman Catholic Church into an important transformation that has brought about changes in its structure and public image even as, at the same time, it began itself powerfully to influence the nature and direction of the ecumenical movement. Ecumenism has changed since the early 1960s.

Among the changes experienced by Christianity during the last century has been a gradual yet pronounced shift: on the one hand, traditional churches, mainly in Western Europe, seem to be stagnant or in decline while, on the other hand, in regions of the world where churches were born as a result of missionary work — Africa, Asia, Latin America, the Caribbean, and the Pacific — new types of Christianity are taking vigorous shape. Today, the Christian communities that are multiplying and growing most impressively are in the southern regions of the world. Among them, charismatic churches and groups are giving expression to new types of spirituality and community even as they are making a strong impact on their own societies.

These expressions of changes in Christianity have a common element: all, in one way or another, are responses to the challenges of modernization. They show that the relationships between Christianity, modern society, and modern culture are far from being settled. It is to be recognized, of course, that as there are different expressions of Christianity so there are different expressions of modernization.[1] While the development of modern societies is not yet finished, some "modern beliefs" or assumptions have collapsed as, for example, the notion of infinite progress. It is also true that the modern faith in the value of reason is increasingly being questioned from a scientific perspective. Moreover, many arguments that support modernization are criticized. For example, it is no longer possible

1. Samuel N. Eisenstadt, the philosopher and social scientist who taught at Hebrew University in Jerusalem, has rightly insisted that "modernization" is a process that has different manifestations and contexts. There is not one unique version of modernization; there are many expressions of it. Even in the case of modern Western societies, there are differences — e.g., in Western Europe secularization and privatization have lessened the influence of religion, while in the United States Protestant fundamentalism is very much alive; the situation of Western Europe seems more favorable to ecumenism than in the U.S. Cf. Samuel N. Eisenstadt, *European Civilization in a Comparative Perspective* (Oxford: Norwegian University Press, 1987), also *Fundamentalism, Sectarianism, and Revolution: The Jacobin Dimension of Modernity* (Cambridge, UK, and New York: Cambridge University Press, 1999).

to say that secularization clearly shows that modern culture prevails in a given society. As a matter of fact, dominant secularization in Western Europe is an exception in the religious situation of the world.[2] This does not mean that the religious dynamism of other societies is not modern; rather that other parts of the world are not following the path taken by Western Europe. In situations other than in the West, interactions between modern culture and tradition often generate other types of modernization which in turn contribute to important changes in the faith and the religious institutions of the people.[3] If, for example, in Western Europe the Christian religion is going through a process of privatization, in other parts of the world, Christianity, Islam, and Buddhism present public challenges to political and social forces. Philip Jenkins asserts that during the past half century, the crucial centers of Christianity have moved to the South, mainly to Africa, but also to Latin America and Asia. For him, this trend is irreversible.[4]

Today there is frequent talk about "the crisis of ecumenism" and there is clear evidence of the reality of such a crisis. For example, at the beginning of the 21st century there is more than one understanding of what "ecumenical" means, a diversity of understanding that obviously impinges on those who engage in "ecumenical social ethics." But the deepest challenge facing ecumenism concerns not so much the sense of being ecumenical; rather it concerns the process of modernization. The ecumenical movement has grown up and exists in contexts of various forms of being modern. The critical period that ecumenism is going through today is mainly a crisis of modernization.

The Crisis of Modernization

In light of all this, clarity about the meaning of "ecumenical" requires an understanding of the directions of different processes of modernization. Hannah Arendt, in her book *Between Past and Present,* published in the

---

2. Grace Davie, *Religion in Western Europe: A Memory Mutates* (Oxford: Oxford University Press, 2000).

3. José Casanova, *Public Religions in the Modern World* (Chicago: The University of Chicago Press, 1994).

4. Philip Jenkins, *The Next Christendom: The Coming of Global Christianity* (New York: Oxford University Press, 2002).

middle of the last century, underlines that a break "between the times" was occurring.[5] This historical fracture was clear to those who had lived through the two world wars of the 20th century. It has, however, been more difficult for later generations — persons who experienced the reconstruction that followed World War II — to perceive that such a break was taking place. What Eric Hobsbawm calls "the golden age" (French historians, philosophers, sociologists, and political scientists use the term, *"les temps glorieux"*) created the impression that humanity was continuing its way forward. A great economic expansion would promote a tremendous growth of world trade. Political trends were expected to lead to a democratization in which "the welfare state" would prevail. These elements, together with the processes of de-colonization and national liberation, concealed the break that seemed so clear to those who lived through the 20th century's two world wars.

By the mid-1970s this "golden age" was coming to an end. It was replaced by the domination of financial capital through deregulation that brought about the end of a bi-polar world where the power of political and economic ideologies was unquestionable. People became increasingly aware of a move away from economic internationalization to globalization. This came about through the rapid development of trans-national corporations, mainly those working at the level of international finance. While the collapse of the socialist regimes of Eastern Europe initially promised peace and justice, it soon became clear that many urgent issues that threatened the life of human societies were not solved at all. Once again people experienced a lack of meaning, both in their social and personal lives.

However, other elements have also contributed to the modernization crisis. In the last twenty-five years or so, human societies have developed technologies that have created new types of relationships with nature, and implemented new forms of production and the creation of wealth. Manuel Castells has called this process "the rise of the network society."[6] Economic globalization has been accelerated by these new technologies. Their impact

5. Hannah Arendt, *Between Past and Future: Eight Exercises in Political Thought* (New York: Penguin Classics, 1977; orig. ed., 1961).

6. Manuel Castells, *The Information Age: Economy, Society and Culture* (Oxford and Malden, MA: Blackwell Publishing), Vol. 1, *The Rise of the Network Society* (1996; 2nd ed., 2000); Vol. 2, *The Power of Identity* (1997; 2nd ed., 2004); Vol. 3, *End of Millennium* (1998; 2nd ed., 2000).

is not limited to economic life: they are creating new types of human communication and they contribute to the "consumption culture" and the "mass culture" typical of modern societies. Where this is taking place, particularly in developing and less-developed countries, the growth of charismatic and especially "Pentecostal" communities is notable.

Another element to be considered is that globalization is not a one-dimensional phenomenon. People who wish to participate in the "global market" and enjoy what it offers, frequently also affirm their particular cultural traditions, their local identities, their specific values. So, although some are convinced that globalization is oriented exclusively by neoliberal economic ideology and try to impose a single frame of thought everywhere *("la pensée unique"),* there are in point of fact various ways by which people participate in the process. Some anthropologists have called this trend the "hybridization of cultures"[7] in which people affirm some elements of their own culture while at the same time accommodating to the behavior and values of a different yet dominant culture.

This socio-cultural process has led to the emergence and development of pluralistic societies. Increases in migration during the last forty years have also contributed to the growth of this social pluralism, which includes a religious dimension. Access to transportation coupled with the realization that there are other societies where, perhaps, life is easier and more enjoyable, have led to increasing numbers of people widening the horizons of their lives. If by the end of the 19th century and the first half of the 20th people moved from East to West (largely from eastern and southern Europe to the Americas), more recent decades have witnessed the most voluminous population flows from the South to the North and West. Migrants arrive with illusions of a new society; some have painfully abandoned their roots. They try to adjust to the prevailing patterns of behavior but they need some elements from their past to prevent them from being totally lost. Some of these elements are found in cultural and religious centers where they can practice their language, share their habits, common values, and expectations with other persons of the same social origin. These migrants experience a strong tension between the impera-

7. Néstor García Canclini, *Hybrid Cultures: Strategies for Entering and Leaving Modernity,* trans. Christopher L. Chiappari and Sylvia L. López (Minneapolis: University of Minnesota Press, 1995; orig. ed., 1989). Cf. also idem, *Consumers and Citizens: Globalization and Multicultural Conflicts,* trans. George Yúdice (Minneapolis: University of Minnesota Press, 2001; orig. ed., 1995).

tives of modernization and the need to remember their roots. For the people who receive these migrants, their presence poses a challenge of welcoming them and understanding their lifestyle. This presents both a social and a moral question, a real test of being. When the peoples of the *oikoumene* come together, no one can remain as he or she was. The modern Western culture cannot continue to be defined only on the basis of Western patterns: "the other" enters our realm of existence and cannot be ignored. Here, again, the break is perceived: the fracture within modern culture.

Alain Touraine, a French social scientist and philosopher, has made clear that in the present phase of modernizations a sharp tension has been created between individuals and the institutions.[8] For Touraine, it is the individual who is the social subject of all processes of modernization. The paradox of modern societies is that individuals are also part of the masses — as consumers, as receptors and reproducers of information, etc. Individuals, while participating in different kinds of mass movements, search to privatize their lives in order to create and preserve meaning. At the same time, they try to share with other individuals, through participation in the mass movements, how they produce meaning. This paradox is one of the elements of the crisis of modernity. People feel that it is difficult to find a "way."

Here too is a dimension of the so-called crisis of the ecumenical movement during the second half of the 20th century. The ecumenical movement initially followed the directions proposed by the Anglican Communion and the mainline Protestant denominations. With the decision of the Roman Catholic Church to become involved in ecumenism, and with the increase in the number of churches of the South that joined the movement, questions about the future, the goal, and the way to proceed multiplied for the ecumenical movement. This diversity, a characteristic of modern societies, has been of considerable consequence for relations between churches.

---

8. Alain Touraine, *Critique of Modernity,* trans. David Macey (Oxford and Malden, MA: Blackwell Publishing, 1995; orig. ed., 1992). Touraine distinguishes four stages in the crisis of modernity: a) the initial movement for human liberation has become exhausted; b) the modern culture has become captive to instrumental reason; c) a more radical stage in the crisis is that modernity questions its own positive goals; and d) modernity, which initially aimed at liberty, has become an instrument of control, integration, and repression.

The Ecumenical Movement and Modernization

For almost forty years, during the latter half of the 20th century, the ecumenical movement evolved in the context of a world where two main ideologies prevailed: one expressed the expectations of liberal capitalism, the other tried to articulate the views of the working classes, the proletariat. During the 1980s, however, real socialism accelerated at a pace that weakened its internal organization and its expectations. The fall of the Berlin wall was a sign that its days were numbered. It seemed, then, that economic neo-liberalism had become the best ideological tool with which to face the future. This economic ideology does not allow space for the inclusion of those who cannot share the benefits of globalization. This presents a serious and unprecedented challenge to the ecumenical movement which, in the years following World War II and through the whole "cold war," had endeavored to be an agent of peace and reconciliation. World tensions were not limited to those generated by the two superpowers and their allies. There were also the aspirations of the South and the "non-aligned nations." The ecumenical movement experienced the tension between its vocation to be at the service of both peace and the struggle for justice for those peoples who had experienced the yoke of colonialism. This context became passé with the acceleration of international political events from the 1980s onwards.

The early 1990s were dominated by neo-liberal orientations. Things began to change following a succession of financial crises that started with Mexico at the end of 1994 and included the national economic crisis in Argentina in 2002-2003. Gradually, neo-liberalism discovered that it could not overcome existing socio-economic contradictions in many societies; in fact, it caused more tension. The failure of the two classical ideologies — Marxist socialism and neo-liberalism — has created a vacuum. Since human societies need "ideologies" in order to operate, the events of recent years have challenged people to fill this vacuum with other ideological proposals. In this situation, some ideological proposals that use religious and cultural symbols have been developed in various parts of the world. This often gives rise to dogmatic and fanatical affirmations based largely on religion. Although the terms are not the same in every part of the world, the phenomenon is growing everywhere. Some conservative Christian groups participate in this, although Islam seems to be the religion most influenced. In this context both modern societies and modern ecumenism are seriously challenged.

For many observers, one of the most important, if not the most important development taking place in the context of modernization is women's emancipation. Women have begun to leave the privacy of the family, where traditionally they found their role. During and after the industrial revolution, when capital directed the economic process in most countries of the world, women began to get involved in industrial production and other economic activities. They became aware that their rights should be respected and that equality with men is a prerequisite for the construction of modern societies. The struggle for women's rights began to introduce radical structural changes in society. These are taking place not only at the level of the social division of labor, but also in the family. Religious groups are facing this new situation with different attitudes; some welcome women's liberation, while others are reticent or negative. The challenge that women put to modernity, and thus to the ecumenical movement, is about the coherence of modern societies, modern cultures, and modern ecumenism. How is it possible to be "modern" when women, more than half of the world's population, and the gender that gives social legitimacy to religious institutions, are not respected and recognized?

As in other critical periods of human history, many now experience what is narrated in the story of the Tower of Babel (Genesis 11:1-9): situations of crisis are periods of disorder, chaos. Many do not realize the potential for positive change inherent in historic crises, and consequently they endeavor to impose their own order, including prescriptions for human behavior. Some religious ideologies, as already mentioned, contribute to this reactionary trend. Power has a tendency to build empires and to institutionalize hegemonic interests in order to govern human societies. Thus, the vocation to freedom and the recognition of the right to diversity inherent in modernization is betrayed. The conflicts provoked by such social and cultural orientations run across the world including the ecumenical movement.

The ecumenical movement is shaken and challenged by these trends. To be ecumenical at the beginning of the 21st century is not the same as it was at the beginning of the 20th, when the vision of an ecumenical utopia began to inspire some Christian leaders. It is also different from the years when the World Council of Churches was founded and Vatican II was convened. It has already been pointed out that in the crisis of modernization many churches and other religious institutions and communities take on conservative, even reactionary positions. Indeed, such attitudes are also expressions of the relation between these religious bodies and modernity. Other believers express disorientation.

Yet, as has been briefly mentioned, there are situations in the world where religions are experiencing strong revitalization, manifesting in their own particular ways a clear intention to join modernity. Christian communities, especially in sub-Saharan Africa, Latin America, and parts of Asia, are growing rapidly. They are developing new liturgies, experiencing new ways of celebration, bringing into being new types of piety, and giving birth to new theologies. Some of these communities keep certain elements of the traditional Christian faith, while others articulate lines of theological reflection that make evident certain discontinuities with traditional Christianity. This is not a phenomenon that happens only to religious bodies or only to Christian communities. It is inherent in the crisis of modernity. This crisis of modernization makes unavoidable a crisis for Christianity, and it also makes a strong impact on the ecumenical movement.

A point that needs to be highlighted is that the ecumenical movement has been successful. Its evolution has called for the creation of new structures within the churches — structures needed for ecumenical relationships that have become extremely important in recent decades. Here we must recognize that the ecumenical impulse and the crisis of modernity go hand in hand.

It is in this context that the question of an "ecumenical social ethics" must be raised. In order to do this with serious reflection, it is relevant to explore the "ecumenical ethos." Is there only one? Or has it diverse expressions? If there is more than one such ethos, how does each care for the other? Is there a dialogue that recognizes ecumenical diversity? Or do some try to impose their views upon the others?

The Ecumenical Ethos in Tension

The history of religions shows a virtually perennial and sharp tension: the need to be faithful to a certain tradition and the imperative to be relevant to the immediate historic context. This is a tension that has often devolved into a conflict between authority and freedom. For some — in most cases the majority of believers — it is part of the *ethos* of a given religion to be loyal to the tradition received from the forefathers. Furthermore, even when it is recognized that the tradition should be revitalized, what matters above all is the tradition *per se*. For others, what is important is to keep alive the freshness of faith amidst the changes of history. *Renewal* is a key word for this group. In the history of the Christian churches we often see this tension present; it has influenced the history of divisions within Christianity. Nor has the modern ecumenical movement escaped this tension — even in its short history. It is clearly present today in the life of the World Council of Churches (WCC) where considerable reflection on the presence and role of the Orthodox churches, with their strong insistence on tradition, in the life of the Council is taking place. Another example of this tension is found in the ongoing debates within the Roman Catholic Church (RCC) about how to implement the reforms called for by Vatican II. These situations are among many that demonstrate that the very meaning of "ecumenical" is being questioned.

The decisions of Vatican II to open the RCC both to modern societies and to modern cultures, as well as to participate in the ecumenical movement, has made a great impact on the whole of Christianity. It could not be otherwise, given the importance of the largest Christian church for the rest of the Christian world. The influence of the RCC on the ecumenical movement has grown continually, although differences between the WCC and the RCC about how to be ecumenical cannot be hidden.

There are differences in understanding ecumenism among the member churches of the WCC as well as between the WCC and the Roman Catholic Church. Thomas Hughson wrote in 1994:

> With understatement so refined as to evoke suspicions of difficult meetings, the Sixth Report of the Joint Working Group between the WCC and the Roman Catholic Church (JWG) writes that "diverse understanding of the ecumenical goal and means of achieving visible unity may affect ecumenical progress." Common understanding of ecumenism among WCC members and between the WCC and RCC cannot be taken for granted — or that the WCC and the RCC are on the same page in the ecumenical movement. Divergence on the goals and means of ecumenism weakens the premises foundational for WCC-RCC cooperation, which in turn can only erode the bases for bi-

lateral and multilateral dialogues. Hence the challenge to seek common understanding of the ecumenical movement.[9]

Since this was written there seems to have developed an even greater divergence between the Roman Catholic Church and the WCC — and also within the WCC — concerning a common understanding of the ecumenical movement.

Two Vatican documents published in September 2000 could be generously described as only reiterating earlier positions, but the spirit of the documents does not seem to be "ecumenical." *"Dominus Iesus": On the Unicity and Salvific Universality of Jesus Christ and the Church,* published on August 6, 2000, by the Vatican Congregation for the Doctrine of the Faith, declares that "the ecclesial communities which have not preserved the valid episcopate and the genuine and integral substance of the eucharistic mystery are not churches in the proper sense."[10] Another document, *The Expression "Sister Churches,"* issued by the Congregation on June 30, 2000, orders Roman Catholic Bishops not to use the term "sister church" in reference to Protestant churches. This document stated: "It must always be clear when the expression *sister churches* is used in this proper sense, that the one, holy, catholic and apostolic universal church is not sister but *mother* of all particular churches."[11]

Both documents pointedly avoid using the word "church" when referring to Protestants, adopting instead the non-committal phrase "ecclesial communities." By restating the long-held view of the Roman Catholic Church on the status of other Christian churches the documents break no new ground, but neither do they fully reflect the deeper ecclesiological understandings achieved through ecumenical dialogue and cooperation during the past three or four decades. Even though the documents are not part of the process inaugurated by Vatican II, the idea that other churches are not "proper church" seems counter to the considerable gains made since the beginning of the 1960s.

Since 1961, at the time of the 3rd Assembly of the World Council of Churches in New Delhi, virtually all Orthodox churches have been mem-

9. Thomas Hughson, article in *The Ecumenical Review* 46, no. 3 (July 1994): 248.
10. *"Dominus Iesus": On the Unicity and Salvific Universality of Jesus Christ and the Church,* in *Origins: CNS Documentary Service* (Washington, D.C.: Catholic News Service, September 14, 2000), Vol. 30, no. 14: 216 (§17).
11. *The Expression "Sister Churches,"* in ibid., 224 (§10).

bers of the WCC and active participants in the movement for Christian unity. At that time, many of these churches lived in situations where the state tightly controlled the different religious confessions. Since 1989, most of these churches have been set free from such control and this new situation has its effects on ecumenism. For example, there are new tones to the voices of Orthodox churches in the ecumenical movement. "The Final Report of the Special Commission on Orthodox Participation in the WCC"[12] describes deep divergences within the WCC itself and raises fundamental questions about the future of that body as a major instrument of the ecumenical movement. The Commission was appointed to address Orthodox concerns and to propose "necessary changes in structure, style and ethos" of the WCC (§A.5), virtually everything that pertains to the Council's life and work. If the proposals of the Commission are implemented they will alter the character and course of the ecumenical movement.

The Commission envisions a Council that will hold churches together in an ecumenical space (§A.11). The question may be asked: is it an expanding space or a shrinking space that the Commission envisions?

The Commission further believes that it is up to each church to shape its own moral teachings. Under "Social and Ethical Issues", the Report states: "Faced with the need to develop Christian ethics that respond to current problems and struggles, it is the responsibility of each church to shape its own moral teaching. At the same time the Special Commission recognizes the WCC as a vital forum for raising and reflecting together on moral issues facing churches and society" (§B.23). There follows an indictment of the way in which the WCC has dealt with social and ethical issues. What was understood as ecumenical social ethics is challenged here both in content and methodology.

The Special Commission was created in part because of dissatisfaction raised by Orthodox and others with the ways in which certain social and ethical issues have reached the agenda of the WCC, and the ways in which they have been treated. Specifically, there has been a perception that churches are coerced into treating issues they deem as either foreign to their lives or inappropriate for a worldwide forum. There has also been a perception that the WCC has on occasion sought to "preach" to

12. "Final Report of the Special Commission on Orthodox Participation in the WCC" (Geneva: WCC Central Committee, 26 August–3 September 2002).

the churches rather than to be an instrument for common reflection (§B.25).

The Report underlines the links between the prophetic and pastoral roles of the churches:

> The churches take on a "prophetic role" when they truthfully describe and react to situations in the world precisely in the light of the Gospel. More reflection is required on what it means for churches in fellowship to engage in this way. A prophetic voice can never be divorced from the pastoral role, which includes building up, encouraging, and comforting (1 Cor. 14:3). (§B.29)

> The way in which a church (or churches together) orders and structures its own decision-making on moral matters is in itself a prime ethical issue. *Who* decides *what* and *by which means?* The forms of decision-making and communication already embody a social ethic, and influence moral teaching and practice. Structures, offices and roles express moral values. Ways of exercising power, governance and access have moral dimensions. To ignore this is to fail to understand why moral issues can be so divisive.

> The WCC needs constantly to monitor procedures for dealing with social and ethical issues proposed for common deliberation. For example, how should it be determined that a given matter is directed to the WCC for discussion by a genuine "church" request, rather than by pressure-group advocacy? (§B.32,33)

In trying to clarify, perhaps even rediscover, the meaning of "ecumenical," two problems must be faced: (1) the variety of perceptions — and misunderstandings — of the word and its meaning. (2) The widespread and strong impression that there is a crisis in the ecumenical movement and in the practice of ecumenism. Clarifying the issue is highly important when our intention is to reflect about an "ecumenical social ethics." Diane C. Kessler, in giving examples of several types of gatherings or enterprises with the label ecumenical, has written: "Unless these initiatives have a reconciling intention among all Christians and their churches — an intention embracing the *fullness* of our life in Christ, indeed 'everything that relates to the whole task of the whole church to bring the gospel to the whole world' — they may be worthy enterprises but they are not *ecumenical* in their aim or their result."[13] This is correct in the light of the definition offered by the WCC Central Committee in 1951, but how do we understand the many "popular," "elastic," "secular," and "revised" meanings frequently given to the term?[14] Further, inter-faith efforts are increasingly called "ecumenical." Ashish Nandy, a well-known Indian thinker, says that the Indian state is an "ecumenical" rather than a "secular" state because it treats all religions equally. He points out that the state pays the salaries of teachers in Christian schools, subsidizes "Haj" pilgrims, and supports many Hindu activities.

The 1951 WCC Central Committee statement shows that the leaders of the WCC had already become aware of the need to make clear — in the context of the history of the mid-20th century: the Cold War, the Korean War, the reconstruction of Europe, etc. — the relationship between participation in God's mission and the concern for the unity of the church. The emphasis on "wholeness" in the committee's formulation came mainly because of criticism, especially from Asians, at the inaugural Assembly of the WCC and even earlier, concerning the lack of such "wholeness." The Asians expressed doubts about whether the new body, the WCC, would manifest the "essential missionary dimension of the ecumenical movement" and they raised those doubts forcefully. In 1939, a few days before the beginning of World War II, D. T. Niles had insisted that the "ecumenical vision revealed indeed God's pilgrim people on the way to the centre and frontiers of the Church and the world," and not just "a Christian fellowship of humanitarian service"; and again, "Our main concern is that the missionary emphasis becomes central to the life of the churches represented within the World Council."[15] A few years later, Stephen Neill wrote

13. Diane C. Kessler, "Ecumenism Defined," *The Ecumenical Review* 50, no. 3 (July 1998): 278.

14. The 1951 formulation is perhaps the best known definition: "It is important to insist that the word (namely ecumenical) which comes from the Greek word for the whole inhabited earth, is properly used to describe everything that relates to the whole task of the whole Church to bring the Gospel to the whole world. It therefore covers equally the missionary movement and the movement towards unity, and must not be used to describe the latter in contradiction with the former. We believe that a real service will be rendered to true thinking on these subjects if we so use the word that covers both Unity and Mission in the context of the whole world" (WCC Central Committee Minutes, Rolle, Switzerland, 1951, p. 65).

15. Quoted in Hans-Ruedi Weber, *Asia and the Ecumenical Movement* (London: SCM Press, 1966), 37.

in the Epilogue to Volume 1 of *A History of the Ecumenical Movement* that "[o]ne of the chief problems of the ecumenical movement in the mid-20th century is that occasioned by the separation between its two essential components. This History has shown at point after point the intimate connection between the missionary work of the Church and the ecumenical ideal. Throughout, the word 'ecumenical' has been used to designate the efforts of Christians to seek and promote unity; but it should by now be plain to the reader that these efforts are not an end in themselves. The aim of Christian union is *that the world may believe.*"[16]

Concerning the "crisis of the ecumenical movement," it is clear that the use of expressions which are often used in religious studies today like "ecumenical winter," "lost in the fog," et al., is increasing. Some would argue that the movement is at a crossroads. There is a decline in the ecumenical impulse and the loss of ecumenical motivation is bound up with a disregard for what has been achieved ecumenically, with a growing uncertainty of ecumenical direction, and with an ambivalence concerning ecumenical accomplishments. In this context, many would argue for a rethinking of the ecumenical enterprise against the background of new and manifold challenges. An effort has already been made to make clear that the ecumenical movement does not develop in a vacuum, simply by its own internal dynamic. Historical, political, social, and cultural factors influence the movement. Ecumenical leaders have consistently insisted, since the beginning of the last century, that ecumenism is called to discern the way to proceed in its ministry of reconciliation, taking into consideration "the signs of the times" through which the Spirit of God is at work.

Subsequent attempts at definition have often emphasized that the object of God's reconciling purpose is not only the church but the whole of humanity, indeed the whole of creation. The WCC's Vancouver Assembly in 1983 spoke of a eucharistic vision that "[u]nites our two profoundest ecumenical concerns: the unity and the renewal of the Church and the healing and destiny of the human community. Church unity is vital to the health of the Church and to the future of the human family. . . . Christ — the life of the world — unites heaven and earth, God and world, spiritual and secular. His body and blood, given us in the elements of bread and

---

16. Stephen Neill and Ruth Rouse, eds., *A History of the Ecumenical Movement*, Vol. 1: *1517-1948* (Philadelphia: Westminster Press and London: SPCK, 1954), 730.

wine, integrate liturgy and diaconate, proclamation and acts of healing. . . . Our eucharistic vision thus encompasses the whole reality of Christian worship, life and witness."[17] At the following Assembly of the WCC in 1991 in Canberra, Australia, the desperate need for a visible and absolute commitment to the reconciliation of God's world was acknowledged: "Our theological perspective convinces us that we need to affirm the vision of an inhabited world *(oikoumene)* based on values which promote life for all."[18]

The 1996 study of the WCC, "Towards a Common Understanding and Vision of the World Council of Churches" (CUV), explores meanings of "ecumenical" and comments: "In the present situation of uncertainty and transition, the ambiguities surrounding the meaning of the term 'ecumenical' will not be resolved by a descriptive — even less a normative — definition which identifies a particular model, strategy or organizational affiliation as criteria for what is 'ecumenical.'"[19] The CUV text seems to resist changing the definition of ecumenism to include "other religious and cultural traditions beyond the Christian community." It speaks of renewal "in the light of the gospel of God's kingdom" and affirms "the Christian hope of life for all."[20] It roots the ecumenical movement "in the life of the Christian churches." "It is committed to the search for visible unity." It points more specifically to the "catholicity of the church" and "is concerned with the true being and life of the Church as an inclusive community."[21]

Multiple Dimensions of "Ecumenical"

Clearly, then, there is more than one meaning of the word "ecumenical."

17. David Gill, ed., *Gathered for Life: Official Report, VI Assembly World Council of Churches, Vancouver, Canada, 24 July–10 August, 1983* (Geneva: WCC Publications and Grand Rapids: Eerdmans Publishing Co., 1983), 43-45.

18. Michael Kinnamon, ed., *Signs of the Spirit: Official Report, VII Assembly World Council of Churches, Canberra, Australia, 7-20 February, 1991* (Geneva: WCC Publications and Grand Rapids: Eerdmans Publishing Co., 1991), 245.

19. "Towards a Common Understanding and Vision of the World Council of Churches" (Geneva: World Council of Churches, 1977), §2.8.

20. Ibid., §2.6; 2.8.2.

21. Ibid., §2.8.3; 2.8.4; 2.8.5.

Unity of the Church

For most Christian people, to be ecumenical implies working for unity between Christians and churches, for reconciliation and peace. These efforts focus primarily on Christian unity. Christian institutions and bodies like the Roman Catholic Church, world confessional families, and the World Council of Churches have for a long time been engaged in seeking to achieve "visible unity." Therefore, dialogues aiming at convergence and, if possible, consensus on matters related to traditional Christian doctrine and order are essential. This has been and continues to be the work of those engaged in what is known as Faith and Order, in which member churches of the World Council of Churches, the Roman Catholic Church, and other bodies and individuals participate.

Renewal and Human Community

This quest for unity, however, does not cover the whole spectrum of ecumenical activities. The word also applies when important documents issued by churches and ecumenical organizations and communities use expressions like "renewal" and "human community." The WCC's First Assembly in 1948 issued a "Call to the Churches" that stated: "Our first and deepest need is not a new organization but the renewal, or rather the rebirth of the actual churches."[22] Since then, the indissoluble connection between "unity and renewal" has been one of the constant formulas of the ecumenical line of thought, both in theory and practice. At Amsterdam it was affirmed, moreover, that unity itself is the ecumenical way to renewal.

This was not an opinion shared by all. Ernst Lange, for example, writing after the Faith and Order Conference in Louvain, 1971, said:

> [T]he controversy over the meaning of "radical renewal" deepens more and more as the ecumenical movement advances. It becomes a controversy between the "younger" churches and the old established churches . . . between the cultures in which the Christian faith has been implanted . . . between the world religions. . . . All the emerging cen-

22. Quoted in Harold E. Fey, ed., *A History of the Ecumenical Movement*, Vol. 2, 1948-1968 (London: SPCK and Philadelphia: Westminster, 1970), p. 9.

trifugal forces in the ecumenical movement produce their rival concepts of renewal.

Renewal is, therefore, to put it bluntly, a thoroughly polemical term. If the union of Christendom depends on its "radical renewal," no wonder the ecumenical movement is still undecided as to its motivations and goals.[23]

Nevertheless, there has been a strong trend throughout ecumenical history that emphasizes the strong links between the unity of the church and its renewal in the service of the human communities where the gospel of Jesus of Nazareth is preached.

The process followed by the ecumenical movement during the last century makes clear that the search for Christian unity has always been linked to the churches' renewal: liturgical, biblical, spiritual, etc. It should be underlined that, especially between the mid-1950s up to the 1980s, the renewal of the churches was related to the renewal of humankind. The connection between these two lines "is one way of describing the mission of the church."[24]

The Unity of Humankind

The concept of the unity of humankind was not, as is usually thought, a product of the 1960s, but was in use in the ecumenical movement prior to and after World War II. Only at the Fourth Assembly of the WCC in Uppsala in 1968, however, were the two poles "church" and "humankind" explicitly brought together under the common rubric of unity. Since its conference at Louvain in 1971, the relationship between the unity of the church and the unity of humankind — or as some would say, between Christian ecumenism and secular ecumenism — has been recognized by Faith and Order. The modern ecumenical movement, to be sure, began as a renaissance of Western Christianity under the impact of modern vi-

23. Ernst Lange, *And Yet It Moves: Dream and Reality of the Ecumenical Movement*, trans. Edwin Robinson (Belfast: Christian Journals and Geneva: World Council of Churches, 1979), 110.

24. John Austin Baker, "The Unity of the Church and the Renewal of Human Community," in Thomas Best, ed., *Faith and Renewal: Commission on Faith and Order; Stavangar, Norway, 1985* (Geneva: WCC Publications, 1986), 172.

NINAN KOSHY WITH JULIO DE SANTA ANA

sions of unity. The modern vision of the world, however, has awakened Christianity to the classical meaning of the word *oikoumene,* "the whole inhabited earth."

Of course, there was, and is, no such a thing as the "unity of humankind." In fact, the modern ecumenical movement emerged from an unprecedented experience of a broken humankind — world war, social suffering — and from the appeal of that experience to the Christian conscience. Although a passion behind the movement that has never completely disappeared has been an eschatological one, a vision holding the kingdom of God and humankind together, the focus on church unity and that encompassing eschatological framework have not always been brought together smoothly, even though they are both indebted to modern thought forms.[25]

It is safe to say that until the 1960s the ecumenical perception of the problem of the unity of humankind was dominated by Western experience and concepts. The paradigm of colonialism lingered for a long time. This perception was shaken profoundly by the new awareness of the pervasive and global nature of injustice, poverty, and racism. The "unity of humankind" in the sense of unity in the struggle against those worldwide evils received high priority in the Christian world and became a focus for theological attention. Within the WCC, as in other ecumenical organizations, the debates at the Uppsala Assembly in 1968 and the Faith and Order Study "Unity of the Church — Unity of Humankind" (1969-1974) typify this priority.

For the Roman Catholic Church, it was the Second Vatican Council's Dogmatic Constitution on the Church's statement that "the Church, in Christ, is in the nature of sacrament — a sign and instrument, that is, of communion with God and of unity among all men" that proved pivotal.[26] Four years after the approval of this text by the Council Fathers, the participants in the Fourth Assembly of the WCC made the following comment: "The Church is bold in speaking of itself as the sign of the coming unity of humankind."[27] In point of fact, the Roman Catholic Church's entry into

25. Bert Hoedemaker, "The Unity of Humankind," *The Ecumenical Review* 50, no. 3 (1998): 307-14.
26. *Lumen Gentium: Dogmatic Constitution on the Church* (Vatican Council II, November 21, 1964), Chap. 1 §1.
27. Norman Goodall, ed., *The Uppsala Report: Official Report of the Fourth Assembly of the World Council of Churches* (Geneva: The World Council of Churches, 1968), 17.

the ecumenical movement strengthened both the focus on the church and its link with the unity of humankind. However, the boldness of the Uppsala Assembly's declaration was neither continued nor given substance. The subsequent Faith and Order project, "The Unity of the Church and the Renewal of Human Community," can be charged with domesticating humankind by its concentration on ecclesiology.[28]

Nevertheless, new perspectives on the unity and diversity of humankind have resulted in a more realistic and more authentically global — less exclusively Western — view of the *oikoumene*. But this has not expressed itself in a coherent ecumenical theology that combines the several and various streams and interests of the whole ecumenical movement. Indeed, after the Uppsala Assembly, church-centered and liberation-centered thinking seemed more in tension than during the formative years of the World Council of Churches.[29]

The crucial point of the term "unity of humankind" is not the attempt to realize this unity at some point in history, but a consistent orientation towards this unity as the "end." Further, the unity of humankind should be understood as uniting humankind not only in its present state, but also with its complex histories of alienation, misunderstanding, hostility, and violence. In the quest for the unity of the church, issues of the unity of humankind continue to assert themselves. If they are not attended to, work for church unity will be frustrated over and over again. *The ecumenical movement is about the unity of humankind; the crucial significance of the unity of the church is based on its relation to that perspective.*

Unity in the Struggle for Justice

Another meaning of ecumenical, closely related to the foregoing, is unity in the struggle for justice. This was another important point made at the WCC's Uppsala Assembly. There is a connection between ecumenism and the unity of humanity that is based on justice. This was perceived at Uppsala as a universal, "catholic" reality that involved a concrete option for justice and peace. From the Roman Catholic point of view, Francis

28. Faith and Order Paper 151, *Church and World: The Unity of the Church and the Renewal of Human Community* (Geneva: WCC Publications, 1990).
29. Cf. Hoedemaker, op. cit.

Sullivan shows why this is so in his examination of post-conciliar ecclesiology and soteriology: "The Church is the sign and the instrument of intimate union with God and the unity of the human race. Salvation is integral, it includes a temporal dimension of peace and justice. This brings church and salvation into confrontation with global injustice. Injustice causes disunity. Indeed the major cause of the disunity of the human race at the present time is the objectively unjust situation in which relatively few people enjoy the advantages of prosperity while the great majority of the people suffer all the disadvantages of poverty."[30]

The nature of the Church and of salvation leads to a quest for the realization of justice for the sake of unity. If catholicity qualifies the cause of ecumenism, then it must tie together faith and justice.

Liberation

During the second half of the last century, different theologies were formulated — each one in its own context — that emphasized the relevance of human liberation in all its dimensions: personal, cultural, social, and political. The point was not new in ecumenical thinking. In his 1959 John R. Mott Lecture at the inaugural Assembly of the East Christian Conference (now the Christian Conference of Asia), W. A. Visser 't Hooft, then General Secretary of the WCC, gave a definition of ecumenism stressing three points:

> First, ecumenism is churches in mutual dialogue in Christ. . . . This inter-church dialogue is necessary for mutual correction and for a common discrimination of the Word of God from human words. It will lead each participating church to an increasingly deeper conversation with Jesus Christ and all the churches to a fuller knowledge of Jesus Christ as their one "common foundation" and "common criterion of truth." It will help to "purify our message and our task" and "discover a common word for the Church and the world" in our time.
>
> Second, ecumenism is liberation of the churches from an idolatrous attachment to outdated values and patterns of life which are passing away. . . . *This spiritual liberation is the path towards ecumenism.*

---

30. Francis A. Sullivan, S.J., *The Church We Believe In: One, Holy, Catholic, and Apostolic* (New York and Mahwah, NJ: Paulist Press, 1988), 133.

"*Churches imprisoned in cultural and social patterns can hardly be ecumenical;* on the other hand, churches which stand on their feet naturally seek to establish fellowship with each other."

Third, this spiritual liberation *from* the bygone world and its idols is liberation *for* a new Christ-centred involvement in the emerging . . . world, with a view to its renewal in Christ. In the Bible, "freedom in Christ is to be available for the work of Christ in the world."[31]

A Dialogue of Cultures

While recognizing ecumenism as a dialogue among churches in Christ, Philip Potter, General Secretary of the WCC, 1972-1984, moves beyond those limits and envisions the ecumenical movement as a universal dialogue of cultures. The theology of the *oikoumene* challenges us to see the whole world as the house of God. Potter affirmed that the ecumenical movement is "the means by which the churches which form the house, the *oikos* of God, are seeking so to live and witness before all peoples that the whole oikoumene may become the *oikos* of God through the crucified and risen Christ in the power of the life-giving Spirit."[32]

The ecumenical movement is a movement engaged in dialogue, striving for mutual understanding, mutual correction, and reconciliation between human cultures. The plurality of cultures, in the perspective of the ecumenical movement, does not mean simply "many cultures." The question of plurality is a question of interrelationships between multiple realities. The ecumenical movement, in the name of Christ, invites all cultures to a common dialogue with the intention of fulfilling a vision marked by unity. This seems to be particularly urgent today as the world is threatened by various ideologies that are permeating the cultures of humanity, using the name of "God."[33]

31. M. M. Thomas, "Ecumenism in Asia: An Assessment," in Ans J. van der Bent, ed., *Voices of Unity: Essays in Honour of Willem Adolf Visser 't Hooft on the Occasion of His 80th Birthday* (Geneva: WCC Publications, 1981), 92-93. Quoted material is from Visser 't Hooft, *A Decisive Hour for the Christian Mission* (London, 1960), 46-71. Emphasis added.

32. David Gill, ed., *Gathered for Life: Official Report, VI Assembly World Council of Churches, Vancouver, Canada 24 July–10 August, 1983* (Geneva: WCC Publications, 1983), 197.

33. Kosuke Koyama, "The Ecumenical Movement in the Dialogue of Cultures," in Pauline Webb, ed., *Faith and Faithfulness* (Geneva: WCC Publications, 1984), 47-51.

An Ecumenical Social Ethics

It is now appropriate to consider the issue of an ecumenical social ethics. Lewis Mudge[34] has written that an attempt to see ecclesiology and ethics together has, in ecumenical circles, produced talk of a new paradigm, one in which the unity of the church is seen as inexplicable apart from God's work in the world, and in which the meaning of the human journey is thought to be adequately signified only in the church's *koinonia* or communion. In the oft-quoted expression of Stanley Hauerwas, "[t]he church does not *have* social ethic; the church *is* a social ethic."[35] This also applies to the ecumenical movement. Duncan Forrester has written: "From its beginnings the modern ecumenical movement has wrestled with the relation between ethics and the being and unity of the church. There has been a steady conviction that there *is* a relationship, but spelling out what it is has continued to prove difficult and controversial. Some people have felt that the only way to progress towards unity is either to set aside ethical concerns, which are so often divisive among Christians, or at least to pursue the two quests independently of one another. Others have found in ethical struggles a new and vital experience of unity and solidarity, even of what it means to be the church, or new and challenging ethical insights emerging from the work of the ecumenical movement and the new experiences of unity that this has brought."[36]

Churches cannot live effectively in solidarity with the suffering when they are themselves divided. *Costly Commitment* puts the issue before us with unmistakable and unavoidable clarity: "Is it enough to say that, if a church is not engaging responsibly with the ethical issues of its day, it is not being fully church? Must we also not say: if the churches are not engaging these ethical issues *together*, then *none of them individually is being fully church?*"[37]

34. Lewis S. Mudge, "Ecclesiology and Ethics in Current Ecumenical Debate," *The Ecumenical Review* 48, no. 1 (January 1996): 11-27.

35. Stanley Hauerwas, "Remembering as a Moral Task" (1981), reprinted in John Berkman and Michael Cartwright, eds., *The Hauerwas Reader* (Durham, NC: Duke University Press, 2001), 341. Mudge also makes reference to Hauerwas, *The Peaceable Kingdom* (Notre Dame, IN: University of Notre Dame Press, 1983 and London: SCM Press, 1984), 99.

36. Duncan Forrester, *The True Church and Morality: Reflections on Ecclesiology and Ethics* (Geneva: WCC Publications, 1997), 27.

37. Thomas F. Best and Martin Robra, eds., *Costly Commitment: Ecclesiology and Ethics* (Geneva: WCC Publications, 1995), 64.

Lewis Mudge takes this discussion on ecclesiology and ethics in the ecumenical movement to the concept of *koinonia*. He points out that the Fifth World Conference on Faith and Order (Santiago de Compostela, Spain, 1993) used *koinonia* as the key term for grasping what *oikoumene* currently means.

> The term denotes a living-together which shares a certain spiritual *substance*, a common rootage in some particular religio-cultural "thickness." . . . We experience various forms of this koinonīa in our different confessions and communions. Our problem is that the comprehensive oikoumene of God, to which our existing forms of koinonīa point, remains a prophetic vision expressed in theological concepts, in various common activities, in certain more or less bureaucratic institutions. These ideas, activities and institutions represent the ecumenical vision in the world. So to speak, they mark it, hold a place open for it. But they are not yet the *substance* of it. The comprehensive oikoumene of God does not yet exist in the world with the kind of tradition and substance and "thickness" that can truly form people ecclesially and morally. Yet there are anticipations of this ecumenical koinonīa. The *nearness* of the comprehensive, inclusive communion which is God's will has been palpable during many ecumenical events.[38]

A Wider Ecumenism

More than two decades ago, Stanley J. Samartha wrote that the nature of the Christian obligation is becoming more complex in an increasingly religiously pluralistic world. "Some of the important issues in this connection are the content and practice of mission, the nature of Christian universalism in situations of pluralism and the purpose of dialogue among people of living faiths."[39] He also said that the time has come to search for a "new style of ecumenism." With a broadening awareness of the global reality of religious pluralism and with several world organizations seeking a greater measure of

38. Cf. Lewis Mudge, op. cit., 21, 22.
39. Stanley J. Samartha, *Courage for Dialogue: Ecumenical Issues in Inter-religious Relationships* (Geneva: WCC Publications, 1981), 29.

cooperation, the spirit of our time is moving us to search for a new style in ecumenical relationships encompassing the whole of humanity, and recognizing at the same time the creative particularities of pluralism.[40]

A number of influential people in the churches hold that ecumenism now calls for a wider understanding of the church than currently held, in respect both to its mission in the contemporary world and its unity in relation to humankind as a whole. This wider understanding calls for dialogue with other religions and spiritual traditions while simultaneously incorporating the perspectives of the poor, of women, and of the oppressed. The number of persons who understand ecumenism in this wider and more comprehensive sense is increasing.

Raymondo Panikkar calls the present understanding of ecumenism "Christian ecumenism." He says: "Christian ecumenism if it is really to be ecumenical cannot be reduced to settling Christian family feuds as it were or healing old wounds. It has also to take into account the entire world situation and find the place of the religions of the world in this 'Christian economy of salvation' without an *a priori* subordination of other religions to the Christian self-understanding."[41]

This call for wider ecumenism was acknowledged in the discussions that took place within the WCC while its document on "Towards a Common Understanding and Vision of the World Council of Churches" (CUV) was being prepared. "More recently, a growing number of voices from the churches, especially in Asia but also in Latin America, have spoken of the need for a 'wider ecumenism' or 'macro-ecumenism' — an understanding which would open the ecumenical movement to other religions and cultural traditions beyond the Christian community."[42]

The CUV document raises several questions in relation to this concept of wider ecumenism: "What is the meaning and the purpose of this movement? Who are its subjects? What are its goals and methods or forms of action? What is the source of the dynamic which warrants speaking of the 'ecumenical movement' beyond its institutional manifestations in the WCC and elsewhere?"[43]

40. Ibid., 34.

41. Raymondo Panikkar, "Towards an Ecumenical Ecumenism," *Journal of Ecumenical Studies* (Fall 1982): 764-65.

42. "Towards a Common Understanding and Vision of the World Council of Churches" (Geneva: World Council of Churches, 1997), §2.6.

43. Ibid., §2.7.

Wesley Ariarajah has taken up the issue:

At the global level, there is an increasing recognition that the world's problems are not Christian problems requiring Christian answers, but human problems that must be addressed together by all human beings. We know that whether it is the issue of justice, peace, human rights or the destruction of the environment, we need to work across boundaries of religions, nations and cultures. . . . So the issue of "how ecumenical 'ecumenical' should be" is no longer a question of semantics or inclusion; it is a theological question. It has to do with a reassessment of our understanding of God, of the scope of God's saving work, and of the agents of God's mission. Such reflections necessarily affect our present understandings of the mystery of the incarnation and the being and meaning of the church as the body of Christ.[44]

In terms of our present discussions on ecumenical social ethics, it also raises questions about our understanding of what is ecumenical and who constitute the ecumenical movement.

About forty years ago, Hans Ruedi Weber offered some reflections on "ecumenical" that are still relevant: "The Central Committee of the WCC received in 1957 a statement asking 'What is ecumenical?' We are in the midst of an ongoing process of a movement which we have come to label with the term 'ecumenical'. Because the process is still developing, the content of the term 'ecumenical' is still developing accordingly. With every new step forward old definitions must be critically reviewed and a more accurate definition must be found. . . ." And he added, "Indeed we are on the way 'Towards the Wholeness of the Ecumenical Movement' and must remain sensitive to what new generations and new developments will contribute."[45]

---

44. S. Wesley Ariarajah, "Wider Ecumenism: A Threat or a Promise?" *The Ecumenical Review* 50, no. 3 (July 1998): 327.

45. H.-R. Weber, op. cit., 40.

CHAPTER 4

Forming Frameworks That Uphold Life:
An Historical and Social-Ethical Approach

Julio de Santa Ana

As this book has already argued, the current period of accelerated economic globalization seems to be prolonging the historical crisis of meanings that first attracted the attention of 19th-century thinkers such as Edmund Husserl, Jose Ortega y Gasset, Hannah Arendt, and others. As in other crisis situations, this is a moment when the various beliefs and assumptions that formerly ensured some measure of common life-understanding for the world's cultures and peoples are being deeply questioned. In different parts of the globe, men and women, young and old, have the feeling that the certainties they held at the beginning of the 20th century, certainties that provided a basis for action and understanding their situations as human beings, are falling apart. Understandings that people have shared for decades no longer make sense. It is hard to find firm ground for efforts to promote the public good. Life seems vulnerable, fragile, and precarious. Many feel threatened by this historic process of change. They seek desperately to preserve life as it used to be. But such preservation is no longer possible. More and more people therefore realize that their views of the world need to change. They know they need new keys for interpreting what is happening around them.

In such times, human societies are challenged to reconstruct many of their beliefs, institutions, codes of coexistence, and values, as well as to reorient their conceptions of communal action. Such reconstruction and reorientation become more than mere exercises of adaptation to new circumstances. They demand the discovery of new frames of reference for personal and social life. New factors and dimensions have been added to human existence, transforming the very conditions of life. There are those, of course, who proclaim that this "new time" (*Neuzeit,* or "modernity") marks the culmination of the historic process of humanity, calling our epoch "the end of history." Francis Fukuyama first used this term, but has now retreated from it. Indeed, life does not stop, and those who are sensitive to the challenges that result from the evolving situation in our societies and cultures, strive to find a path that will help human beings, in harmony with their environment, to uphold a better quality of life for all.

It should come as no surprise when we note that, in such situations, religions and theologies have been, and continue to be, challenged to renew themselves as well. The foundations of these spiritual dimensions of life seem to remain the same, but the perception, and above all *the interpretation* of these basic human beliefs go through a process of reformulation and transformation. Those aware of the emergence of new life-contexts need to give special attention to the relationships that exist between faith and society. Transformations in this realm do not come from heaven; they happen in response to technological and other sorts of innovations, imperceptible changes and vicissitudes, long social processes, and even sudden or abrupt happenings such as terrorist attacks or natural disasters.[1] In the ecumenical movement there are some who are ready to reconsider ecumenical social ethics in the midst of circumstances like these, while others resist taking them into account in the name of preserving age-old forms of life.

Lessons from the Bible and the History of Christian Thought

The history of Christian theology helps us recall various periods when, challenged by dramatic historic developments, some Christian communities and theologians have experienced as crucial the challenge to rework the elements of faith-reflection that provide believers with a firm ground on which to follow the way of Jesus.

1. Fernand Braudel, *Civilization and Capitalism,* trans. Sian Reynolds, 3 vols. (Berkeley: University of California Press, 1992 [pb. ed.]).

Paul

The case of St. Paul is an example. Paul gave new and refreshing dimensions to the beliefs of people who had become members of the early Christian communities. His theological reflections focused on the experience of sin and grace and on the tension that exists between them. This tension led him to reflect on another: that between law and gospel. In the Epistle to the Romans, after he had developed his thought on "life in the Spirit" (Rom. 8), Paul reflected on the relations between Israel and the Gentiles according to his understanding of God's economy of salvation for the people of the *oikoumene*. He then developed his views on *ethics* (chapters 12–14). He did this fully conscious of the time in which he was living. Paul was aware of the historic *kairos* being lived through by peoples around the Mediterranean. Disturbing transformations were influencing the existence of the young Christian communities just beginning to emerge. A new interpretation of the biblical faith, taught basically by Jesus of Nazareth, was one expression of this transformative process. The relationships that had prevailed for three centuries between the communities of faith and that part of the world under Roman domination, needed to change. In Romans 12, Paul began his reflections on ethics. He told the followers of Jesus: "do not be conformed to this world." In other words, do not adjust to the structures of this world. He went on to urge them to renew their minds and offer their bodies as a living sacrifice: thus fulfilling the will of God. This was a clear proposal for change! Paul's argument implied a question: what could Christians contribute to renewing the existing social order? Using symbols that were accepted by "official" historians of Rome, he affirmed that the transformation he was talking about meant building a communitarian *framework* that would ensure the practice of genuine love (Rom. 12:9). For this purpose he offered the image of the body of Christ. Even more, these communities should urge people to avoid resentment: "Do not repay anyone evil for evil, but take thought for what is noble in the sight of all" (12:17), to which he added: "Do not be overcome by evil, but overcome evil with good" (12:21). "Good" for Paul meant to live in grace and love; to live "in the Spirit" (Rom. 8:9-27).

Paul was clever enough to realize that, maintaining such a communitarian radicalism, the very existence of such new communities would be under threat from the power of Rome. Therefore, this new framework for upholding life needed stronger elements of external reference; among them a recognition of the authority and function of responsible govern-ment: "Let every person be subject to the governing authorities," Paul wrote. And then he made a surprising affirmation: "For there is no author-ity except from God, and those authorities that exist have been instituted by God." He continued to develop this reflection: "For rulers are not a ter-ror to good conduct, but to bad" (Rom. 13:3). One of the several faces of Paul, in this case his status as Roman citizen, came to expression at this point. Yes, Christians have to do good, to pay taxes, to submit to the gov-ernment "not only because of wrath but also because of conscience" (Rom. 13:5) "for the authorities are God's servants, busy with this very thing" (Rom. 13:6). The framework within which the fragile and socially weak early Christian communities could continue following the way of Jesus of Nazareth did not mean *for Paul* that life in visionary "grassroots commu-nities" could replace the Roman order. Instead, the prevailing political and juridical order, in Paul's view, ensured the preaching of the gospel.

But such interacting frameworks (community organization, Roman authorities, Roman law, etc.) were not sufficient in themselves. The most important thing was "to love one another," because "love is the fulfilling of the law" (Rom. 13:10). Following this Paul wrote: "Besides this, you know what time *(kairōn)* it is, how it is now the moment for you to wake from sleep. For salvation is nearer to us than when we became believers; the night is far gone, the day is near. Let us lay aside the works of darkness and put on the armor of light" (Rom. 13:11-12).

For Paul there were also other institutions needed as frames of refer-ence for Christian life: the family, and above all the wider, organized Chris-tian community. With the evolution of the critical historic process of the Roman *oikoumene,* other New Testament writers proposed other frame-works to be considered by believers. This is neither the moment nor the place to discuss such other proposals, each of which had its own contextual validity. At this point, our interest is to indicate that, when human societies experience radical historic transformations, such changes, in one way or another, impact the beliefs, symbols, and interpretations of religious com-munities and not only Christian ones! It seems imperative then, in every age, to construct or reconstruct frames of life that enable people to con-tinue "on the way."

Augustine and Chrysostom

A few centuries after Paul, when Christianity had been incorporated into the Roman Empire across the whole Mediterranean world, St. Augustine in the West and St. Chrysostom in the East were deeply concerned with the need to give fresh interpretations of the relationships between God's believing people and an empire now living under changed conditions. In the West, Alaric's troops had invaded Rome in 410 C.E. In the East, the growing power of the Byzantine authorities was creating the risk that the Christian faith could become an instrument of political domination. The arguments offered by these two theologians were not the same. Contextual conditions account for many of the differences. Augustine, whose insight perceived that the Western Roman Empire was falling to pieces, reflected on this process in *The City of God*.[2] In this book the Bishop of Hippo opposed the *civitas Dei* to the *civitas terrena*. He affirmed that, in history, they cannot be separated. The main challenge he faced was this: how could Christianity continue to be alive, on the way, in spite of the decline and fragmentation of the Western Roman Empire? Here we need to recall that after the Decree of Milan (313) — and the controversies concerning it that followed among Roman authorities — the ideological formulation of Eusebius of Caesarea became the official view of the relationships between the Roman State (both in the West and East) and the Christian church. By the end of the 4th century the marriage between these two institutions had been consummated. Thereafter, there was a real danger that the fall of the Roman Empire would correspondingly impact the life of the church. St. Augustine felt a challenge to respond to questions about the reinforcement, and even the survival, of the church in the light of the dramatic changes happening in his time. His main concern was not the survival of Rome. In his book he describes the heavenly city in contrast to, but interacting with, the earthly city. From this it is clear that what he had in mind was that, in and through the church, according to his understanding of the Christian faith, Roman society (where churches were very much present) would continue to have the necessary institutional *framework* (perhaps even the basis!) for sustaining life. The church, in Augustine's view, was a figure of, and model for, human society as intended by God.

2. St. Augustine, *The City of God*, ed. J. E. Rotelle, *The Works of St. Augustine: A Translation for the 21st Century* (New York: New City Press, 1990-), 1.6-7.

This understanding of frameworks for upholding life was not given to Augustine by revelation. Rather, it was a construction based on his own reflection. A similar thing happened, from a different perspective, to St. Chrysostom. On the Eastern side of the Empire, the challenge was to see how the church could avoid falling captive to Byzantine power. As Patriarch of Byzantium, Chrysostom confronted the vested interests of the different political parties active in the powerful galaxy of that part of the Roman Empire. The option he chose was clear: the church should work to ensure a life with dignity for the poor and the underprivileged, classes not respected by the existing powers. According to him, the church was called to construct a network of institutions to take care of the victims of social injustice. This led Chrysostom to consider the organization of social assistance centered around orphanages, houses for the poor, hospitals, hospices, schools, and so on.[3] Such social radicalism was not tolerated by the Byzantine court: Chrysostom was twice obliged to go into exile. He died a martyr during the second exile. Most surely, his particular, contextual, proposals for the construction of frameworks for social care would not be adequate for today's societies. But no one can deny that his intention was motivated by deep Christian love and responsibility. And it must be said that the institutions created in *Chrysostom's* time to sustain the victims of social injustice continue to play a role among deprived people in that part of the world today. We may think they are anachronistic, not responding to the imperatives of our own time. Nevertheless they still provided a service *(diakonīa)* to those lacking a decent and satisfactory life in the 5th century.

The situation in Western Europe following the death of Augustine was characterized by fragmentation and increasing social differentiation. The East continued under the control of the Byzantine Empire. In Western Europe, by the end of the 12th and the beginning of the 13th centuries, further changes began to take place. In this context we should consider St. Thomas Aquinas. He taught theology at a time when great demographic transformations were taking place in central and Western Europe. For one thing, the population there almost doubled in less than sixty years.[4] As

3. Demetrios J. Constantelos, *Byzantine Philanthropy and Social Welfare* (New Brunswick: Rutgers University Press, 1968; rev. ed. 1991), 43-65.

4. Statistical data from Amedeo Molnar in Jean Gonnet and Amedeo Molnar, *Les Vaudois au Moyen Age* (Turin: Ed. Claudiana, 1974), Vol. 1, 18.

usually happens, population growth went hand in hand with an increase in the number of the poor. A variety of movements emerged within Christian circles as expressions of, and responses to, the claims of the dispossessed: the Waldenses, the Humiliati, the Franciscans, the poor of Lombardy, are some examples. Some Christians became aware of the need to care for these "other" people, an awareness that had already arisen in eastern Christianity.

And there was another important element of change. Islam, by that time the most dynamic religious movement in the Mediterranean region, had gained an overwhelming influence in southern Europe. Muslims dominated North Africa and were influential in the south of Spain and Portugal. They continually threatened the Byzantine Empire. Moreover, Islamic thought, based mainly on Aristotelian philosophy, seemed more appropriate for a period of history when new technologies and new forms of trade began to develop. Western Europe (and therefore, the Latin church) was severely challenged by the faith and culture of Islam. Christianity was in a newly precarious situation, devoid of adequate means for facing this growing political and cultural power. The Augustinian pattern of thought was exhausted; it had become anachronistic.

Thomas Aquinas

By this time, as well, feudalism had taken over Western Europe and the institutional church had become one feudal actor among many. Christian feudalism as a social system was unable to compete with Islam and its institutions, above all in the development of knowledge and trade. Feudal lords, to accomplish their ends, appealed mainly to force. In this context, some Christian thinkers started to reflect on the need to overcome Augustinianism as an intellectual context for grasping the role of the church in the social order. Aristotle, so important for the articulation of Islamic thought, had also begun to be studied in Western Europe. Based on the insights that this teacher produced, theologians like Peter the Great, Peter of Lombardy, and Thomas Aquinas introduced some of the most important Aristotelian notions into Christian theology. This happened at both the level of reflection on revelation as well as that on creation and social organization. Among such notions, the concept of *natural law* played (and for Roman Catholics still plays) a major role. Aquinas found a scriptural basis (later strongly criticized by theologians of the Reformation) for the use of human reason in doing Christian theology. This newly unrestrained use of reason in theology began a general process of de-sacralization in several other fields of knowledge. A few centuries later this move provided a basis for the development of modernity and secularization. In Romans, Paul had written:

> When Gentiles, who do not possess the law, do instinctively what the law requires, these, though not having the law, are a law to themselves. *They show that what the law requires is written on their hearts,* to which their own conscience also bears witness; and their conflicting thoughts will accuse or perhaps excuse them on the day when, according to my gospel, God, through Jesus Christ, will judge the secret thoughts of all. (Rom. 2:14-16, emphasis added)

Following Aristotle, Aquinas affirmed that God created a rational world. Reason, therefore, is a privileged instrument for understanding life and organizing it. Natural law is not exactly the same as the eternal, divine Law of God. The latter, for St. Thomas, is related to the divine government of the natural world and of human societies, while the natural law is a form of participation by reasonable creatures in the process oriented by the eternal Law. This participation finds expression in the different positive laws of societies. According to this view, human beings are thereby called to collaborate with divine providence. It is God himself who instructs us by the law and who also sustains us by his grace. Grace does not suppress or deny nature, but corrects it when necessary.[5] The use of this natural law enables human beings (Christians and others) to look for the *common good* and to construct better societies. This task demands an exercise of virtues, which in turn orient the natural inclinations of human conscience to do good, to take care of one's own being and the being of others, to seek sexual union in marriage, to see to the education of children, to search for the knowledge of truth, and to develop a social life.[6] Here it is possible to perceive the relevance of the notion of "moral consciousness" in St. Thomas's system of thought: such consciousness is manifested when human actions are decided by practical reason (Aristotle's *phronesis*), gathering as much in-

5. St. Thomas Aquinas, *Summa Theologica,* Q. 90, a. 1.
6. Ibid., Q. 94, a. 2.

formation as possible (scientific knowledge, experience, moral insights, convictions, and even different opinions) in order to articulate practical and normative judgments. "Moral consciousness" participates simultaneously at the level of theoretical knowledge and at the level of practical life. It is thus able to fulfill its role in terms of both theological and natural virtues. Natural law provides human beings with sufficient and necessary instruments for organizing family life, providing for governance, making laws, and searching for knowledge. These domains are parameters, or frameworks, that help men and women find and follow the right paths for upholding life.

Martin Luther

Further important and historic changes began to take place in Western Europe beginning in the second half of the 15th century. These changes were influenced by a multitude of factors: among them the expansion of trade, developments anticipating modern science and technology, growing autonomy in the use of reason, the gradual emergence of the bourgeoisie as a dynamic and influential social class, political transformations like the centralization of power in some emerging states, relationships of Western Europeans with other cultures, the rediscovery of the thought of ancient Greeks, the impact of new inventions, and still other factors. Likewise, changes in the arenas of artistic expression, social behavior, and academic life prepared conditions for a transition to a new historical situation. The bourgeoisie of Western Europe led this transformation over a period of more than three centuries. Unavoidably, Christian communities were challenged to participate in this process. Some Christians resisted the new orientations and reaffirmed traditional positions, mainly in relation to the exercise of power and political domination. Others became involved in new historic paths that involved all spheres of life: cultural, social, economic, political, and religious. Some Christian thinkers decisively furthered, in many respects, these new historic trends in social relationships, governing institutions, developments of science and technology, philosophy and theology. By the beginning of the 16th century, the reformation of the church in Western Europe had definitively begun. Martin Luther, Ulrich Zwingli, Martin Bucer, John Calvin, John Knox, Johan Heinrich Bullinger, Philip Melanchthon, and Johannes Comenius were among those who clearly influenced this new period of Western European history. All of them, in one way or another, made significant contributions to the creation of frameworks that could provide orientation to societies for the upholding of life.

The theological genius of Martin Luther highlighted the point that human beings do not effect justice by themselves. Men and women live by the grace of God. In Jesus Christ, and by Jesus Christ, we are called to live in freedom. Luther had in mind the words of St. Paul in the Epistle to the Galatians: "For freedom Christ has set us free. Stand firm, therefore, and do not submit again to a yoke of slavery" (Gal. 5:1). According to Paul's line of reflection, the freedom to which we are called is manifested in love for our neighbors: "For you were called to freedom, brothers and sisters; only do not use your freedom as an opportunity for self-indulgence, but through love become slaves to one another. For the whole law is summed up in a single commandment: 'You shall love your neighbor as yourself'" (Gal. 5:13). For Luther, Christian liberty is experienced in paradoxical terms. Following Jesus, living in the Spirit, we are servants of all, moved by love for all. At the same time, when human beings live with "love, joy, peace, patience, kindness, generosity, faithfulness, gentleness and self-control," they experience this liberty because "There is no law against such things" (Gal. 5:22-23). This liberty is the fruit of the grace given to those who live, following Jesus, "in the Spirit." To live in this way is not an obligation, but an expression of freedom. This does not mean that Christians will always be righteous and do good. According to Luther, following Paul, we are not justified by the quality of our works, but by faith. Justification by faith is thus the true foundation for ethics in Luther's thought. Human beings are not subject to the yoke of any law; they *are not obliged* to seek to be perfect. This distinguishes Luther's ethic from the scholastic ethic of the Middle Ages. Human beings are saved by God's grace: a grace that is given only by God and that can be lived freely by faith alone. We are justified by faith, not by good works. In other words: for Luther, the law, with its imperatives, is not a means to salvation. "Faith makes the person."[7] Faith is more than belief: it is also courage for action, courage to be free! However, freedom does not mean that we can do whatever we want. The house of freedom is human conscience, and conscience orients and judges our ac-

7. Martin Luther, *D. Martin Luthers Werke. Kritische Gesamtausgabe* (Weimar, 1883-), 391, 282.

tions. At this point the distance between the thought of Luther and that of the scholastic tradition, for which freedom was related to the exercise of human will *(libero arbitrio),* is evident. Luther affirmed: "Christian or evangelical freedom is therefore freedom of conscience."[8]

In a period of Western European history in which the emerging bourgeoisie claimed the right to be free, the Augustinian monk who animated the Reformation of the Western church nevertheless held, up to a certain point, conservative political positions. He was articulating theologically the world view of the new social subject, but with caution and care. He was formulating important questions: How to be free in societies dominated by strong powers? How to be free without falling into or encouraging anarchy and disorder? Luther was aware that the *corpus christianum* of the Middle Ages, that which both the Roman Church and the Emperor Charles V wanted to preserve, was in process of fragmentation and change. The peoples of Western Europe, influenced by the new *Zeitgeist,* were increasingly self-conscious about the meaning of their lives. Luther's thought made room for this self-consciousness, for the realities of this new historic context. For Luther, the preferred way to follow Jesus was no longer the monastery. The path of those who wanted to be disciples of Jesus was to be found amid the realities of the world. "This world is one of the realms where Christian liberty may be exercised; the other realm is spiritual."[9] It is in the latter realm that Christians live by the grace of God, in the liberty of the Spirit. In the worldly realm, Christians are called to fulfill their vocations through their professions. Christians must do this with respect toward the powers that have institutionalized some of the "orders of creation" that ensure that believers can witness and practice their faith: the family, political authorities, the church.

Dietrich Bonhoeffer

In the history of churches of the Lutheran confessions, interpretations of these "orders of creation" have generated hot debates. This happened when

8. Martin Luther.
9. This is a short and quick way to express the Lutheran doctrine of the Two Kingdoms. It also demonstrates the influence of Augustine on Luther, who at the start of the Reformation was an Augustinian monk.

the *"Deutsche Christen,"* who supported National Socialism in Germany between 1933 and 1945, based their interpretation on Luther's doctrine and insisted that Hitler's government should be obeyed by the church. A minority of evangelical and reform-minded people opposed that interpretation and launched the so-called "Confessing Church." Dietrich Bonhoeffer, who was deeply involved in this movement, struggled to give a different understanding to Luther's insight. In his *Ethics,* he introduced the notion of *mandates.*[10] According to Bonhoeffer, there are four mandates indicated by Jesus Christ: work, marriage, governance, and church. Human beings are called to relate to each of these spheres or structures. Bonhoeffer wrote that these mandates "are not a product of history." Nor do they manifest laws inherent in the structures of creation. He said that he spoke of "mandates" rather than of "divine orders," because the word "mandates" refers more clearly to divinely imposed tasks rather than to determinations of the nature of being. Mandates do not emerge naturally from historical contexts, but they illuminate them, contributing to the situations we experience a necessary organization: "The practice of the Christian life can be learned only under these four mandates of God." Bonhoeffer insisted — and Karl Barth applauded the martyr-theologian when he commented on this point[11] — that these mandates are, indeed, "divine . . . only because of their original and final relation to Christ." They are clearly indicated in the Bible: *labor* (Gen. 2:15), through which human beings participate in the action of creation, and *marriage,* "a great mystery" (Eph. 5:32), that enables human beings to produce "new life," entering into the will of Creator in sharing the process of creation. Furthermore, "The divine mandate of government already presupposes the mandates of work and marriage." Bonhoeffer had a rather conservative understanding of government, which "itself cannot produce life or values. It is not creative. Government maintains what has been created, *in the order that was given to the creation by God's commission*" (emphasis added). "By establishing justice, and by the power of the sword, government preserves the world for the reality of Jesus Christ. Everyone owes obedience to the government — according to the will of Christ." Finally, writing about the mandate of the church,

10. Dietrich Bonhoeffer, *Ethics,* trans. R. Krauss, C. C. West, and D. W. Stott, *Dietrich Bonhoeffer Works,* Vol. 6 (Minneapolis: Fortress Press, 2005), 68ff. Quotations from Bonhoeffer in the text of this chapter are from these pages.

11. Karl Barth, *Church Dogmatics* 3/1, trans. Geoffrey Bromiley (Edinburgh: T. & T. Clark, 1958), 194-96.

Bonhoeffer stated that it is different from the other three. "[T]he divine mandate of the church is the commission of allowing the reality of Jesus Christ to become real in proclamation, church order, and Christian life." The church is not a mandate given exclusively to Christian believers; it is extended to the whole world. It is about the eternal salvation of human beings and of creation. Mandates are necessary for men and women to obey the will of God. Through them, we are enabled to participate in the achievement of the divine will. Collaboration in God's creative work through the tasks indicated by these mandates becomes conscious action by faith in Jesus Christ. But, what about those who don't live confessing that Jesus of Nazareth is the Messiah (Christ) of God? They also experience, in different forms, the desire to give more substance to life through labor, family life, and governance. Bonhoeffer said that we, Christians, perceive "a great mystery" in the orientations and aspirations of human beings to uphold life through these mandates. Some theologians (Augustine, Thomas Aquinas, in some ways Luther, and up to a point Friedrich Schleiermacher) have thought that it is inherent in the nature of human beings to search for the fulfillment of these orders given by God. Other theologians (Calvin, Barth, Bonhoeffer) have underlined that to get involved in social action for the improvement of the conditions of labor, family, government, and church is something that human beings do in obedience to God's will, even if it is not in their nature to do so.

It is appropriate to raise the question whether this debate about orders of creation and mandates has to do with real substance, with actual forms of life, or whether it is mainly a question of semantics, strongly influenced by contextual situations, in which the theological imperative "to understand in order to affirm our faith" finds different sorts of conceptual response. The theologians mentioned above, and others too, in the end were focusing on the question of the social-ecclesial conditions needed for upholding life. They were doing this according to the dictates of conscience, never in abstract terms, and always in ways rooted in their own particular realities.

John Calvin

This was especially the case for John Calvin, the French Reformer who, from Geneva, irradiated an understanding of the content of the Christian faith that contributed to revolutionary changes in Western Europe from the 16th century onwards. We must note that Calvin's theological formulations — according to his "Note to the Readers" in the *Institutes* — were not articulated only for "those who must work hard to serve the Christian congregations to have a better doctrinal understanding of their faith." Calvin did give priority to ministers of the church in the task of theological formation. For this purpose, he focused his work in Geneva on writing commentaries on the different books of the Bible. But Calvin also said that his intention in writing the *Institutes* was to prepare and instruct those who wanted to understand Christian theology better and who could read well the Holy Scriptures "going ahead for the right way without falling out from it."[12]

So *The Institutes* were mainly addressed to the laity. In the context of the transformations that were taking place in Western Europe and in other parts of the world in the run up to the 16th century, the construction of new social structures and institutions, as well as the development of a new lifestyle in the emerging society that followed the Middle Ages and the Renaissance, the laity were called to play a crucial role. The universal priesthood of believers was one of the emphases of the Reformed confessions of Christian faith. Laymen and laywomen were called to witness to their faith and to fulfill their vocations *in the world*. As all the Reformers did, Calvin stated strongly that human beings are saved only by grace, that they are justified by faith. However, he never disqualified the theological relevance of the law. This is one point at which he developed a different understanding than Luther. Perhaps his training as a jurist and his interest in social questions, whether in France or in Geneva or in other parts of Western Europe where he was concerned that the Reformed faith be propagated, motivated him to perceive the connections between "the three uses of the Law" and different dimensions of the Christian faith.

As Augustine had done already, Calvin affirmed that human beings cannot have a "natural knowledge of God." He appealed to the notion of the "providence of God" to affirm that God keeps order in the world, negating the thought that it could be dominated by "chance, destiny or fortune." This is important: good works are not part of the way to salvation. It is God's providence that ensures that some men and some women can

12. John Calvin, *L'Institution Chretienne*, Book I (Geneva: Labor et Fides, 1955), xviii. (Not included in English editions of this work.)

JULIO DE SANTA ANA

be saved. This does not mean for the Reformer of Geneva that ethics has no importance in Christian life. Ethics is not disqualified because it is through actions and works that Christians witness to their responsibility and that they are on the way to salvation. In *The Institutes, Calvin* recognized that "natural ethics" is acceptable within the limits of earthly realities such as social order, political life, the way human beings manage family life, deal with new inventions, conduct economic activities, and so forth.[13] Through these provisions, God's "general grace is limiting the corruption of nature."

Calvin underlined the *triplex usus legis. In its first use,* the Law makes evident human moral weakness. Human creatures cannot affirm any longer that, with only our natural virtues, we can be saved. It is only by God's grace that we receive salvation. The Law calls us to repent and change our life, trusting only in God. The *second function* of the Law is to point to the moral conditions for human coexistence and how those who don't respect these conditions will be punished. This is the civil use of the law, necessary to keep a social order and without which anarchy would prevail. The *third use* is the most important: it has a theological dimension. The Law in this use makes understandable to redeemed men and women what is the will of God, what God commands us to do. Thus, the Law tells us that even in the state of salvation we must not trust ourselves in moral matters. The Law gives order to human relationships and at the same time, it calls us to practice justice. In these three dimensions, the Law guides Christians to sound social action.

To sum up, Calvin's ethical concerns are about human sanctification, social responsibility, and a pedagogy for human growth. His distinctions among the "three uses" should not make us think that these uses can be clearly and neatly isolated. They form a complex whole. Being attentive to these three uses, Christian believers can fulfill their vocations, both as disciples of Jesus Christ as well as in society. Personal commitment to do the will of God, to improve the political construction of institutions and forms of life that ensure progress of justice in society, to set limits to human greed in the economic realm, to make efforts to bring moral order to sexual life and family relationships, all these things are expressions of Cal-

13. John Calvin, *Institutes of the Christian Religion,* trans. Ford Lewis Battles, Library of Christian Classics, Vol. XX (Philadelphia: Westminster Press, 1960), Book II, Ch. 1, Paras. 4-7.

vin's ethics of responsibility. At the same time, his commitment to establish a legal code in Geneva that would not exploit the poor proved that, for him, solidarity could not be separated from the practice of a responsible life. Nevertheless, it must be remembered that Calvin's rigidity where "responsibility" was concerned often led him to emphasize "law and order" more than the care of other persons.

John Calvin did not write a treatise on "ethics." Nevertheless, his ideas on this subject — perhaps even more than his doctrinal views — were very influential in the development of the moral life and values of those societies that adhered to the Reformed faith. Millions of Reformed believers contributed decisively to processes of political and social transformation in different Western societies. Committed to bear witness to the saving grace they believed they had received, they constructed frames of reference for social action which, in spite of their unavoidable provisional and ambiguous aspects, contributed to upholding life.

Living and Reflecting in the Modern Ecumenical Movement

The history of the modern ecumenical movement is an expression of how churches and religious communities have tried to respond, in different times and places, to the challenges of situations that called them to give witness to their basic assumptions and convictions. As Chapter 2 has shown, they have made this response in multiple, even diverging, ways, yet they have recognized one another as being participants in the same movement. This is one of the paradoxes of ecumenism in our time. Local churches and communities try to make clear their response to the calling to do justice and seek reconciliation in contexts that are not the same. Inevitably, they act in different ways. But they are able in most cases to recognize one another as pursuing the same calling. This happens when, in their respective ways, they work for peace, or when they combat racism and other forms of exclusion, or when they defend and promote human rights, or when they claim that economic growth must take place within the framework of a just, participatory, and sustainable society.

Contexts and Frameworks

How can we illumine this ecumenical paradox? Let us begin by making a distinction between the contexts in which we live on the one hand, and the frames of reference we devise for human action on the other. By "contexts" I mean the settings in which churches and ecumenical communities proclaim and witness to the message of the Christian gospel. By "frameworks" I mean the social constructs that churches, Christian communities, and believers think are necessary to support ways of acting that uphold life. It is a fact that we human beings do not choose where we are born or the societies to which we belong. We are projected into a world that is already there. We have to live in it as it is. This is *the context* whose structure, cultural forms and institutions condition our existence. Churches and ecumenical communities experience this unavoidable dimension of their existence. Contexts therefore influence the social thought and action of ecumenical agents. However, churches, ecumenical communities and others also feel that there is a chasm between the realities in which the churches live and the vision of a world ruled by the will of God. The reality and the vision seem incommensurable. Aiming to bring the world closer to the vision of faith, ecumenical churches and communities seek to build up social conditions that improve life. This calls for the creation of new institutions, for the introduction of new legislation to make life more just, for reaffirming old values where necessary and for envisioning new ones.

Yes, contexts are there, but they can be transformed. This may be done by introducing new frames of reference for organizing human life. Such frames of reference are always provisional. The need to change frames of reference becomes urgent in situations of historic crisis, such as those we experience today. The effort to construct frames of reference for our common life is always risky. The frameworks we devise quickly become anachronistic, and new frameworks must be sought. Contexts are the places where we must walk, following the way as disciples of Jesus of Nazareth. Frameworks are the indications, the signposts, that indicate the path we must follow in order not to lose the way. Therefore, the search for the good life prompts us to analyze the contexts and the frameworks where these goals are realized. This analysis involves all sorts of aspects and dimensions of human existence on earth, from basic subsistence and reproduction of life to the organization of historical institutions (professional, ethnic, national, international) and modes of life (culture, politics, economy, community life, personal life, and so forth).

The distinction we have made between contexts and frameworks serves this process of analytical-ethical reflection. Most often, we are so much involved in action and decision-making, that it is not easy to discern what makes the difference between context and framework. Nevertheless, it belongs to ethical reflection to act on the basis of real facts and not to forget reality or fall into high-minded abstractions. Ethics is grounded on what is real, not on abstruse idealizations. Dietrich Bonhoeffer made this clear in his *Ethics*, writing that we must approach this realm of life with "simplicity" and "wisdom." It must be recognized, at this point, that the real world in which we live is both complex and at times self-contradictory. Nevertheless, it is decisive for us to become aware of the multiple dimensions of our concrete situations. Ethical reflection does not start with things as they should be, but with things as they are. "The person is wise who sees reality as it is, who sees into the depth of things. Only that person is wise who sees reality in God. Knowledge of reality is not just knowing external events, but seeing into the essence of things. . . . Wisdom is recognizing the significant within the factual. . . . There is no true simplicity without wisdom, and no wisdom without simplicity."[14] We must acknowledge the hard facts of our existence. Many human beings try to transform the conditions that contexts impose on their lives. They try to create new frames of reference for their lives. Doing this can create moments of high tension for human life. Other persons adjust to the conditions imposed by their contexts. Still others strive to build up new values, new structures, new institutions, new codes of behavior, with the aim of correcting injustices and social unbalances. Sometimes, change is actually brought about. For a while such change may help to improve the conditions of life. However, as we have said before, these constructions are seldom definitive. When they lose validity, still further changes in the frameworks of life become necessary.

We perceive these notions of context and framework as ingredients for a shared understanding of how globalizing developments and our aspirations for a good life are related to each other. This relationship entails not only that the existing order of things (or context) supports a certain view of, or framework for, what the human community should be like and

14. Dietrich Bonhoeffer, op. cit., 81-82.

JULIO DE SANTA ANA

what its place in the world should be. It also entails a need to assess how existing frameworks serve the purpose of sustaining life, or need to be changed for that purpose. These formulations reflect the two strains of tradition in (Christian) religious thinking: on the one hand, efforts to postulate, discover, or devise features in the structures of experience (personal, collective, historical) that uphold a good and peaceful life; on the other hand, the view that God's work and revelation must be discerned as already present in the events of history and in the acts of commitment of those who struggle for a better life for all. Each of these positions, as articulated, leads to the search for a framework for the good life, and to a need to "read" social reality in order to find there both the signs of actual processes of change and life affirmation, and the limits of existing structures for securing fairness in social relationships and the provision of basic needs for all.

Some questions must be raised here: what is the actual relationship between context and framework? How do the elements of framework actually appear in concrete situations? Do they evolve? Can we do without them? Can we change their form or content? Are frameworks by definition historically situated? Up to what point does our framework represent the *telos* of our actions? To start with, it is a mistake to identify frames of reference with static and all-encompassing conceptions of the good society. A significant breakthrough in contemporary social consciousness can be identified in the rising awareness of the value of plurality, of difference, and of the importance of public spaces for the negotiation of demands and the affirmation of rights. Faced with the experiences of terror, totalitarianism, war, dictatorships, economic oppression, all combined with the social and cultural discrimination that deeply marked the last century, people from North and South have struggled hard to ensure their survival, freedom, material well-being, and mutual recognition as human beings.

These struggles were the expression of people who wanted to change their prevailing, unbearable, situations. These people generated movements, collectives, and organizations. They managed — with different degrees of success and of wider influence — to institutionalize their demands by political and social expedients. They interpreted these processes of change as the result of struggles for liberation and salvation, not as mere instances of disorder and disobedience.

The Element of Desire

Such efforts to change our contexts are expressions of our aspirations, of our *desires*. The notion of "desire" has been extensively developed by thinkers in both East and West. They have underlined the influence of needs, appetites, preferences, and desires in the development of individual persons. Poetry and other works of the human imagination have sought to articulate this factor of desire, sometimes captivating our thinking, in ways that science could never do. One can say that we must satisfy our basic needs in order to exist. Through the satisfaction of our needs, we become increasingly aware of our preferences. But needs that create appetites and preferences are not yet desires in the philosophical sense.[15] Our desires move our very beings to seek things we see as necessary for the fulfillment of life itself. Such desires can bring satisfaction, but also pain. For Siddartha Gautama, also called "the Buddha," "the Illuminated One," human beings experience, in one way or another, a deep, unending malaise, because their visions and dreams can never be fully fulfilled. For Gautama, the deepest cause of this unease in human beings is found in the fact that we are people who *desire*. It is not possible to affirm convincingly, of course, that desires are the only causes of our pains and sorrows; Buddha also said that desires are, at the same time, both causes and effects of our human predicament.

In ancient Greece, Aristotle underlined the crucial importance of desire, whose expression, he argued, should be guided by moral virtues and by the discernment that comes from knowledge and wisdom *(sophia)*. Desires motivate human beings, either as persons or as members of the *polis*, to search for the "chief" or "highest good." The human *psyche* has, on the one side, a rational dimension, while on the other side manifests a desiring orientation. Many centuries later, at the dawn of the European enlightenment, Spinoza developed the notion of the *conatus*. He saw desire as inherent in human beings: "each thing, in itself, strives to affirm its own being." For Spinoza, desire is the manifestation of the human self in its depth.[16] Desire is the deepest expression of the human way of being: desire to af-

15. René Girard, *Les Origines de la Culture* (Paris: Desclée de Brouwer, 2004), especially 61-102.

16. Baruch Spinoza, *Ethics*, trans. Edwin Curley, *The Collected Writings of Spinoza*, Vol. 1 (Princeton: Princeton University Press, 1985), III, 6-7.

firm one's own power, thus to exist as fully as possible, and also to enjoy life as much as one can. During the 19th and 20th centuries, other Western thinkers continued to underline the importance of desire for understanding the human mind. (See also Hegel[17] and Freud.[18]) Desire thus is one of the most important expressions of human conscience. No action can be envisaged without the presence of desire. The Book of Proverbs says it in these words:

> The appetite of the lazy craves, and gets nothing,
> while the appetite of the diligent is richly supplied.
>
> (Prov. 13:4)

When we talk about desires we must avoid generalizations. Some desires are personal, others are social. Some are passionate, others search for peace and quiet enjoyment. But it is possible to affirm that the wish to construct frameworks that uphold life belongs to the category of desires with a social dimension. Now it also seems to be relevant to highlight the relationships between desires and beliefs. In many ways beliefs help shape our desires, by reorienting, correcting, or affirming them. Lack of satisfaction with what they wish for motivates some people to resist certain desires and develop their imaginations about a world in which they could fulfill their higher expectations. In order to make that possible, they must construct new frames of reference. Although building up such frameworks has not been at the heart of ecumenical social ethics, it seems that this is one of the decisive steps needed for a way ahead.

Human beings are living organisms who have given concrete proof that they are not closed in upon themselves. Nature indicates that humankind is in a stage of evolution, always open to new ventures. Living organisms search for and receive information, on the basis of which they explore paths for the further evolution of the world. Life is, in each living organism, an exercise of self-affirmation that wishes to have more life, to live better. Through this process, human beings bear witness that this sort of

17. G. F. Hegel, *Hegel's Phenomenology of Spirit,* trans. A. V. Miller (New York and Oxford: Oxford University Press, 1977), 366-69, §602-3. Cf. Alexandre Kojeve, *Introduction to the Reading of Hegel: Lectures on the Phenomenology of Spirit,* assembled by Raymond Queneau, ed. Allan Bloom, trans. James H. Nichols Jr. (New York: Basic Books, 1969).

18. Sigmund Freud, *Civilization and Its Discontents,* trans. James Strachey, The Standard Edition (New York: W. W. Norton, 1961).

wish motivates behavior. It also motivates the invention of new devices that can ensure the fulfillment of desires. Unfortunately, however, this sort of search very often puts life under threat. Human desires, seeking to affirm life, can produce unintentional effects that threaten life or harm it. There are situations in which it is difficult, if not impossible, to discern how to move forward. Our decisions are often uncertain and problematic. Our best intentions do not ensure that the best possible world can be achieved.

It is significant that such challenges are present in the thought of certain contemporary biologists. One of the most respected among them, the Chilean Humberto Maturana, wrote that the culmination of the human venture (which, for him, is human liberation — that is, the creation of conditions for living free of imposed constraints) takes place when conscious human nature encounters, in depth, expressions of human nature that are different from its own. For Maturana, this brings about an encounter of the human being with other expressions of itself: *"Conscientia ens sociale."* He adds that it is not possible to reach this level of meeting others when we try to annihilate or suppress those others, particularly when they do not live or think as we do. To follow the line of suppressing the other is "the way of war," which for Maturana has multiple painful dimensions. "The way of freedom is the creation of circumstances that liberate in the social being his or her deepest impulses of solidarity with no matter whom among other human beings."[19] Creation of "liberating circumstances" is not possible unless human beings experience a strong desire to move towards freedom. Nevertheless, for Maturana, human consciousness can lose itself on the road to freedom; often, taking that way, we become oppressive and destructive.

How can we move to uphold life (that is, seek "liberation") and yet avoid getting lost in the labyrinth of the diversity of our desires that, unfortunately, often move us to behave in ways that lead to destruction and even death? Another biologist, the Australian Charles Birch, who has been one of the leading thinkers in ecumenical social ethics for the last 30 years, reminds us that the Nobel Prize physicist Erwin Schrodinger wrote a book in 1944 with the title *What Is Life?* He offered two themes: "order from disorder" and "order from order." The first emphasized that life feeds on neg-

---

19. Humberto Maturana y Francisco Varela, *El Árbol del Conocimiento* (Santiago de Chile: Ed. Universitaria, 1984), xvi.

ative entropy. This is a way of saying that whereas the universe as a whole is becoming less ordered (positive entropy) life creates greater order (negative entropy). Schrodinger's second principle, or "order from order," is about "how information raises a series of big questions."[20] The history of humankind is full of experiences that show that human beings do not face these big questions concerning their existence. Or, that they do so in such a way that their responses to these challenges are already biased, moving human beings, communities, and societies onto wrong paths. What matters for our present reflection is that our intention or interest in responding to such challenges is always grounded in our desire to affirm life, to live better.

Consequences for Moral Formation

We now come to moral formation. The World Council of Churches a few years ago launched a discussion of this particular theme. It is urgent to give orientation to the desires and sentiments that shape the decisions we take in trying to make our actions both better and more efficacious. The theme of moral formation addresses this challenge.[21] Moral formation aims at moral growth. Education is imperative for human beings who want to be grown up, to become adults. Each human being has a potential that can be developed. Moral formation tries to develop this potential. In the age of the pre-Socratic thinkers of ancient Greece, Pindar told the young people of Athens: "Become who you are." These words were recalled by Nietzsche as the culture of the 19th century neared collapse. We are living beings who always wish to enjoy more life. Unfortunately, we often dilute our possibilities, or use them in ways that do not help to uphold life as it could be. When some of us become aware of this, or when we perceive that we are losing the way, we need to reorient our actions so as to go on trying to be who we can be. This includes building pedagogical processes that will help us grow as human beings. A society's provision for moral formation is thus one of the frameworks that help to make life better, that help to fulfill it.

20. Charles Birch, *Biology and the Riddle of Life* (Sidney: University of South Wales Press, 1999), chap. 1.
21. Duncan Forrester, *The True Church and Morality: Reflections on Ecclesiology and Ethics* (Geneva: WCC Publications, 1997).

Throughout human history, different peoples of the "whole inhabited earth" *(oikoumene)* have tried to build up such frameworks to help them achieve, even provisionally, at least enough stability to develop their moral potential. One clear example of such a framework is *the family.* While it is not our purpose here to consider the whole shape or form of human parenthood, it is important now to recognize that "the family" is the place where we begin to learn and come of age. It is one of the most important institutions that contribute to moral growth. Jesus of Nazareth highlighted this dimension of human life. This point is clearly made in Mark 10:1-12, and also in Matthew 19:1-9. Some Pharisees came and tried to test Jesus on the topic of divorce: "Is it lawful for a man to divorce his wife?" Jesus responded by asking his questioners to remember what Moses had taught about divorce. The Pharisees' answer was right, according to the letter of the Torah. But Jesus immediately gave a deeper meaning to their question, saying: "Because of your hardness of heart Moses wrote this commandment for you. But, from the beginning of creation, 'God made them male and female. For this reason a man shall leave his father and mother' and be joined to his wife, and the two shall become one flesh.' So they are no longer two, but one flesh. Therefore whom God has joined together, let no one separate." Later, talking to his disciples, Jesus radicalized his position: "Whoever divorces his wife and marries another commits adultery against her, and if she divorces her husband and marries another, she commits adultery." Eric Fuchs, who taught ethics at the Faculty of Theology of the University of Geneva, interprets this passage as Jesus' challenge to each human being who, at a certain moment of his or her life, must prove that he or she has come of age.[22] The couple forms a new family. This institution is, then, part of the framework that contributes to the moral formation of parents and children.

Other parts of the New Testament move in the same direction. For example, in the Epistle to the Ephesians it is written: "We must no longer be children, tossed to and fro and blown about by every wind of doctrine, by people's trickery, by their craftiness in deceitful scheming. But speaking the truth in love, we must grow up in every way into him who is the head, into Christ (that is, Messiah), from whom the whole body, joined and knit together by every ligament with which it is equipped, as each part is working properly, promotes the body's growth in building itself up in love"

22. Eric Fuchs, *Le Désir et la Tendresse* (Geneva: Labor et Fides, 1989).

(4:14-16). With a poetic tone, the Epistle to the Colossians agrees: "we have not ceased praying for you and asking that you may be filled with the knowledge of God's will in all spiritual wisdom and understanding, so that you may lead lives worthy of the Lord, fully pleasing to him, as you bear fruit in every good work as you grow in the knowledge of God" (Col. 1:9-10). This kind of formation is more than a matter of "spirituality": it is sustained by the creation of instances (cultural settings and values, structures, institutions, legal orders, artifacts that contribute to healthy human relationships, communities of moral support, and so on) that are not "natural" in themselves. Rather, they are products of human imagination and creativity that aim at upholding life.

Seeking a Better Life in the Midst of Our Inner Conflicts: The Risk of Doing Harm

How can we be faithful to God, the creator and animator of life, when we try to place the signposts that can help direct and sustain our actions toward a better life? In spite of our best intentions, nothing ensures that what we do will help resolve the conflicts inherent in human existence or respond to the deep questions that persist within society. Not even the decision to follow Jesus, or the inspiration that he gives us, will save us from doubt and anxiety. Dietrich Bonhoeffer made clear that nobody can prove what is the will of God on the basis of his or her own resources. In moments of moral decision-making, we are inspired by the life of the son of Mary, but we also feel that we are very vulnerable in the face of the contradictions and ambiguities of the contexts in which we live. "Possibilities and consequences will be considered carefully. In short, in order to discern what the will of God may be, the entire array of human abilities will be employed. But in all of this there will be no place for the torment of being confronted with insoluble conflicts, nor the arrogance of being able to master any conflict, nor also the enthusiastic expectation and claim of direct inspiration."[23] We are part of the dynamics of life, and these are not always moving in one and the same direction. Opposing, uneven, and even disparate trends are seen among the forces of the universe. Our human existence, either at the personal or the social level, is not exempt from these tensions.

23. Dietrich Bonhoeffer, op. cit., 324.

The words that Goethe put on the lips of Faust are well known: "There are, alas! two souls combating in my heart." It is also possible to say that in many cases there are more than two! Human beings live out the anxieties generated by the challenges of urgent problems demanding moral action. Often we feel deeply torn by having to make painful decisions. Different desires confront each other. We feel perplexed, not knowing where to go or what to do in order to make things right. The situation may become dramatic, as with the man possessed by demons in the country of the Gerasenes. He was suffering to the point where "he was always howling and bruising himself with stones. When he saw Jesus from a distance, he ran and bowed down before him; and he shouted at the top of his voice: 'What have you to do with me, Jesus, Son of the Most High God? I adjure you by God, do not torment me.' For he [Jesus] had said to him, 'Come out of the man, you unclean spirit!' Then Jesus asked him: 'What is your name?' 'My name is Legion, for we are many'" (Mark 5:1–13). The end of this narrative is well-known: Jesus liberated this man from his unclean spirits, who were then sent into a great herd of swine feeding nearby. The animals rushed over the steep bank, fell into the sea, and were drowned. The self-contradictory behavior of this man possessed by the forces of evil and disruption was clear. When Jesus arrived, the man immediately came to him. He recognized Jesus as one who could heal him. He bowed down in front of Jesus. Yet at the same moment, trying to put distance between himself and Jesus, he shouted, "I adjure you by God, do not torment me." He wanted to be healthy, and at the same time wanted to continue in his sickness. About his name, he said: "My name is Legion." He was living the human experience of being both one and another at the same time.

St. Paul also wrote in Romans of an experience which, although it was not the same as that of the man among the Gerasenes, indicated the deep complexity of human existence. He wrote about the inner conflict in our consciousness: we want to do the right thing, but we cannot escape doing the very wrong that we abhor. Even when men and women try to submit themselves consciously to the "teaching" received as revelation through generations, they cannot avoid being trapped by their orientations to act in ways that they think are inappropriate.

For we know that the law is spiritual; but I am of the flesh, sold into slavery under sin. *I do not understand my own actions.* For I do not do what I want, but I do the very thing I hate. Now if I do what I do not

81

JULIO DE SANTA ANA

want, I agree that the law is good. But in fact it is no longer I that do it, but sin that dwells within me. For I know that nothing good dwells within me, that is, in my flesh. I can will what it is right, but I cannot do it. For I do not do the good I want, but the evil I do not want is what I do. Now if I do what I do not want, it is no longer I that do it, but sin that dwells within me. So I find it to be a law that when I want to do what is good, evil lies close at hand. For I delight in the law of God in my inmost self, *but I see in my members another law at war with the law of my mind,* making me captive to the law of sin that dwells in my members. Wretched man that I am! Who will rescue me from this body of death? Thanks be to God through Jesus Christ our Lord! So then, *with my mind I am a slave to the law of God, but with my flesh I am a slave to the law of sin.* (Rom. 7:14-25, emphasis added)

The apostle to the Gentiles excelled in the exercise of his theological imagination and dialectic in order to make "understandable" to his readers what he himself confesses he does not understand, but that causes him deep distress. He perceived theologically the conflict between spirit and flesh, between *pneuma* and *sarx,* between good and bad desires, as a confrontation between law and grace. The good news brought by Jesus, Messiah of God, calls us to believe and live by faith because, in spite of our permanent failure in doing what is bad, we are forgiven, saved, and able to reorient our existence ("conversion"). What matters here is to note that Paul was aware that in his own self, mind and body, this confrontation between different, opposite, and even contradictory desires always takes place.

Reflection on this issue motivated Paul Ricoeur to write one of his most insightful books, *Oneself as Another.*[24] One of the intentions of the French philosopher was to highlight that the presence of "the other" is not only of that one who is outside of ourselves, but of the one who is also within each of us. The way that we care for the different others inside ourselves has consequences for our behavior in society. Ricoeur organized his text into a series of studies; in the last one he put a question about our being: *Toward what ontology?*[25] His view is that we, as human beings, are aware of ourselves *(ipséité),* but at the same time we recognize, with per-

24. Paul Ricoeur, *Oneself as Another,* trans. Kathleen Blamey (Chicago: University of Chicago Press, 1992).
25. Ibid., Tenth Study, "What Ontology in View?" 297-356.

plexity, that our being is manifested through multiple dimensions. The difficult problem is: how to *care for* the relationships between oneself and "the others" who are also oneself ("soi même *comme* un autre!"), and very often are in contradiction among themselves. Ricoeur reflects on "the recognition of the other" (a theme to which he has come back to again in one of his most recent writings: *The Course of Recognition*).[26]

This is a topic that has also received attention from some of the most important philosophers of the last century. For example, Heidegger, for whom the goal to achieve at the level of our moral existence is to be authentically oneself (a notion that strongly influenced the theology of Rudolf Bultmann). It is a call to be efficient and powerful at the same time. For this purpose, the self ("the existant") needs to suppress "the others" that hinder his or her fulfillment. It is a matter of conscience and discipline at the same time. It is also not to recognize "the others" that share existence with "oneself." Instead of such a militant disposition of the self against the others, Ricoeur remembers the position of Spinoza and his notion of the *conatus*. The "others" must be cared for in them, in the concrete things of our lives, as Spinoza wrote in his Ethics, "God's attributes are manifested in a clear and determined way." God is in some way present in these other(s).[27] The way that we care for ourselves (including the multiple dimensions of each of our particular beings, either as individuals or as participants in social life) is indicative of how we are disposed to treat others and the "others" with whom we share the social and the natural environment.

The problem of the orientation of our desires is always complex. Especially when our wishes involve other persons. Emmanuel Levinas was attentive to this dimension of the human being, and Ricoeur considers the Jewish philosopher's notion of *"l'altérité radical,"* radical otherness. Levinas made the point that to be open to the other is indicative of a break with the primordial egoism of the human being. "The other" challenges and threatens my own self in its vulnerability: therefore *to respond* to "the other" is unavoidable (either welcoming him or her, or rejecting his or her presence). The identity of one's own self becomes open to "the other." In some way or another the self becomes either like a host, or like a hostage,

26. Paul Ricoeur, *The Course of Recognition*, trans. David Pellauer, Institute for Human Sciences, Vienna Lecture Series (Cambridge, MA: Harvard University Press, 2005).
27. Ibid.

to the other. It is at this point that, instead of suppressing those who challenge and question us, the notions of *responsibility and solidarity* become relevant. This point will be looked at in more depth in Chapter 9. As we become aware of "the other," our own self is conscious of its presence in the world. *Présence* is a key notion in Levinas, and one that Ricoeur also recognizes as extremely important. The presence of "the other," who challenges me to respond and to care, is an enrichment of myself. To be responsible and to share who we are and what we can have (e.g., solidarity) makes human life more full, more abundant. It is not by self-affirmation that I follow this path, but rather by being attentive to the movement of the other toward myself. This disposition to be compassionate and responsible urges me to be attentive and at the service of those who, loudly, or silently, call for our service and companionship.

Again, Constructing Frameworks to Uphold Life

What is the relationship between these arguments and the construction of frames of reference to uphold life? Ricoeur says that the way to follow requires us to be aware, conscious as much as possible of our complexity. He uses the German word *Gewissen,* which indicates a praxis of reflective discernment that enables the human being to accomplish responsible works. Ricoeur, following Hegel, calls us to accept the dialectic between the acting consciousness and the judging consciousness. Very often, moved by the impulse and motivation of our action, we don't accept the verdict of our judging consciousness — or conscience — about what we have done. In other cases, our judgment has no mercy on us, reminding us of what we could have done (either as individuals or as communities), but did not. Ricoeur affirms at this point that "the 'forgiveness' that emerges from the mutual recognition of both antagonists (the 'souls that combat in our breast'), confessing the limits of their points of view and resigned to the claims of their respective partialities, indicates the authentic phenomenon of the consciousness." And, at once, he adds: "It is on the way of this recognition (reconnaissance) that takes place the criticism of the moral vision of the world."[28] Nietzsche, a few decades earlier, followed this radical line of thought about the human being: when we are challenged to make moral

28. Ibid.

84

decisions, the consciousness of the self has to be strong, responsible, and caring. It is not enough that our action aims at accepting and responding to "the other" (including our mutual environment). The upholding of life invites us to create the conditions for responsible and sharing decisions. These constructions are frameworks that human action needs in order not to lose the way: caring for oneself in our inner complexity (including such indispensable "forgiveness" among the differences that coexist within each of us and our communities and our societies), caring for "the other" whom we must welcome, listen to, and care for, and being always consciously responsible and ready to act in solidarity: these are the guidelines that we need to consider when we decide how to act in order to make a better life for all.

Some of the frames of reference needed for this purpose are: governance that administers the order that enables life to continue to grow, legal forms whose purpose is to give guidance to our social coexistence, community that contributes to our development, culture that helps us deal with the forces of the world, an organization of labor such that each human being can fulfill his or her vocation in society, a construction of artifacts (for example, markets and other economic instruments — money, financial institutions, and so forth) that contribute to the wealth of our societies; an organization of people's associations that contribute to human wealth and that monitor the administration of power. In the following chapters more attention will be given to the construction of these elements of frameworks to uphold life. Nevertheless, there is one point that must be highlighted here: the decision to construct such frames of reference cannot be imposed on others by those who feel enlightened either by their knowledge or by the power that they enjoy. Frameworks for life must not come into existence by arbitrary decisions, but rather through exchange of opinions, reflection, and the construction of transitional social contracts.

In spite of all this it needs to be said that there have been processes through which, in different situations and different historic circumstances, human beings have constructed these frames of reference for action and for life. For example, at a period of history when the peoples of Western Europe were killing each other for irrational motives, some thinkers, like Thomas Hobbes, began to develop the notion that it was morally imperative to move from "the state of nature" involving the "war of all against all" *(bellum omnium contra omnes)* towards a State of Law. At this moment, the modern nation state began to take form. Hobbes, Locke, and later Rousseau insisted on the need for social contracts. In our time, we observe that states are evolving into new forms. Few people in the world believe that this instrument of governance is unnecessary. Furthermore, as our societies look *consciously* to the future, they experience the need to develop states that care for freedom, human rights, justice, and peace. The form, role, and function of the State in our time are under intense discussion. The form chosen depends on the historic, social, and cultural conditions of each nation. The ecumenical movement and many Christian laity involved in it contributed to the development of nation states as they were reconstituted after World War II. Following this line of thought, we can also say that the construction of international organizations during the last century was a step towards the affirmation of life. Of course, these institutions as they stand are not satisfactory. But the world would lose a lot if they did not exist! Their service to the cause of peace and international stability cannot be denied.

Something similar can be said about the relevance of the family, and of the value and organization of human labor. In these and other spheres of life we continue to appreciate that, although cultures are different, we can learn from the forms of life, traditions and values of others. Unfortunately, forces and powers continue to exist that do not recognize the presence of "the other" or of other cultures and religions. Often, these forces enjoy such power that many men and women of our time are pessimistic about the future. The attitudes of such powers are in themselves a challenge to the construction or reconstruction of frames of reference that care for others' cultures, not looking at them as enemies, but as "others" who can enrich our lives. Among human constructions that play a major role today we must mention the market and the organization of financial life. Careful consideration will be given to these constructions in the following chapters. For now, our perception is that "the social contract" that gathers and keeps together most of the peoples of the world in our time is the modern global market. However, among those who participate in that market there is a growing awareness that its present situation cannot continue. On the one hand, markets demand an aggressive and competitive attitude toward others. On the other, poor nations on the periphery of the world economic system get poorer, while the rich diminish in number but get richer. Therefore, this particular frame of reference, the global market, is one that needs careful and responsible consideration.

Having said this, we have to recognize that there is also a tension between responsibility and solidarity. Ecumenical social ethics worked with both these guidelines or criteria during the 20th century. Sometimes, responsibility prevailed over solidarity, at other times the reverse was the case. The problem now is not to choose between them. It is possible to renew and refresh ecumenical social thought and action in such a way that we do not create unnecessary tensions between "the responsible self" and the solidarity that is an expression of grace, but rather make the two principles work in collaboration, amalgamated if possible. Max Weber, in a series of lectures given in Vienna in 1920 on "The Profession and Vocation of Politics,"[29] radicalized the tension between an "ethic of conviction" and an "ethic of responsibility." Today, it is clear that both convictions and responsibility are necessary to ethics. Although they are in tension, they do not contradict each other. It is a challenge to ecumenical social ethics to reflect on how to take both into account. This seems to be the way to follow in a time of increasingly plural societies and a multiplication of interreligious relationships.

Can we develop markets and systems of financial exchange that simultaneously contribute to consolidating social and political structures and avoid harming the underprivileged? Can we develop a new type of State that encourages and embodies new relationships among nations? Can we participate in the dynamics of civil society through critical dialogues with governments/states, economic corporations, and other powers? Can we approach the issue of governance by limiting the new imperial manifestations of Leviathan? These are some of the questions that challenge ecumenical social ethics in our time. In the following chapters we try to respond to specific questions — in economics, politics, and the construction of civil society — as they relate to the need to construct new frames of reference. These responses may help churches, religious communities, and ecumenically committed people not to lose the way, to do good, and to uphold life.

---

29. Max Weber, "The Profession and Vocation of Politics," in Peter Lassman and Ronald Spears, eds., *Weber: Political Writings,* Cambridge Texts in the History of Political Thought (Cambridge, UK, and New York: Cambridge University Press, 1994), 309ff.

PART II

Globalization and Its Discontents: Examining the Spheres of Economic, Political, and Civic Life

As seen in Part I, the current wave of globalization has presented new challenges for ecumenical social ethics. Living conditions have dramatically changed to those experienced three or four decades ago. The direction and progress of ecumenical thought and action are now under closer scrutiny, resulting in a loss of orientation and sharpness. So far this book has demonstrated the close connection between the gospel and ecumenical tradition and between the response to God's call and a fair (and critical) assessment of the current situation. No social ethic can afford to lose this connection.

In order to make sense of God's work among us and God's demands on us as ambassadors of Christ and stewards of creation, ecumenical social ethics must take account of and respond to the human context. This means taking action, but not without due reflection. It also means knowing how, when, and why things appear to us as they do. We must avoid idealism. Nevertheless, we are not mere detached observers of the world; we are directly involved and implicated in it. It does not then suffice and it is no longer appropriate to assume that the world is simply "out there," ready to be described and experienced. As human beings, we do not simply *see* the world, we also *tell* the world: we participate by constantly interpreting it and projecting our expectations and anxieties onto it.

So, our next step is to provide a number of entry points into our situation, by exploring the dialectic between context and framework suggested in Chapter 4. To do this we offer an analysis of present-day globalization that gives a balanced description of the complex set of dimensions and flows that define its dynamics, and evaluates its distortions and achievements in the light of our understanding of the necessary frameworks for upholding life. Globalization must be understood both in terms of its prevailing *project* (which attempts to shape every aspect of human experience according to the logic of the capitalist market) and of its countervailing forces. This is done through three main topics: the modern roots of economic globalization emergence (i.e., the *process* of globalization) — in Chapter 5; the political dimension of some current global changes — in Chapter 6; and the implications for culture and society of the tremendous impact economic and political changes have brought about — in Chapter 7.

The Modern Roots of Economic Globalization

Bob Goudzwaard with *Julio de Santa Ana*

Introduction

We have been considering, in both ecumenical and historical terms, the need for social frameworks to uphold life in all its fullness. Now we must deal with certain dynamic processes — economic, financial, and socio-cultural — emerging in the frameworks of today's global reality. These processes may either support or erode the social arrangements needed for fostering the fulfillment of life according to God's purposes.

Understanding these dynamic influences calls for an in-depth analysis of the *process of globalization*. This process has functioned in our investigation as a compass for comprehending a broad range of economic phenomena. It still functions in that way. What we are calling "globalization" has broad implications at every level of our life on this planet. The entry-point for our analysis must therefore be an attempt to go to the roots of this process. Trying to understand the process of globalization in depth brings us into several different fields of controversy. At present, globalization is seen by many as mainly an economic, technological process, charac-

An earlier working draft of this chapter was published in India as an article by the present authors under the title "Globalization and Modernity" in Ninan Koshi, ed., *Globalization: The Imperial Thrust of Modernity* (Mumbai: Vikas Adhyayan Kendra, 2002), 1-32. The authors also wish to thank Rob van Drimmelen of Brussels, Belgium, for his valuable contributions to the preparation of this chapter.

terized by the internationalization of markets and the spread of modern technologies. Other observers see globalization in far broader terms: social, cultural, environmental, psychological, or even spiritual. Closely related to this debate is the question of how far globalization is just an extension of existing (economic) processes, or a new historical phenomenon altogether. For one group of authors globalization is just a factual process for which no alternative is at hand and which therefore has to be seen as value-neutral. For another group globalization is a fully value-laden enterprise with a neo-liberal project at its heart.

In a book such as this it would be irresponsible to take *a priori* any particular position in these debates. We have to get to the heart of controversies that go back to two prior but not sufficiently well-discussed themes. The first theme concerns the understanding of globalization as a *modern* phenomenon. Its roots lie no doubt in the origins of the modern era and, in its present form, it has many modern traits. But what, exactly, is implied in words like modern, modernity, modernization? Are we speaking about facts or values, about processes or deliberate value-laden projects?

The second concerns understanding globalization as a *market-oriented* phenomenon. Markets in some form are, or have been, present in almost all human societies or cultures. Does that imply that the kind of dynamic market-mechanism that functions now in the globalizing context is of the same flesh and blood as traditional markets and so just grew out of the latter in a natural way in the course of historical events? Or is today's global market mechanism a new and deliberate artifact?

This chapter wrestles with questions such as these. First we ask why and how far the process of globalization has a distinctively modern character. We try in the second section of this chapter to analyze the historical roots of words and concepts like modern, modernity, modernization, to detect the dilemmas inherent in such terms. This is followed by an analysis of the historical process through which Western society became a "modern" society. Then we take up the phenomenon of modern markets in general, and follow this with an overview of globalization in its relationship to global markets, and especially to global financial markets. These considerations lead us to ask how far the present process of globalization evinces fully the traits we have assigned to modernity. A final section deals with concerns about all these matters that arise from the viewpoint of ecumenical ethics.

The Origins of Modernity

> Tis all in pieces, all coherence gone
> All just supply, and all Relation
> Prince, Subject, Father, Sonne are things forgot
> For every man alone thinks he hath got
> To be a Phoenix, and that then can bee
> None of that kinde, of which he is, but hee.

These lines, written in 1610 by the English poet John Donne,[1] give a vivid impression of the sense of uncertainty, and even brokenness, of life in Europe in the early 17th century. At that time, the continent was convulsed by wars between nation-states fueled, among other factors, by strong religious tensions. Both tested the sense of belonging and loyalty felt by many if not most Europeans. Uncertainty ruled, both socially and economically. The feudal system, which combined extreme forms of inequality with elements of social protection — for instance the "just supply" or price mentioned in Donne's poem — was breaking down. A young but harsh capitalism was gradually taking its place, starting from the free cities in northern Italy, France, and Flanders.

The idea of public morality was also in process of change. Machiavelli had already written his *Il Principe* and his *Discorsi*, stating that even the highest moral standards are corrupted by power in daily political practice, so that it is meaningless to bother about good intentions: results are decisive. The political and economic drive towards expansion and world-wide conquest, characteristic of the Renaissance, added to the insecurity. Stories were written about the existence of other cultures not founded on Christian principles but well-organized and stable — at least before they were conquered. Last but not least, traditional views concerning the entire physical world were coming under attack and withering in the process. Galileo, born in 1564 in Pisa, was forced by the Inquisition to deny what he had written as "contrary to the Christian belief." Galileo's findings turned the everyday certainties of simple Christians upside down. You could no longer trust your own senses when you saw the sun move up-

1. John Donne, *An Anatomie of the World; the First Anniversary,* quoted in Robert N. Bellah et al., *Habits of the Heart: Individualism and Commitment in American Life* (New York: Harper & Row, 1986), 276.

ward and go down again. Scientists too were looking for new certainty and security. Indeed, Donne was right: things were "all in pieces, all coherence gone." No wonder this was a time of shaking foundations and existential questions: What can I believe? Where do I belong? What can I know? What is good?

In recent years a shared conviction has grown among historians and philosophers that modernity can be seen as the answer society found for this 17th-century crisis. They see the period from about 1600 to 1720 as the age in which a new, modern, awareness of security and certainty appeared in Western Europe; though they differ about the precise turning point and about the identity of those who caused it.[2]

For us, such differences are of secondary importance. It is the commonly shared conclusion of scholars that before the 18th century the basis was laid for a new, rationalistic way of thinking and acting, which started from individual personhood but also had the potential for generating the notion of a parallel, mechanistic reconstruction of human society.

The basic characteristics of this emerging modernity can be summarized in the following three principles, which in many ways still shape our thinking today:

(1) *The Galileo-Descartes principle of the primacy of the mathematical method,* which implies the possibility of reducing the natural world to a series of calculated entities, which, because they are ideal, cannot be shaken. This "archimedization of nature" is directly linked to the operational or instrumental side of modernity and its fondness for mechanical metaphors.

2. Stephen Toulmin, the author of *Cosmopolis: The Hidden Agenda of Modernity* (Chicago: The University of Chicago Press, 1990), places the turning point between 1590 and 1640, when Descartes wrote his *Discourse de la Methode,* which laid the base for the rational construction of a new city of man — paving the way for the later contribution of Baruch Spinoza (1632-1677), who introduced in his *Tractatus Theologico-Politicus* the "modern" conception of intentional instrumentality in human behavior. The Dutch philosopher Hans Achterhuis in *Het rijk van de schaarste* (Baarn: Ambo, 1988) sees, however, the years around 1650 as the turning point, when Hobbes laid down in his *Leviathan* the foundation for seeing human society as a continual process of eagerness, rivalry, and acquisition. Paul Hazard (*La crise de la conscience européenne, 1680-1715* [1935]; Eng. trans., *The European Mind: The Critical Years 1680-1715,* 3 vols.; 1953), locates the turning point towards modernity between 1680 and 1715. For then John Locke formulated his great synthesis between basic freedom and equality before the law for all men.

(2) *The Hobbes-Rousseau principle of social-constructive rationality,* which starts from natural law and finds a base for a (re)construction of human society, according to the rules of the new natural sciences. This breaks down existing social reality into its simplest elements (atoms, individuals) in order to rebuild it in a creative, rational way. Here lie the foundations of the creation of the "heavenly city of 18th century philosophy" (Dawson).[3]

(3) *The Locke-Spinoza principles of human autonomous freedom and equality.* These start from the recognition of individual rights (including property), and are related to a positive appraisal of self-interest.[4] Spinoza wrote that every individual has a sovereign right to seek and take whatever he thinks useful "whether by force, cunning, entreaty or any other means."[5] He also stated in his *Theologico-Political Treatise* (1670) that life is best secured in a democracy, for "thus all men remain equals, as they were in the state of nature."

This last principle was elaborated by Immanuel Kant. In his dissertation *What Is Enlightenment?* (1784) he refers to the right of human beings to take rational decisions (they are in the state of *Mundigkeit,* i.e., "of age," and hence may "dare to think," *sapere aude*). Thus modernity and the emancipation of human beings became inseparable. Such principles found their way into constitutional formulations at the end of the 18th century (the American Declaration of Independence, the French Constitution) and into a new structuring of economic life, for which Adam Smith provided the intellectual basis.

These three stated lines of intellectual development can thus be recognized in the early origins of modernity, that is, predominantly during the time of the Enlightenment. Each had, and no doubt has, its own significance. But these directions of thought could also be combined as theoretical and practical building stones for still further developments. Two examples of such combinations illustrate this possibility.

3. Christopher Dawson, *Progress and Religion: An Historical Inquiry* (London: Sheed & Ward, 1929).

4. For a detailed critical analysis of Locke's views see Ulrich Duchrow and Franz J. Hinkelhammert, *Property for People, Not for Profit: Alternatives to the Global Tyranny of Capital* (London: Zed Books, 2004).

5. Baruch Spinoza, *Theologico-Political Treatise* (1670), in Elwes, ed., *The Chief Works of Benedict de Spinoza* (London, 1903), p. 16.

The first shows what happens with the coming of modern views of the *conquest of nations* outside the western hemisphere. The Enlightenment philosophers differ about the legitimacy of such conquest. Kant writes, not without sharpness, that visiting other nations is for Europeans equal to conquering them: "treating those countries as if they belonged to no one, so starting a process of continued oppression of the original inhabitants."[6] But Locke formulates the way out by combining the aforementioned second and the third strands of modern thinking. He chooses the inalienable right of private property and contract as his starting point. Uncultivated land, he writes, can be seen as belonging to a still empty space; people are free to start new political communities in all *vacuis locis*.[7] Of course Indians in America have a right to property: the fruits they gather and the deer they kill are theirs. But gathering and hunting do not lead by themselves to property rights in the land as such. Only the labor of cultivation does; this represents a higher step of culture. In this way, from the 17th century all the way to the 20th a rational (re)construction of society on the basis of newly established property rights could become the formal, modern legitimation of an ongoing process of colonization of the world by Western countries.

A second illustration relates to the modern idealization *of the market.* Adam Smith in his analysis of the market-phenomenon sees the market as the utmost expression of freedom and equality, the third line mentioned above, but he also sees it as well-ordered and self-regulating, the first. The market mechanism starts from individual self-interest, but has the inbuilt capacity to overcome scarcity and bring wealth to all nations, the second line. In his *Theory of Moral Sentiments* Smith wrote that nature has ordered it that way so that it keeps "in continuous motion the industry of mankind."[8]

At the time of the Enlightenment the desire to construct a better human society begins to permeate all rational and social action. This permits us to speak of the birth of a separate fourth line in modern thinking:

(4) *The Utilitarian, Benthamite line.* Jeremy Bentham is the first thinker to use a *felicific calculus* — a mathematical method — to check all

6. Immanuel Kant, *Zum Ewigen Frieden* (Towards eternal peace), 1795.

7. John Locke, *Two Treatises of Government* (Cambridge, U.K.: Cambridge University Press, 1690), Treatise II, §121.

8. Adam Smith, *The Theory of Moral Sentiments* (London, 1790), Part III, §5.1.7.

types of social reconstruction with the *adagium* of "the maximum happiness for the greatest number." In that way he relates the ordering of society to the fulfillment of human wishes as its ultimate goal.

It is important to see that any combination of these lines increases the ambivalence present in modernity. For how far can you go in the rational (re)construction of your own free (Western) society if it is built on the denial of the equality of all human beings? And, how far can you, and should you, strive for the promotion of the public good in terms of the "greatest happiness for the greatest number," if that effort violates the fundamental premise of the freedom of the individual? Bentham used the totalitarian formula of the *pan-opticum* in his proposal to create a large number of productive industry-halls in England.[9] Modernity is about freedom, equality, the organization of well-being and emancipation. Where these elements do not spontaneously fit together the modern era cannot exclude *a priori* the practice of oppression and inequality.

These deep dialectical tensions within the Enlightenment were highlighted by Adorno and Horkheimer in their *Dialectic of Enlightenment*,[10] but the ambiguity was named earlier in the first part of Goethe's *Faust* ("there are two souls combatting in my heart"). In time this ambivalence in modernity drove an intensive search for escape-routes. The hope for, and trust in, the *making of a better future* began to be fuelled by technological, economic, and intellectual achievements. Such perspectives began to provide a "roof" for the modern social edifice that held all its "walls" or lines of thought (1 through 4) together. Reflection on modernity teaches us one important lesson: modernity is not a neutral phenomenon. It appeals to values such as:

- the promotion of human rights;
- the search for democracy and emancipation in place of authoritarianism;
- the potential for creating higher standards of living.

But it is also accompanied by certain shadows:

9. Jeremy Bentham, *The Panopticum*, 1st ed., 1791.
10. Max Horkheimer and Theodor W. Adorno, *Dialectic of Enlightenment* (London: The Penguin Press, 1973).

- the risk of oppression by controlling societal mechanisms;
- the lack of respect for non-Western civilizations;
- the march into unrestrained forms of individualism.

Thus modernity is value-laden. That implies that globalization, *as far as it can be proven to be modern in its features and outlook,* should also be seen as value-laden. *This is an important conclusion, for it negates the widely held view that the process of globalization is a value-neutral process for which no alternative exists.*

Modernity and the Transition of Western Society

There is no doubt a connection between the original motives or elements of modernity that arose in the 17th century and the concrete features of Western society in the 20th and 21st. But it is a complex connection. For new ideas never steer societies simply by their own force. There is always the influence of traditional values, the geographic situation, the character and diversity of the population, the results of scientific research (in the form of inventions and technological innovations), and the original distribution of property. Last, but not least, are the enormous effects of the use of economic or political power that led to the enclosure of common land in 18th-century Great Britain, and to the European colonial empires. At least two circumstances show how the process leading toward 20th-century Western society was triggered by the power and spirit of modernity.

First, the deep influence of "ideological transfer." Hannah Arendt makes use of this notion in her books *On Revolution* and *The Human Condition,*[11] explaining how human beings, who know that they can never become absolutely free, tend to transfer what freedom they have to institutions or mechanisms like the state, the market, and the party. Indeed, only in such terms can we understand why, especially in the 18th century, the majority of Europeans started to perceive that radical changes in the political and economic orders could benefit them. Freedom and welfare became political goals that could be achieved as part of the meaning of public life.

11. Hannah Arendt, *On Revolution* (New York: The Viking Press, 1975), also *The Human Condition* (Chicago: The University of Chicago Press, 1973).

Modern political ideologies like Liberalism and Socialism contributed powerfully to the implementation of such goals.

Second, the remarkable role of faith in "progress." In the 18th century this faith was present mainly in academic circles, but later deeply influenced many more hearts and minds. The achievements of the natural sciences, the adoption of new technical devices, the small beginnings of improvement in the general standard of living, could all be seen as signs that better times were coming and that civilization was going forward. All this was paralleled by an increase in public knowledge and a seeming improvement in human qualities as such. This faith in, hope for, and love of progress began to permeate the whole of Western society in the second half of the 19th century. It suffused existing ideologies in evolutionary or revolutionary ways. In this same period, the great industrialist Andrew Carnegie wrote his *Gospel of Wealth,* a book that ends with the sentiment that peace will return fully to earth if we "obediently" follow the path of progress.[12]

After 1850, ideological transfer and dynamic faith in progress together bring about a more or less permanent change in the interpretation of modernity itself. Modernity begins from this time to function primarily as a continuous dynamic *program.* That program can be called *modernization.* A common belief of the time is that humanity can and will go forward in all aspects of life, so long as it sustains the forces of progress (technology, economy, and science), and maintains the new institutional mechanisms of modernity: free markets and democracy.

We can therefore speak of the rise of a new *ideology of modernization.* Here all four ideational lines of modern thought — the mathematical/mechanical perspective, the belief in social/rational reconstruction, the autonomous search for freedom and/or equality, and the search for common happiness — return ideologically in a dynamic, spiritual form.

This ideology of progress also paved the way for looking at society as a mechanistic or rationally ordered universe of interacting parts (*ordre et progrès,* Comte). Progress toward liberty and the fulfillment of all wants gave soul to the mechanisms of society. Thus, after about 1850, the idea of continuous societal *evolution* justifies claims for the necessary social adaptation of individuals and the contribution of all to the struggle for life. For while the idea of progress was still connected to the realm of self-made hu-

12. Andrew Carnegie, *The Gospel of Wealth and Other Timely Essays* (Cambridge, MA: Harvard University Press, 1962).

man subjectivity, the notion of evolution encompasses all aspects of the human being from the outset. Man becomes an object, compelled by history to move forward.

Before analyzing the modern market from the perspective just offered a short ethical reflection on the notions of ideology and progress as the two basic components of modernization theory may be useful.

An Ethical Comment on Ideology

The first thinker to use the term "ideology," the French reformer Destutt de Tracy, was aware of its double nature. He saw it as "the purest of all sciences" (the objective knowledge of the formation of human ideas) and as "the greatest of all arts."[13] Ideology seen as an art refers to the very possibility of forming ideas in the human mind. Destutt, as an educator, was in favor of such a pursuit, especially if the ideas of children as well as adults could be changed to the benefit of society as a whole.

This classical view of ideology brings us back to the ambivalence of modernity. Usually ideals like freedom, solidarity, truth, justice are upheld or cherished by people for their inspirational significance, their power to motivate actions. But what if these ideals become tools in the hands of others and are bent out of shape so as to effect preconceived and extrinsic social goals? Then they no longer receive their value from their spiritual backgrounds but from the ends to be achieved, or from the interests to be (pre)served. Such ideas can then become instrumentalized so as to function as moral legitimations for political actions, including totalitarian ones.

In the context of the Benthamite vision of modernity this still may look acceptable, but not so from a Christian point of view. If the word "ideology" is used and understood as J. L. Segundo did, as a way of combining people's own ideas that puts their faith to work, there is no ethical problem. All human beings think and act in such terms. But that changes if, under the instigation of a ruling ideology, the chosen goals begin to radiate ultimate meaning, becoming so absolute that only consequences count.

13. See Emmet Kennedy, *A Philosopher in the Age of Revolution: Destutt de Tracy and the Origins of Ideology* (Philadelphia: The American Philosophical Society, 1978).

Modernity does not in itself imply an adherence to one or another type of consequentialist ethics. But it is fair to say that the risk of leaning in that direction has always been present. For modernity, as we saw, rejected reliance on insecure, outside sources of meaning, and had to create meanings from within itself. Jürgen Habermas wrote, "Modernity can and will no longer borrow the criteria by which it takes its orientation from the models supplied by another epoch; *it has to create its normativity out of itself*" (italics by Habermas).[14] So the question becomes who or what steers that autonomous creation of new *normativity?* To answer such a question is to show that results are possible that conflict with the basic theonomous vision of the ecumenical movement.

An Ethical Comment on Progress

In discussing the role of progress, especially in Western society, it must never be forgotten how deep was the poverty of most people in Europe at the time of the rise of modernity and the Enlightenment. Hunger and social deprivation abounded, especially in rural France and England. Here, the average life-span was less than 40 years. People daily suffered under the power of the elite classes. So a political and economic breakthrough was urgently needed. Without the coming of modernity and the Enlightenment that breakthrough would have been unimaginable.

The struggle against economic scarcity and political inequality in Western society was, however, a mixed story. Deep forms of economic inequality arose in the new market economies. Colonialism, with all its depredations, was seen as a natural phenomenon, a kind of modern necessity. Damage to human health and the environment accompanied the Industrial Revolution from its beginnings. Global problems of poverty and environmental destruction preceded the present process of globalization. But all this took on new dimensions altogether toward the end of the 20th century. Such side-effects of modern development, on such a scale, pose an ethical question. We must now ask whether continuous economic and technological progress should ever serve as a lasting and decisive orienta-

14. Jürgen Habermas, *The Philosophical Discourse of Modernity: Twelve Lectures,* trans. F. G. Lawrence (Cambridge, MA: MIT Press and Oxford: Polity Press/Basil Blackwell, 1987), 7.

tion point for the direction of society as a whole. Only a synthetic-logical approach, resting on a very restricted and reductionist view of reality, can lead to such an ethical *a priori*. Nevertheless, such an approach is often defended today as a naturally self-evident position.

The Jewish philosopher Walter Benjamin gave an explicit comment on this issue in his *Theses on the Philosophy of History*,[15] written when Fascism was on the rise in Europe. In these theses he accused Western society of being so oriented to its own project(s) for a better future that it tended to neglect the values of the day and was therefore no longer capable of giving due recognition to the past. As a metaphor for this insight Benjamin used Paul Klee's sketch, "The Angel of History." The angel tries to bless the present and the past, but is blown away by the stormy winds of progress. So what can be done to combat the human suffering that arises as a consequence of striving for a better future? Faith in progress alone will see such suffering as unavoidable sacrifice for the sake of the modern project.

Benjamin's implicit ethical critique is important. Even more so if faith in such self-engendered progress gets the chance to crystallize in the main political and economic structures of society. For then the frameworks of society themselves begin to enforce the pursuit of progress, with all its corresponding human sacrifice. Progress then turns into a binding law for all. It asks continuously not only for physical and mental adjustments, but also for often heavy spatial-ecological ones too.

It should not be forgotten that humankind's relationship with *nature* has always been a vulnerable point in the thought and practice of modernity. In an age of deep uncertainty, as soon as security was sought and found in autonomous human reasoning, nature, almost by definition, was relegated to an inferior position in relation to the human will and intellect. Nature became a domain that could not only be explored by the human mind, but one that had to be mastered or controlled. Such exploration and mastery was seen as the principal way in which the human race could better its own condition and elevate itself. Nature thus became an object to be conquered in and through human progress — indeed nature came to be seen as empty space. This created an attitude toward nature that should trouble us. Traces of this attitude still remain today.

15. Walter Benjamin, *Über den Begriff der Geschichte in Gesammelte Schriften* (Frankfurt am Main: Suhrkamp Verlag, 1972), Part 1, p. 697; see also "Theses on the Philosophy of History," in idem, *Illuminations: Essays and Reflections* (New York: Schocken, 1969).

The supposed emptiness of nature led, as we saw, to a defense of colonial imperialism. But in the history of modernity women were also often seen as mere parts of an exploitable nature, more oriented to romantic feelings than to rational insight, and therefore in need of continuous cultivation and control by the mature male intellect. To see nature as something of intrinsic value remains difficult for the modern mind.

The Modern Market

No doubt the modern market economy is an essential manifestation of modernity and hence of the march of nations into the modern world. But what makes markets modern? Before we can discuss globalization as not only a modern, but also as a market-related phenomenon, we need to know the answer to that question.

One of the main differences between modern and traditional markets lies in the way prices for goods and services emerge. In traditional markets price is usually negotiated day-by-day. Price decisions are thus reached by parties dealing face-to-face with each other or are set by some authority or community. It is only since the end of the Renaissance period — the beginning of the modern era — that a new type of market has emerged: one in which prices are allowed to move freely.

Looking deeper into this makes clear that the modern type of market is only feasible if at least three conditions are fulfilled. The first is that a large number of participants are present on the supply-side as well as on the demand-side of the market. The second is that the potential trading partners deal with homogeneous or homogenized goods. The third condition is that they together accept only one kind of intermediary (money) as the common standard and means of exchange. These conditions are not spontaneously met in traditional societies. They require for their existence a modern setting of uniformity and homogeneity so that prices begin to take an independent course, free from the will and power of any of the individual trading partners. Only in such a setting will any difference that arises between the quantities of goods offered and of those demanded generate price-movements that lead mechanically to a new equilibrium between supply and demand. The word "mechanical" is specifically chosen because this type of market functions on the base of an in-built feed-back mechanism. Prices automatically rise when more is demanded than is offered, and they go down if the opposite is the case.

It is important to observe that such free markets only function if already existing trade-relations are first deliberately broken down into at least two separate parts. The first can be called price-supply; the second price-demand. In the modern era each part begins to stand on its own feet. The price-supply part deals with the meeting of any potential supplier with a given price (in fact the price which matches at a certain moment the total supply and the total demand in a balanced way). Sellers sell their produced goods from that moment on, not primarily to a known person but to the market itself, as to a separate social institution. On the other side of the free modern market something similar takes place: those who demand a good buy it from the market, regardless of who the supplier is. This has important cultural implications. From this time onward market-behavior no longer exists primarily in the sphere of *I-you* relationships (Buber), but enters the sphere of *I-it* relationships.

Something more needs to be added. When at the beginning of this modern process several free markets emerged it became clear that these two parts of the market can gainfully be separated from each other in place and time. You can produce for future clients elsewhere whom you do not know, and consume from these remote suppliers whom you will never meet. *The modern market therefore gradually emancipates itself from the will of the joint trading partners.* It functions seemingly autonomously! But only seemingly so — for at first sight an unimportant element of dependency remains. The market cannot function in this way without the willingness of at least some persons or institutions (such as banks) to bridge the gap in space and time. A specific money-input is needed — we call it capital — to finance the gap between the potential demand and supply.

Nevertheless, the emerging modern free markets were enthusiastically welcomed, especially by a group of academics whom we have already met: the so-called classical economists. Of course, the free market was not their invention. Long before they wrote their essays, dynamic markets had entered Western society where, alongside money, credit was introduced (in order to bridge the gap in time). We know of important and stable markets for colonial products (bridging the gap in time and space) that contributed to the enrichment of some Western European countries from the 17th century onward. What fascinated classical economists was the idea of self-regulating markets. These held a promise of being able to turn the free market into a model of rational re-construction. The economists saw them as an organizing ideal which functioned like an autonomous mechanism. This insight corresponded with the enlightened insights offered by the new equilibrium-analyses of the natural sciences. The self-regulating market was even more the economists' ideal because of its supposed inherent capability, if correctly and broadly implemented, to function in the service of a dominant political purpose: namely, to contribute to the diminution of poverty in Western society and to promote the material progress of Western countries. The new epoch of the *wealth of nations* had come.

So the deliberate project of rational *re-construction of economies* enters the story of Western society. In the free self-regulating market, economists and economically-interested politicians detected a mechanism that could lead to an increase in the supply of basic goods for the people. They were also aware that this perspective (later on called mass-production) could only be realized under one specific condition: that of a continuous cheap supply of capital, specialized labor, available land, and more advanced production technologies. This implied the need to apply the same market model to land, to labor, and to capital. Deliberately, by the abolition of guilds, support for the enclosure-movement, and the institution of holding shares in newly formed companies, artificial markets arose for all those factors of production.

The institution of factor-markets can be seen as the real and decisive act of modernization for traditional economies.[16] The institution of such factor-markets was in turn inspired by the new scientific universalism and by dreams of reconstructing the essentials of modern Western societies. This development can be seen as the starting signal for the implementation of the principles of the Industrial Revolution.

Two critical observations should be made here. First, if self-regulated markets are installed in society in the form of coherent separate domains, they will tend to grow as separate, autonomous parts, but not, as we saw already, as domains without external dependency. Enough intermediary capital, or supply of money, needs to be present or available to let them function in that way. This dependency starts from the will of the holders of

16. For a similar but more developed argument see Karl Polanyi, *The Great Transformation* (Boston: Beacon Press, 1957).

private capital, together with the creation of sufficient amounts of money by banks or by the state, to let the system function smoothly. The first traits of modern capitalism begin to become visible!

The second critical comment concerns the evolution of free markets in time. The dream of the classical economists centered upon the universal application of market principles, with wide possibilities for cost-reduction, mass-production, and the sharing of benefits by all. This economic dream presupposes a competitive climate, the closing-down of less efficient firms, an increase in the average size of production-units, and, in the end, a reduction in the number of competitors. It is the dynamic of rapid economic growth itself that eliminates full and free competition. Oligopolies and even monopolies emerge, becoming visible actors on the market scene! At first sight this looks beneficial: the realm of anonymous markets and of purely *I-it* transactions is diminishing. We should, however, not ignore the fact that these new actors are not identical to the former non-anonymous market-parties. They think and act differently because they act in a separate autonomous sphere or sector of society which has its own goals (efficiency, profit) and its own yardsticks (quantitative, financial, shareholders' value). These goals will often not correspond sufficiently with the broader distributive yardsticks of a democratic society, especially if their power accumulates and their will becomes decisive.

Globalization and the Global Market

It is now time to focus on globalization itself, especially on its intrinsic relationship to the role of modern, global markets.

"Globalization" is one of the most-used words of our time. So it is not surprising that it is described in various ways. Some examples:

- Joseph Stiglitz, in his book *Globalization and Its Discontents*,[17] uses a short-cut definition. Globalization is "the removal of barriers to free trade and the closer integration of national economies."
- Manuel Castells, in his impressive study *The Information Age: Econ-*

17. Joseph Stiglitz, *Globalization and Its Discontents* (New York: W. W. Norton and London: Allen Lane, 2002).

omy, Society and Culture,[18] puts globalization and the global market in the broader framework of the rise of a network-society.
- Barnet and Cavanagh, in their book *Global Dreams,*[19] speak of four dimensions of globalization: the rise of global information and images, the emergence of a global shopping mall (including armaments), global working places, and global financial markets.
- For the Group of Lisbon, in its report *Limits to Competition,*[20] globalization primarily relates to the rise of mega-infrastructures for world production, finance, and services, and to the emergence of world markets characterized by strong competition between mainly transnational firms.

These descriptions — the list could easily be extended — make three things clear:

(1) Globalization is seen by most authors as an interlocking process with a dynamic nature. (2) Technological and economic developments are central to the process, but always in close relationship with markets in general, and with the rapidly developing world of (global) finance in particular. (3) The definition of the globalization process is sometimes limited to market-related phenomena, but it always recognizes wider (political, social, and often cultural) connotations.

These common elements suggest at least two things. First, it is not wise to suppose from the outset that nothing new can be found in globalization. It has to be recognized that the global scene has become more than just the outworking of activities begun locally or nationally. The globe has now become a kind of platform from which world-wide economic activities are directly launched. Globalization can therefore be compared with a planetary satellite, which after being launched on the rockets of modern technologies — a common monetary system and free trade — now moves partially under its own inertial energy, in its own orbit around the world.

Second, the globalizing of markets is not a one-dimensional phenomenon. Several markets now have the whole earth as their home base. They are related to almost all kinds of goods and services, including intel-

18. Manuel Castells, *The Rise of the Network Society,* Vol. 1 of *The Information Age: Economy, Society and Culture* (Oxford and Malden, MA: Blackwell Publishers, 1996).

19. Richard J. Barnet and John Cavanagh, *Global Dreams: Imperial Corporations and the New World Order* (New York: Simon & Schuster, 1994).

20. The Group of Lisbon, *Limits to Competition* (Cambridge, MA: MIT Press, 1995).

lectual property. All the named authors furthermore mention explicitly the relatively new and important role of the *financial* markets. These form the most dynamic component of the present globalization process and often have a steering role.

In this time of accelerated globalization the growing degree of autonomy of the financial markets is both striking and fascinating. It seems as if these markets are opening a new additional sphere of autonomy in modern society. Or, to put this in the form of a question, are the global financial markets not emancipating themselves from the joint will of all actors in the real economy, including most national governments?

This is both an intriguing and an important issue. There are at least two indicators that point to a *growing dominance of financial markets over the real economy.*

First, the important role of international clearing houses. These handle the technical side of the millions of international financial transactions that take place each day. They run the books of their client-banks, archiving transactions, and compensating the international debt-positions of their clients by the amounts of their credits. The amounts involved in these transactions are enormous: Trillions of euros and dollars are transferred by them each day.[21] Clearing houses can open non-published accounts for their clients in, for instance, countries that play small financial roles in the global system. Huge amounts of international liquidity leak away like this and stay outside the domain of public control or taxation.

What matters here is that global capital today largely chooses its own taxation level. Such capital has become free, emancipated, even from the will of national states. This development has been helped by the new type of money: virtual, abstract, electronic, anonymous de-materialized, showing up and declining in fractions of time like atomic particles. The time when the majority holders of capital had specific relationships or bonds of loyalty with investments and business life in their own countries has gone. Increasingly the owners of capital look to the whole world to choose the most profitable investments. This has made the real economies of the world highly vulnerable to the whims of global capital flows. George Soros observes correctly in his study of the relationship between globalization and financial markets: "Financial global markets are inherently unstable. Instead of acting like a pendulum, financial markets have recently acted more like a

21. Denis Robert and Ernest Backes, *Révélations* (Paris: Les Arènes, 2001).

wrecking ball, knocking over one economy after another."[22] This tendency towards volatility is directly related to the whims of subjective financial expectations: "If people seek to be guided solely by the (financial) results of their actions, society becomes unstable. Financial markets are given to excesses." Soros summarizes: "It is market fundamentalism that has put financial capital into the driver's seat" (p. 20).

Second, perhaps the most important indication comes from a quite different realm, and points to the possibility of an *inner logic* which adheres to the world of money and finance. The notion of an inner logic is vulnerable and should be treated with care. But it is too important to neglect. Consider Hans Christoph Binswanger, who wrote an impressive study on the relation between "money and magic" in the light of Goethe's Faust.[23] In Faust II, Goethe, a one time finance minister of the German state of Weimar, gives us a lively picture of a magician, Faust, who, against the price of his soul, enters into a contract with Mephistopheles, the devil, who can realize all Faust's earthly wishes. Instead of the unsuccessful alchemy of gold, the successful alchemy of printed money is suggested to Faust by Mephistopheles: this to realize Faust's vision of infinite economic and technological progress. It is a magical path. It opens the possibility of a continuous growth of wealth without a corresponding increase in effort. But this newly created money changes the world like the philosopher's stone, for "by reducing the world to the quintessence of money the world becomes augmentable. It grows with economic growth." In Binswanger's interpretation of Faust's words: "The deed is everything" (*Die Tat ist alles;* cf. John 1:1). The economy gains "the transcendental character (i.e., surpassing all limits) which man formerly sought in religion." The logic of the domain of money and finance is thus infinity and control: "Money is by its nature an order for the future." This is, however, possible only if finance takes the lead in and over the real economy: "Money can be increased more quickly and easily than goods that must be laboriously obtained. The tendency is therefore first to produce money and then, lured by profit, to grant this money additional value through a corresponding expansion of imaginary demand."[24]

22. George Soros, *The Crisis of Global Capitalism: Open Society Endangered* (New York: Public Affairs, 1998), xvi.

23. Hans Christoph Binswanger, *Money and Magic: A Critique of the Modern Economy in the Light of Goethe's Faust* (Chicago: The University of Chicago Press, 1994).

24. Ibid., 89.

The parallel between Goethe's Faust and the worldwide dynamic of global enrichment and impoverishment today is striking. The world economy is now narrowly geared to the ups and downs of the financial markets and these markets set in motion the dynamics for global enrichment and global impoverishment by their selectivity in terms of short-run financial profitability. Another indication of the emancipation towards autonomy of the financial markets is that these markets have created new institutions (like derivatives, tax-free rewards, and safety-havens) and have shown their capability of promoting and feeding off neo-markets and neo-scarcities. The real economy now seems to dance to the enchanting flute-tones of a new piper who has no other horizon than that of a lust for infinite acquisition.

Money can be a wonderful servant. But it has also the hidden capacity to push this finite world and its inhabitants over the border of its limited capacities. Blinded by the new light, Faust rejects the possibility of a caring economy; he simply cannot accept "the ephemerality and frailty of earthly things."

Parallel to our critical ethical remarks on faith in progress and on the ideology of modernization we now have to add a third, more actualized, concern. It is the risk of an increasing bewitchment of society by the illusion of infiniteness maintained by these financial markets. There is an explicit lie in this perspective, because it can never remove the world's real limitations. But if this lie is believed, the illusionary growth that drives the financial markets can push the real world over the edge of its real possibilities.

If we combine this insight with the sketch given earlier of the characteristics of modern markets, we can draw the following conclusions on the place of markets in and during the present process of globalization.

(1) It is beyond doubt that globalization is a further implementation of the modern market as previously analyzed and explained. A similar growth is visible in market autonomy, but now this goes on internationally. Globalization is, however, more than an extension of self-regulating markets. For these markets are all checked by a growing dependence on capital as it functions through the markets maintained by financial institutions. *Globalization now works increasingly as a piece of coherent financially driven machinery.* It develops its own global market constellation.

(2) In this constellation, strongly oriented to global competition, international factor markets play an important role. But there are differences

between land, labor, and capital. The global capital market, as we saw, works with almost no restraint. The possibilities for investment in land and resources are also broadening; rich Western countries are eager to buy land, resources, and even so-called emission-rights in less-developed countries. But a global labor market is absent or not working. Migrant labor is present but meets often several forms of discrimination.The outsourcing of labor, which implies shifting parts of the labor-process to other countries, is increasingly seen as an efficient alternative.

(3) Remarkable too is the growing ambivalence of the nation state. On the one hand Western states use their power globally to protect the economic interests of their investors and their access to basic resources like energy. Parallel to this is the continuing strong protection by those same governments of their own markets: especially for agricultural products where high barriers continue for all imports from the South. On the other hand, many governments now feel obliged to minimize their social safety nets in order to increase the attractiveness of their economies for foreign investments. So, while we see among the richer nations the protection of vital economic interests and the growing role of the state, we also see economic globalization weakening the position of national governments. Governments become more geared to and dependent on what happens in the global and national economies.

(4) Behind all these processes and structural changes there are always actor-perspectives. Sometimes these become clearly visible. Transnational companies do not hide their intentions. They control many markets and at the same time try to set the national and international rules on trade and property for their own advantage. They merge with other companies to gain competitive strength and, in cooperation with strong banks, even try to manipulate their own share values and standards of accountancy. Next to those actors there are the still powerful roles of international money and aid institutions like the IMF and the World Bank, which surely do not work outside the direct influence of the US Treasury.[25] And there is also the role of personal action. Thousands of people work inside these structures as managing directors and financial executives. They are confronted with the risks of power-play, corruption, the secrecy of financial life and

25. See Ariel Buira, *Challenges to the World Bank and the IMF: Developing Countries' Perspectives* (London: Anthem Press, 2003), 18; also George Soros, *George Soros on Globalization* (New York: Public Affairs, 2002), 120.

transactions, and by the temptation to look at their own actions as nothing more than forms of obliged instrumentality within "given" rules — rules set by others as "normal" but which often lack any kind of ethical quality. People of faith living in such worlds may be torn between divergent loyalties.

Globalization and the Test of Modernity

In the second section of this chapter we listed the main characteristics of modernity and in the third section, those of the modernization process. Now we compare the concrete traits of globalization with these previous formulations, to see if there are the similarities between them. We use the four "lines" of modernity (1 through 4, pp. 94-97 above) as our guide and checklist.

(1) From its origin, the spirit of modernity adhered to the *mathematical-mechanical method* as the best way to obtain certainty and security. It is interesting to note how often today's globalizing world is perceived and painted in terms which remind us more of a piece of well-working machinery than a living body. Mechanisms do not register emotion or pain, they just work; it is good that they function in that way. This is evident in the global markets. A cold-hearted calculation of risks belongs to the essence of those markets. The mathematical-operational approach also shines through a word like derivatives.

In the context of the mathematical-mechanical approach it is also striking to see that the adjustment programs which the IMF designs for weaker or heavily indebted economies are still primarily formulated in terms of numerical targets, quantitative restrictions, and the use of mechanical instruments. The targets of the so-called Comprehensive Development Framework state in percentages the levels of growth, inflation, export, investments, which have to be reached, on the basis of mechanisms like devaluation, deflation, and deregulation. Globalization is thus enforced under the guidance of a clear, specific type of modernization policy.

(2) Modernity was from the beginning also characterized by a drive towards *rational social-economic (re)construction*. This drive was led by the principle, set forth by the then-new natural sciences, that reality had to be broken down into its smallest parts (numbers, atoms, individuals), before it could be rebuilt according to the rules of functional rationality. Moder-

nity, and especially modernization, has thus an intrinsic link with the project of constructing programs for a better future — preferably in empty spaces.

If we compare this drive for socio-economic reconstruction with the call for ongoing globalization, as made by international agencies and transnational businesses, we notice some similarities. Firstly there is the *adagium*, that traditional markets of course have to make room for modern ones even if the traditional markets are deeply imbedded in cultures and intertwined with existing social relationships. The vision of the globe as an empty space for joint economic action is still with us. Obviously in these programs the modern market mechanism is seen as both autonomous and culturally acceptable, and thus is allowed to cross all cultural borders. In addition traditional forms of economic participation still existing in other cultures are seen by the new global actors and institutions as hindrances to modern efficiency and transparency; and therefore to be treated as inferior to modern mechanisms.

In this mood of socio-economic restructuring there is present a typical vision of the future. It can best be described as tunnel-vision — a concept which has its origin in the thought of J. M. Keynes.[26] The tunnel metaphor stands for those economic visions in which the goal of a continuous rise in material standards of living is substituted for the perennial human longing for general well-being. In human society this goal of raising material living-standards demands that priority must always be given to efficiency, rising productivity, and rentability. This corresponds with the future-focused goals of the ideals of modernization, as criticized by Walter Benjamin. Even more surprising is that this philosophy is present in official papers, where the merits of ongoing globalization and further expansion of international trade are explained. The WTO and the IMF adhere regularly to this kind of tunnel-vision in defending their views. This is why, for instance, the IMF refuses to discuss restraints on the free movement of international capital, and why the WTO declares that the world will always need a maximum rather than an optimum flow of international trade to reach its economic needs. Only through this tunnel, itself a metaphor of construction and reconstruction, is there for these organizations the perspective of daylight.

In this context it is remarkable how often present forms of globaliza-

26. J. M Keynes, *Essays in Persuasion* (New York: Harcourt, 1932), 372.

tion are presented with the pretension that they are unavoidable: that they are social and political necessities. The WTO has implicitly accepted the expression "there is no alternative" (TINA) — originally coined by Margaret Thatcher — as its leading slogan. A similar choice has been made by Royal Dutch Shell. Any step designed to promote a market-oriented type of modernization is affirmed to be a necessity for all.

(3) Modernity from the beginning has been related to the notion of *autonomous individuality,* with a striving for equality seen as a possible restraint. Here it is striking how far the present style of globalization is permeated by the logic of autonomous will and individualistic self-determination on the part of the most important actors. The element of power and the struggle for power are so overwhelmingly present in today's globalization ideology, that the respected authors of the Group of Lisbon in its book *The Limits of Competition* speak of "a new type of war: the competitive techno-economic war for global leadership." "The new global economy," they state, "looks like a battle among economic giants where no rest or compassion is allowed to the fighters."[27] "The competitiveness of a country is now the primary concern" in a world where "competition [has become an] imperative among firms and among nations."

This combination of the autonomous use of power and the factor of competition is striking: as it has been from its beginning a combination characteristic of modernity. The first element, power, expressed the pole of individual freedom; the second element, competition, stood for the pole of the supposed institutional equality of participants in the market. At the same time, as history proves, this has been a combination that easily leads to situations of oligopoly and monopoly. And did Locke not already legitimate economic and military conquest, if it takes place in empty spaces? The market sees the world as a new, open, empty space to be exploited.

(4) In the later development of modernity, we noted also the strong utilitarian element which permits growing intervention in society so long as it can claim to serve the promotion of well-being for all (the maximum happiness for the greatest number). But we also noted how strongly this utilitarian move contributed to an ambivalence at the heart of modernity and enlightenment, in that it allows for forcing people to be free in your way, on your terms rather than theirs.

It is remarkable how this ambivalence returns in the debate on the

27. The Group of Lisbon, op. cit., xii.

nature and effects of globalization. It comes to the fore where the WTO, the IMF, and the G7 set their agendas according to their own best intentions, but are repeatedly surprised by those who reject their well-meant proposals. This begs the question if ever a Western, utilitarian calculation of the long-run benefits for others of ongoing globalization can act as sufficient reason for accepting violations of rights and freedoms. Such utilitarian calculation is even more problematic at a time when many local groups are searching for better ways of expressing themselves economically. The present crisis in global communication of goals between cultures obviously has its roots in the ambivalence of modernity itself.

These four analogies between the present pattern of globalization and the spirit of modernization are strong and clear enough for us to conclude that deep similarities exist between them. Globalization *can therefore be seen* not only as intrinsically value-laden, but *as the highest expression of modernity* till now *in human history.*

This conclusion leads to two further consequences, both related to power and the use of power. First, modernization was at least partially based on the power to include some in (colonialism), and to exclude others from, its possible benefits. If we see globalization as a new phase of modernization, then we should not be surprised that these dimensions of inclusion and exclusion are returning. The power of inclusion is, for instance, visible in the claim that all nations and economies of the world should be open, or be opened for, the forces of modernization, and should be forced to comply by detailed programs of adaptation (e.g., via the Comprehensive Development Framework of the IMF or the World Bank, or via the WTO arrangements on trade and investments). We could call this *inclusion in the dimension of breadth.*

Next to that there is *inclusion in the dimension of depth.* This comes to the fore — in the South as in the North — in the efforts to draw a growing range of segments of human culture — communications, the arts, education, sports — within the domain of globalizing technology and economy. Dan Schiller speaks of "a deepening of the market both for commercial home entertainment and education: Cyberspace itself is being rapidly colonized by the familiar workings of the market system."[28] A new cultural context is being constructed (hybridization), which has its

28. Dan Schiller, *Digital Capitalism: Networking the Global Market System* (Cambridge, MA: MIT Press), xiv.

spearhead in the fascination with endless growth and continued material progress; a message which is also spread in the hearts and minds of modern consumers.

The power of inclusion is accompanied by growing forms of *exclusion*. This implies that as soon as poor countries are included in the modern world economy they find themselves on the lowest rungs of the international ladder. For governments in the rich countries increasingly give in to the demands of their own middle-classes rather than to the interests of the world's poor. Western states continue to protect their own markets with high protective tariffs, and orient their voting at the international level primarily to their own economic interests. If the poor countries are not willing to adapt their economies to the standards of the international rich community they are either discriminated against or simply ignored. In addition, discrimination against the poor takes place through exclusive property-arrangements (patents, and intellectual property-rights primarily). The large majority of the patents in the South are in the hands of Western transnationals.

The second connotation relates to the power of capital. The expansion of the volume of capital is built on the expectations of further economic growth — especially in the already rich economies — but it also promotes and directs this growth for the sake of higher rewards for capital. It is the empirical evidence for this development itself that points toward the conclusion that a new phase has begun in the development of *capitalism*. A financially-led, globalized type of capitalism is structurally evolving, strongly supported by advanced means of electronic communication.

An Ethical Evaluation

This chapter began by speaking about globalization as a phenomenon not easy to define. This phenomenon has at least three layers that do not fully overlap:

- the spectrum of growing economic, social, and cultural *processes of interaction* around the world, for which "mondialization" may be a better word;
- the smaller layer of globalization as an outward, dynamic *project or strategy* of modernization, made possible by the instruments of tech-

nology and finance. This project bears conquering traits as well as both an inclusive and an exclusive nature;

- a more inward ideological or spiritual dimension of *faith in global progress,* which is built on trust in the tunnel perspective of an endless expansion of markets that work for the benefit of the world as a whole.

How can such a complex phenomenon be evaluated from an ecumenical, ethical point of view?

Let us start from the positive. The thesis can be defended that the process of globalization includes a whole range of world-wide economic and technological developments that not seldom have a capacity to work for the benefit of all, especially where they open up creative possibilities. If, for instance, the knowledge of how to help and cure patients grows impressively today due to an increased global exchange of medical information, this can be seen as a blessing for humankind. So what is the problem with globalization? Does its dynamic form not imply the presence of an enormous wealth-creating capacity, needed so badly in a time of growing poverty? Could such a promise be realized if that potential were combined with codes for good business behavior and a more positive appreciation of the significance of human rights?

In answering these questions we should return to the ethical comments made earlier on the prevailing attitude in modernity toward ideology and toward faith in progress. We need to see how far these comments are also valid for globalization today.

Ideology

A general globalizing ethos is present today with intentions that can often be discussed in positive terms. A globalizing ethos of this kind should in our view be distinguished from a full-grown globalization ideology. Are there visible ideological traits in globalization as it exists today? Two elements can be mentioned as possible indicators: the language used, and the degree of illusion or narrowing of mind involved.

The language aspect of the present dominant style of globalization is remarkable. Often a specific rhetoric is used which not only blesses the free market and unhampered competition, but supports turning these two factors together into a compass for the future of the whole world. "To be competitive," states the Group of Lisbon, "has ceased to be a means to an end; competitiveness has acquired the status of a universal credo, an ideology."[29]

Such an ideological choice has implications. It is interesting to see that the references made to the freedom of the market are increasingly double-faced and even hypocritical. The present process of globalization does not remind us of free markets as described in neo-classical textbooks. Even where powerful oligopolies dominate, traditional free market language is preserved, for that language provides these oligopolies with their most important ideological legitimation. The soul of neo-liberalism, with its roots in the (neo-)Austrian school of economics (Von Hayek, Schumpeter), leads this economic program. But as a by-product it creates a *"bricolage,"* as Levi-Strauss called it. A new culture is built up from the bits and pieces of what came before.

There are still more indicators in the language that point to a possible ideological content. References are often made to the sacrifices that are unavoidable if the process is to be continued. These sacrifices often take the form of employment cuts or higher costs of living for the poor, which nevertheless have to be accepted in the name of a better future for all. In practice this expected better future is built on the anticipated fruits of higher degrees of competitiveness and more freedom for capital flows. The absence of an awareness of social duties by owners of capital is thus legitimated by the argument that these sacrifices are in the long run good and economically healthy for the general public. However, this presupposes that the resulting burdens on the poor must first be rationalized as necessary sacrifices. It is a shame-blame game that hides a shifting of burdens from the strong to the weak. A similar trend can be observed in the current debt regimes for the poorest countries, where the banks and countries that profit most are those that ask the highest sacrifices from the people.

It is important to notice that the reference to sacrifices brings a (pseudo-) religious element into play. Walter Benjamin referred explicitly to those forms of suffering imposed on humankind in the name of hope for a better future. The reference to sacrifices is an undeniable sign that rationalizing ideologies are actively at work.

A second indicator of the presence of full-grown ideology in the

29. The Group of Lisbon, op. cit., Introduction.

practices of globalization is the element of illusion or fascination. A seemingly convincing type of magic often accompanies faith in the power of new technological and financial inventions. These induce a kind of fascinated fear in people's minds. Remarkable is the reference to the word "submission" *(soumission),* which is even used by respected authors who deny the characterization of globalization as a new phase in the development of capitalism. Pierre Bourdieu sees globalization first and foremost as a kind of rhetoric, but adds to it that this *rhetorique* helps governments to justify their voluntary submission to financial markets; their *soumission volontaire aux marchés financiers.*[30] The word "voluntary" gives a further impression here that a kind of fascination is present. There may be a fascination, similar to that mentioned earlier, with the notion of an endlessly growing level of production and consumption.

Fascination is a challenging phenomenon. In literature it related to forms of sacralization. As soon as power becomes visible it no longer continues to be sacred: it shifts to the profane. To avoid such de-sacralization, taboos and prohibitions are imposed on human consciousness, together with elements of hidden fear. Without these elements, without fascination, voluntary submission to globalization ideology remains inexplicable.

Here again a connection can be made with certain particular characteristics of globalization. In its *dynamistic universum* fear is overwhelmingly present as the fear of being left behind. The fear of losing foreign capital, and of what the financial markets can do to them, motivates governments to drastic fiscal measures.

Usually, modern intellectuals, politicians, and educated consumers are not expected to succumb to manipulative efforts. But as François Brune stated in *Le Monde Diplomatique* (May 2000), let us not forget how strong "the powers of fascination" are becoming in the present economy: "Be different, drink Pepsi," we read. Brune speaks of a "submission in the head," which takes place in a "fascination without ending."

These observations confirm that a strong spiritual, ideological power is present and active behind the present trend of globalization. Alain Touraine wrote about an ideology of globalization, "that considers it as a natural force reducing societies to economies, economies to markets, and markets to financial flows."[31] That force has the capacity to lead human

30. Pierre Bourdieu in *Le Monde Diplomatique* (May 2000): 6.
31. Alain Touraine, *La Globalizacion como Ideologia.* El Pais (Sept. 16, 1996), as quoted

beings into a drastic narrowing of mind and spirit. Many people are willing to accept interference in their private lives in exchange for the prospect of an increasing set of consumer attractions. Western society is, according to J. K. Galbraith, "one in which a rising standard of living has the aspect of a faith."[32]

Globalization, seen in this way, stands for a system of *seduction*. It has the power to bewitch; to lead people into forms of enslavement. Here it should be remembered that some kind of hypnosis has always been a basic component of every full-grown *consequentialist* ideology. For if an ideology becomes so strong that its goals radiate ultimate meaning, then the necessary means to realize those goals also take on a spiritual dimension. They begin to act like gods because they are seen as infallible guides to a better future.

Progress

"The global capitalist system," says George Soros, is "far from seeking equilibrium. It is hell-bent on expansion."[33] The prevailing Western view of the world stands in the perspective of a dynamic, global tunnel-vision economy with the capacity to create streams of utilities for everyone. But there is more. This *dynamis* seems now to act like a new *archimedic* point for most human activity, especially in the West. It looks as if the dynamic itself has become the new point of rest, so that speed itself stands for stability and everything that does not move at the same speed is perceived as lagging behind.

This narrowing world-view lurks behind the mainstream phenomena of globalization. It reveals itself in deep irritations among global agents about all that is static, and therefore likely to hinder the self-made dynamic process of globalization. For years a dynamic view thought to be superior has been behind such expressions as "underdeveloped," "developing," or "third-world." These terms usually refer to countries with cultures

by Manuel Castells, *The End of Millennium*, Vol. 3 of *The Information Age: Economy, Society and Culture* (Oxford and Malden, MA: Blackwell, 1998), 325.

32. John Kenneth Galbraith, *The New Industrial State* (New York: New American Library, 1968), 174.

33. George Soros, *The Crisis of Global Capitalism: Open Society Endangered* (New York: Public Affairs, 1998), 104.

older and wiser than those of the West, but regarded as inferior or lagging behind if they are measured and judged from the vantage-point of modern dynamism. This allegedly superior dynamic view of history reveals itself also when *limits to growth* are discussed. It is a standpoint from which nature is seen primarily as a hindrance; as something which places restrictions on our will to go forward. If and where this outlook on the globalizing world becomes a platform for further dynamic achievements, then everything given to us in more static forms — from the gifts of community life and cultural heritage to the factors of time and nature — is then fundamentally no longer safe. In one way or another these elements may be treated as inferior or as barriers to the realization of the new *constante:* the ever more productive, progressive economy. To be able to survive, the state itself has to become dynamic and competitive: a theme which inspired Michael Porter to write his famous book *The Competitive Advantage of Nations.*[34] Politically this leads to the tendency to see everything which in market-terms is not dynamic enough as ending up on the losing side. This new dynamic reality inevitably decides for the end of the welfare state.[35]

From this perspective we now look first at the fate under globalization of the countries and peoples of the South, and secondly at the fate of nature.

(1) From the viewpoint of the dynamics of economic progress, most of the countries of the South are seen as lagging behind: especially so if they "hinder" their own future development by prioritizing their traditional home markets (markets that are usually narrowly related to fulfilling the basic needs of their populations). For, in the prevalent globalizing view, they should give priority to developing new markets that can attract foreign capital. The tunnel-view is thus not only prescriptive for rich countries but has become the prescribed outlook for poorer ones too. What are the consequences? The resources for economic development in the South are no longer primarily geared to what is mostly needed there, but are tied to a continuous export scenario, directed toward the North.

The formula for progress under the obligations of globalization has thus become a *dynamistic* duty that is often contrary to the real interests of

---

34. Michael E. Porter, *The Competitive Advantage of Nations* (New York: The Free Press, 1990).

35. Kenichi Ohmae, *The End of the Nation State: The Rise of Regional Economies* (New York: The Free Press, 1995).

Southern Hemisphere nations. In the present globalization context they are at least partially excluded from the possibility of real progress for three reasons:

- because their economies do not have direct access to the creation of international money or liquidities. If they want these they have either to increase their exports or borrow;
- because the sale of their products is hindered by the protective barriers of the rich countries, so that even if they choose the export scenario the results are absent or disappointing;
- because their debt burdens remain so heavy that year after year official aid and free donations together amount to less than the interest and amortization which have to be paid back to the North.[36]

Progress for these nations under globalization is therefore characterized by a distributive dynamic that often makes the poor poorer as the rich get richer. Somehow the rich are simply taking what is not theirs, consuming the houses of the poor.

(2) The fate of nature. A debate is raging worldwide about *global sustainable development*. This is a terminology that might imply a recognition that future economic and technological processes should permit the enduring preservation of human life and nature, and so should obey clear restraints on the use of the environment and of all scarce resources. For it is beyond doubt that the environmental carrying-capacity of the earth is limited. And feeding the hungry in the context of a growing world population will also have a strong impact on the still available resources. The United Nations Environment Program–Global Environmental Outlook Report for 2000 states explicitly that "it is widely recognized that a tenfold reduction in resource consumption in industrialised countries is a necessary long-term target if adequate resources are to be released for the needs of developing countries."[37] A tenfold reduction in the use of resources in the industrialized countries obviously implies that the present continuous rise of income and consumption levels in those countries can no longer be seen as sustainable. But, remarkably, this is not the conclusion of the above-mentioned re-

36. The (British) Institute of International Finance estimates this deficit to amount to 35.7 billion U.S. dollars (Report of January 19, 2005).
37. UNEP-GEO 2000 Report, New York, 1999, chap. 1.

port. It is also not the conclusion of the international reports on this issue of the World Trade Organization, the IMF, the World Bank, and the International Chamber of Commerce. On the contrary, hope is heaped on what a further march of technology can bring in the form of a lesser use of resources and of the environment, and so solve these global consumption problems and the related one of accelerated climate change.

It is beyond doubt that in our economic and technological development, all feasible possibilities should be used to make production and consumption more sustainable in terms of less energy use, less input of material resources, and lower emission of CO_2. But it is an illusion to suggest that the magnetic pole of further technological expansion can take the responsibility for the preservation of nature away from us. It is simply a modern superstition to expect that sustainability can be realized by trusting ourselves to new technological devices. Sooner or later people who live in this *dynamistic universum* have to accept that they are limited creatures, in spite of the bewitchment inflicted on us by the mass media, which suggests that even the sky does not pose a limit on our ambitions.

Concluding Remarks

In this chapter we have tried to follow the path of modernity and modernization to what we see as its highest contemporary expression: the process and project of globalization. A critical analysis like this is not without risks. The impression can easily grow that from an ecumenical ethical viewpoint modernity and modernization have to be seen as wrong avenues, which includes a negative judgment about globalization as their fruit. So we want to underline at the end of this chapter that in our view, as "modern" persons, modernity, modern, and modernization are not entirely closed concepts. They are subject to differing construals — even now. But at the same time we want to stress that the potential shadow sides of modernity and modernization — like their tendency to subject the world to rational reconstruction and to trust self-made mechanisms from here to eternity — are not only with us temporarily, but reach a kind of culmination point in the present globalization process. This we see as extremely risky for humanity, particularly from an ecumenical ethical point of view. For this process can only lead to poverty continuing on this globe in spite of all possible good intentions, to the community and spiritual life of different cultures being gradually demolished, and to the earth itself, together with its living species, being threatened with death.

This suggests that churches and Christians today should not try to find their hope and strength in new forms of idealism. They should above all choose reality and stand at its side — breaking through and unmasking all unrealistic illusions of infinite progress and trust in self-made institutions and mechanisms. For according to our faith it is God who lives and works in reality, and it is this, God's reality, that is at stake.

CHAPTER 6

Tensions and Dilemmas in Today's Global Politics

Robin Gurney with *Leopoldo Niilus and Ninan Koshy*

Introduction

From the late 1980s and throughout the 1990s, the word "globalization" became, somewhat superficially, common currency. In the minds of many that same period began with a global image, or perhaps a nostalgic feeling, of people reacting to the effects of the events that were taking place during these years: the breaking down of the Berlin Wall, the break-up of the Soviet Union, the demise of Communism throughout Europe and the diminishing of its influence around the world. At the beginning of the nineties, the emergence of the United States as the world's sole superpower had not been widely assessed. The partnership between the U.S. and the countries of Western Europe, the backbone of the transatlantic alliance for over fifty years, still seemed intact.

By September 2001 the global image was of the hijacked jetliners felling the twin towers in New York, a global war on terror, a cooling of America's transatlantic relationship with at least two of the major European powers, France and Germany, and an apparently impotent United Nations.

Then a series of events took place, which increasingly began to add chaos to confusion. To mention some (not chronologically): the Iraq war and its aftermath — elections, the new Assembly, writing the constitution, etc.; the Israeli/Palestinian conflict — building the wall, settlements, death of Yasser Arafat, the revival of the peace process; popular uprisings and/or unrest in Georgia, Ukraine, Moldova, Kyrgyzstan, Lebanon, Egypt, Sudan,

Congo, and elsewhere. Also notable was a "socialist resurgence" in some key countries in South America and a purported militarization of Venezuela. Europe was dominated by controversies around a constitution for the European Union.

Many, if not most, of these happenings have somehow been generated, manipulated, or controlled by powers outside the immediate areas in which they are taking place, but they also both perplex and challenge those same powers. Many unexpected things are happening in world politics that seem to resist being fitted into traditional and long-cherished parameters. They apparently lack "rational patterns" and do not respond to any known "logic." This poses a number of dilemmas, i.e., unsatisfactory but unavoidable political choices in which no clear course of positive action presents itself that does not also have negative alternatives that tend to lead to paralysis.

Conflicting Social Structures and Institutions

The dramatic and often unanticipated changes in Europe at the end of the 1980s did more than bring political and social relief to millions of people. They also pointed to the end of a period when particular ideologies reigned supreme, whether National Socialism or Communism, both of which at one time in the 20th century appeared to define the future. However, there is need for caution in proclaiming the end of all secular ideologies. The jury is still out.

It needs also to be pointed out that the visions which many people held throughout the latter half of the 20th century — a world dominated by a social structure that would create conditions of greater justice for all people, a restructured socialism perhaps, or a true "welfare society" — also disappeared. Since the 1980s we have witnessed the rise of a neo-liberal ideology that proclaims the supremacy of the worldwide "free market" system. Obviously, this ideology is based on the belief that markets are better instruments for the management of society than the nation-state.

So began a period of total free market control, leading to the current situation in which consumerism is king and the new temples are suburban hypermarkets with their glittering array of goods. The majority of those who share a certain affluence do not recognize the fact that the gap between rich and poor is as wide or even wider than ever. The temptations of the market have also created another social phenomenon, that of larger and larger personal debt that can swamp both those bewitched by the market's temptations and those who are among the ranks of the unemployed and poorer sectors of the population.

The end of the Cold War at first seemed to promise a better functioning international system. Addressing a joint session of the U.S. Congress after the 1991 Gulf War, then U.S. President George H. W. Bush announced that the allied action which had evicted Iraq from Kuwait had actually been a war which enabled the United Nations to "fulfill the historic vision of its founders. Now we can see a new world order coming into view. A world in which freedom and respect for human rights find a home among all nations." The end of the Cold War was one of those moments in history when such hopes were kindled.

In fact, the end of the Cold War highlighted the words "freedom" and "choice" but also brought into prominence another two words, "fear" and "uncertainty." The "certainties" of the Cold War gave way to the uncertainties of a world in which things were changing daily. No longer was there a balance of power, as seemed to exist when the two superpowers — the USA and the USSR — managed international tensions. Instead, the one remaining power, the United States, emerged as a kind of "global empire" or "hegemonic power," equipped with unimaginable military power and undergirded by "neo-conservative" thinking and the clout of financial markets.

The U.S. developed a foreign policy, marked by a doctrine of preemptive intervention. In the shadow of this policy and America's overwhelming might, certain parts of the world recovered the sense of certainty that had been lost in the previous ten years. But at the same time, this certainty for some did nothing to lessen the impact of fear and uncertainty among so many others around the globe. The influence of the U.S. on current political events in certain "crisis" areas of the planet cannot be denied (e.g., the Middle East), yet it is also evident that people there do not experience security.

The never-ending Israeli/Palestinian conflict illustrates a region where fear and uncertainty prevail. Here, the Hebrew Bible practice of "an eye for an eye and a tooth for a tooth" prevails. Revenge and further isolation continue to face both parties. Commenting on the Israeli project of building a barrier of concrete and steel which will enclose 40 percent of the West Bank, Gadi Algazi said: "This would not be the first time that fear had

127

been used to justify a political project that creates a dangerous long term situation in the name of short-term security."[1] It is hoped at the beginning of 2005 that efforts and apparent changes of attitude shown by both parties directly involved, as well as the USA and the Europeans, may turn out to be the first effective steps toward breaking the deadlock. The long history of this conflict may induce one to pessimism although hope must never fail. In this situation particularly it needs to be asked, over and over again, what role, if any, do the "religions of the book" have in injecting positive dynamics for a permanent solution.

This raises questions of the extent to which overwhelming physical force is capable of true control and domination, especially in a world characterized by uncertainty, fear, and fragility. Physical force, however awesome, may result in being not only destructive but also self-destructive. The end of the Cold War does not signify that old and traditional geopolitical power games have disappeared or become obsolete. They are still alive both among traditional rivals and newcomers to the game. The emergence of the United States as a global hegemonic power has invited strong reactions and caused positive and negative repercussions. There are those who want to challenge the "supreme power" with violence, terrorism, or competing economic systems.

Another challenge comes with the emergence of new blocks of states where the changing status of the notion of the nation-state can be seen: for example, the European Union, where member states have voluntarily relinquished elements of their national sovereignty in submission to majority voting decisions; MERCOSUR which was created in 1991 by Argentina, Brazil, Paraguay, and Uruguay to build a common market/customs union between themselves; NAFTA, the North American Free Trade Association, which was set up to resolve disputes between the national industries and/or governments of Canada, Mexico, and the USA. Other such efforts between states are in the making.

So, in a globalized world, should the idea of a nation-state be given up entirely? The idea of subsidiarity has emerged from the European Union, as states voluntarily surrender some of the elements of the historical nation-state. This opens up the possibility of a new type of nation-state becoming both a catalyst for a new type of economic actor, and a place

1. "Israel: A Contemporary Ghetto," by Ghadi Algazi, in *Le Monde Diplomatique* (English Edition), July 2003.

where new parameters for economic action can be hammered out and agreed upon. It is from this type of nation-state that a new framework for social action could emerge, and where the concept of public/private partnerships could lead to a new social contract.

There have been periods and cases in history marked by justified disillusionment with the state's capacity to deliver all that it promises. Totalitarian states pretending to handle almost everything either finished in catastrophe, as did Germany's Third Reich, or became incapable of handling anything, e.g., the USSR. The in-between cases have seen welfare states of an exacerbated character, like Sweden at one point, where any individual or private initiative was almost strangled as the overall economy crumbled.

Nevertheless, we would contend that in the context of today's world the idea of the nation-state should not be given up. We believe that here the key lies in the observation by Eric Hobsbawm of the crucial importance of "what the population think or are prepared to do." Having said this, it is important to recognize that, at the same time as politics re-enters the awareness of people as something relevant, vast sectors of public opinion express a growing distrust in politicians.

Values and Visions: Turning Politics into Theater

The title of this book affirms that we must go "beyond idealism." Other chapters, to be sure, have noted that we are not against "ideals." Ideals set standards for human behavior. The problem arises when such ideals are perceived as absolutes, isolated from concrete historic situations. Human language often exemplifies this trend to idealism. How far can the use of such expressions as freedom, liberty, participation, elections, democracy, human rights, sovereignty, and other important political terms be used to convey the notion that something good is being used as a political smokescreen? Everyone speaks with appreciation of human rights while, in actual fact, in today's world they are the most trampled upon values. Instead of describing or changing reality they have become a shibboleth. Free and democratic "elections" are another ideal, but they guarantee little unless what happens substantively on the ground is taken seriously. And, what happens in different places shows how diverse the political contexts of the peoples of the *oikoumene* are. "Peace" is another notion that can be totally emptied of content. The biblical context goes far beyond the political understanding of peace as the absence of conflict and the provision of security. Biblically, peace involves total well-being — prosperity, wholeness, health, as well as, of course, salvation.

When language turns into idealism, it creates false certainties. We move away from the real world where men and women struggle to survive, where they wish to live better lives with justice, receiving the respect that should be given to their dignity. In other words, the political task is about how to respect the worth and honor of each human person, recognizing the peculiarities of human life in each society.

Scenarios in different parts of the world indicate that, while people want to improve the political conditions of their societies, they also feel that it is imperative to find ways to uncover and denounce the increasing skill of politicians — particularly the more conservative ones — at "framing" issues in populist ways that hide their vital interests. The use of beguiling rhetoric and the manipulation of traditional symbols happens daily. In short, politics is turning into theater.

This increasingly theatrical nature of politics is not only cynical and dishonest, but more importantly, it gives rise to dangerous and sinister dynamics. People come not only to despise politicians; they also withdraw from politics altogether. In countries where authoritarian regimes prevail, where dictatorial governments rule, where people are prohibited from participation, the dynamics are somewhat different and people are already cynical and resigned. The real danger lies in states and nations where people can participate in political affairs but no longer want to. Here the consequences may be devastating, both for political life and eventually for the politicians themselves. It may also kill any attempt at a functioning nation-state.

To give an example: one only has to look at how the majority of the world's people today want peace. Most politicians, to be sure, also affirm their support for the concept of peace. However, prevailing geopolitical conceptions, as formulated since the Cold War ended, insist that the world is characterized by conflict. Cultural values, including those of religions, whose differences with each other cannot be denied, are perceived as being in conflict. Instead of seeing such differences as opportunities for cultural enrichment, they are interpreted as the basis for new confrontations. Governments with this understanding of international politics follow the road of *Si vis pacem, para bellum,* "if you want peace, prepare for war." It is important to remember what the prophet Jeremiah said to the priests and prophets of his day, who were saying "peace, peace, when there is no peace"

(Jer. 6:14; 8:11). When those who have political responsibility say one thing but do another, when they manipulate popular symbols for their own interests, then values become only rhetoric and visions are turned into falsehood. This is not idealism. It is hypocrisy, and sooner or later such persons will be brought to account.

The Re-emergence of Religions
within the Context of Cultural Tensions

Does this mean that there are no longer any truthful frames or reliable points of reference for political action? Are we becoming prey only to unpredictability and fragility? Are we at the mercy of those who follow the advice of Machiavelli (1469-1527), who wrote in *The Prince* that the politician has "to learn how to use evil, according to what is necessary"?[2]

Centuries ago, the political philosopher Thomas Hobbes (1558-1679) observed that total lawlessness in human society is difficult to imagine, asserting that a total absence of order is tantamount to universal violence. Hobbes wrote *The Leviathan* in the context of religious wars in Western Europe, specifically in Great Britain. He perceived that a strong state could manage the social situation in such a way that life rather than death is affirmed. Hobbes, like others, was aware that religions, although they preach peace, could also be agents of war and violence.

The thinkers who developed the notion that social and political progress cannot exist without a strong base in a social contract also perceived the important function of religious beliefs in construction of social covenants. Jean-Jacques Rousseau (1712-78) in his famous text on *Le Contrat Social* stated that such a contract needs religious belief to support it. In the eighth chapter, Rousseau talks about "the civil religion" shared by a nation's citizens no matter what their confession or denomination. In the second half of the 20th century, Robert Bellah, the North American sociologist of religion, made valuable contributions on the nature and use of civil religion, not only in the U.S., but also in other countries such as Japan and Italy. His books, such as *The Broken Covenant*,[3] emphasize that the af-

2. *The Prince*, §19.
3. Robert Bellah, *The Broken Covenant: American Civil Religion in Time of Trial*, 2nd ed. (Chicago: University of Chicago Press, 1992).

firmation of democracy in a given society needs some set of commonly shared beliefs — in other words, a civil religion — among the people. The concept of civil religion is clear evidence of the relevance of religion in public life.

The end of the 20th century was a period in which the influence of religion on public life became clear. The 1979 Islamic revolution in Iran, the impact of liberation theology in Nicaragua and many other countries in Latin America, the influence of the Roman Catholic Church in Poland in sustaining the political struggle of the Solidarity movement against communism, the growing civic power of conservative religion in the USA from the beginning of the 1980s — these are some examples of what alerted the world that religions were not losing influence in society as a whole, as seemed to be the case in Western Europe. Today it is not possible to accept the validity of the theory of secularization as formulated by Max Weber and his successors such as Brian Wilson.

At the end of the 1970s, Shmuel Noah Eisenstadt of the University of Jerusalem began to draw attention to important religious phenomena in today's world that need to be considered in the context of the processes of modernization. He pointed out that there is more than one version of such processes. Simply put, the birth and evolution of modern society in Western Europe is different from the modernization that has taken place or is evolving in other parts of the world. One of the main features of these processes is the growing force of fundamentalism. This religious manifestation is often considered anti-modern. Eisenstadt says that contemporary fundamentalist movements express heterodox utopian trends. The dogmatism and intolerance that characterize most fundamentalist groups is a consequence of the appropriation of Jacobin totalitarianism.

This phenomenon points to the close relationship between some religious trends that impact and influence contemporary cultural, social, and political life, and the cultural and political project of modernity. Martin E. Marty has studied many current trends in fundamentalism.[4] For him, there are many close links between public religion, politics, and other aspects of religion that belong to both private and personal areas of life. He insists that public religion must be handled with care, or it can become threatening, even dangerous.

4. Martin E. Marty and R. Scott Appleby, eds., *Fundamentalisms Observed* (Chicago: University of Chicago Press, 1991).

At the same time, aspects of public religion contribute to the public good. Traditional institutions — parishes, congregations, denominations, ecumenical agencies — offer the opportunity for public expression of what religious people think and feel. Marty suggests that, for the construction of a good society, religious people should join the political conversation and be involved in political activities.[5]

We recognize how fluid the notion of "the common good" is; religions do not always make this clear. There is a real danger that public religion becomes more of an ideology than an authentic expression of religious faith. For public religion to play a positive role in social life, Marty proposes that new theological work needs to be done so as to avoid disturbing, confusing, and messy interrelationships between public religion and political action.

A major contribution from a sociological perspective on "public religion" was formulated by José Casanova in his book *Public Religions in the Modern World*,[6] where he considered five cases of two different Christian traditions, Roman Catholicism and Protestantism, in four different countries, Spain, Poland, Brazil, and the United States. Casanova analyzes the changes that Roman Catholicism in Spain, Poland, and the USA has experienced in the second half of the 20th century, then goes on to examine the role that Protestant fundamentalism and evangelicalism has played and continues to play in the new American Christian right.

It seems clear that these public manifestations of religion, which impact the political life of society, are not exclusive to Christianity. They can be seen in Judaism, Islam, Buddhism, and among other religious communities, even in religious trends influenced by Confucianism. Conflicts in the Middle East, Iraq, and Sri Lanka; tensions with Syria and Iran; problems between the government of the People's Republic of China and the majority of the population in Tibet — all are examples pointing to an exacerbation of the public role of religion in recent times.

For some, the 2001 terrorist strikes at the United States were a moment of universal violence somehow involving religion. This event created seminal changes in many attitudes, actions, and reactions throughout the

5. Martin E. Marty with Jonathan Moore, *Politics, Religion, and the Common Good: Advancing a Distinctly American Conversation about Religion in Our Shared Life* (San Francisco: Jossey-Bass, 2000).
6. José Casanova, *Public Religions in the Modern World* (Chicago: University of Chicago Press, 1994).

world, including a sharpened focus on what was already beginning to be seen as the re-emergence of religion as a major factor in social life.

The re-emergence of religion in public life has critical implications for churches and Christian communities which participate in the ecumenical movement. It is the role of the church to engage with "the Other," including powerful media conglomerates which shape our images of friends and enemies, as well as "the stranger in our midst." Ecumenical social ethics must be prepared to open itself to dialogue with a wider range of opinion and thought than could previously have been imagined.

Challenges to Governance — Local, Regional, Global

"Globalization" *latu senso* is Janus-faced. It is not, *per se,* either totally negative or totally positive. It is a human construct that can produce effective instruments which the more effective they become have increased potential for destruction. Are cellular phones positive? Yes, if used, for example, to organize democratic resistance against dictatorial regimes. No, if applied to trigger bombs in trains full of passengers, as happened in the Madrid terrorist attack of March 11, 2004.

To some extent this also applies to instruments of governance. Strong countries' imposition of policies on weak countries is also a sign of our times. How can this state of affairs be challenged? Could the United Nations provide an answer? The ecumenical movement has keenly supported the UN throughout its lifetime. Indeed in many ways, the developments of the UN and the World Council of Churches have paralleled one another over the last fifty years. That both institutions feel themselves in some crisis today is perhaps an indication that all institutions need renovation after half a century.

It has been claimed that the UN is the only real institution of global governance to which states pay any heed. The current UN Secretary General, Kofi Annan, has called for the remaking of the institution to fit the geopolitical realities of the 21st century.[7] This is important as it comes after continual flouting of UN authority in international affairs, and after a widespread failure to implement international treaties.

7. Felicity Barringer, "UN Senses It Must Change Fast," *New York Times,* September 19, 2003.

While it is important and necessary to support the UN, it is questionable whether this is the most effective instrument for governance, global or otherwise. In a world of constant change, the question must be asked: Is the United Nations the only form of global governance that we should have? After all, powerful countries as well as less powerful ones can flout the will of the UN and ignore treaties even after they have prominently backed them at world conferences. The Kyoto Accord, the treaty on global warming, is an example. And if countries flout such treaties, where can they be held accountable?

Today there are multiple layers of governance, all aspiring to some form of global perspective. The UN is at the top of the pyramid but then comes regional governance — the European Union and similar projects already mentioned; world alliances such as the (British) Commonwealth; sub-regional alliances, transnational activities by mega industries that are often larger and certainly more powerful than many independent nation-states; nation-states themselves, often with sub-states. Do we need even more governance or could some be subsumed into others? Would that contribute to extending democracy?

Another area affecting governance is how local and regional infra-structures are implemented and maintained — the public-private partner-ships. Here, there is a clear redrawing of boundaries between private power and the public authorities who have a duty to oversee the "good life" of people. In many cases private enterprises exert more power than a weak and politically divided public authority and thus dictate decisions to national governments. This raises the question: In what industries should the public good be given more importance than private entrepreneurs? This is clearly relevant to the provision of water and energy, among other important issues.

What Are We Called to Do Living in a World of Uncertainty?

Throughout this book, but particularly in this chapter, it has been apparent that change has brought about uncertainty. Frequently there has been a feeling of being lost. Where this has happened, signposts have been pinpointed to enable us to move ahead. However, there are many areas where immediate answers are lacking.

The death of secular ideology seems to some to have been a touchstone for the use of religion as an ideological tool in the struggle for social change. For ecumenical institutions the re-emergence of religion into the public domain presents real challenges. How, for instance, can these institutions deal with, or come to terms with their heritage and also go forward to seek a new vision, a vision which will necessarily encompass the changing social situation, the new threats to life and liberty, and the possibility of being in the media spotlight rather than in the shadow of world events?

In this age of uncertainty it is too easy — and dangerous — to fall back on false certainties. It may be too much to suggest that the rise of extremism in religious belief is doing just that. That many people today are having their hopes raised by false prophets cannot be disputed. The words of the wise Pharisee Gamaliel come to mind: "[I]f this plan or this undertaking is of human origin, it will fail; but if it is of God, you will not be able to overthrow them — in that case you may even be found fighting against God" (Acts 5:38-39). Today, ecumenical social ethics, like individual Christians, is thrown back on the cushion of Christian hope.

Paul K. McAlister, in the *Marshall Pickering Encyclopedia of the Bible*, describes hope as "An expression or belief in the fulfillment of something desired." He goes on: "Present hurts and uncertainty over what the future holds create the constant need for hope. Worldwide poverty, hunger, disease, and human potential to generate terror and destruction create a longing for something better. Historically, people have looked for the future with a mixture of longing and fear. Many have concluded that there is no reasonable basis for hope and therefore to hope is to live with an illusion. Scripture relates that being without hope to being in the world without God."[8] The Apostle Paul addresses this issue in Ephesians: "you were at that time without Christ, being aliens from the commonwealth of Israel, and strangers to the covenants of promise, having no hope and without God in the world. But now in Christ Jesus you who once were far off have been brought near by the Blood of Christ. For he is our peace" (Eph. 2:12-14).

There are concrete tasks ahead. Earlier in this chapter it was shown that there is an urgent need to uncover and denounce the schemes that generate false certainties, to dispel political smokescreens, and to pinpoint human dignity within society. There is a need to give new legitimacy to notions of value, to combat political disenchantment, to liberate the con-

8. *The Marshall Pickering Encyclopedia of the Bible.*

science of communities in order to use politics for the good. In all of this, however, there is a need to be cautious on at least two fronts. First, for Christians and Christian communities these tasks stem from an imperative in our understanding of the Christian faith. Excuses about small numbers or perceived weakness are unacceptable. Secondly, in these tasks we neither possess a monopoly nor can we claim exclusiveness. We must give full cooperation to "the Other," whether within the nation-state or the scientific community. We must also highlight what the challenges presented by change mean to "the Other." Persons and communities who advocate ecumenical social ethics must support and applaud those people who, notably in the United States, are questioning the unceasing expansion of military might and the headlong rush into technological change. The "Other" must also be kept in mind where the ceaseless race to keep up, to innovate, and to develop is paramount.

CHAPTER 7

The Framework(s) of Society Revisited

Joanildo Burity

It is an ecumenical truism that, faced with a God who acts in and through history, who takes up the human condition in Jesus Christ, any response to God's call must take the situation where we are into account. From this comes the insistence on knowing human and nature's realities, on probing the position from which we search for signs of God's work, but also for signs of opposition to and neglect of God's designs. Commitment to life comes from life-giving experience that liberates, empowers, and calls for action and solidarity. Having received graciously given life from God, we feel compelled to extend it toward as many people as possible, always with an understanding that in each time and place there are distinct experiences of what life in abundance means. In each case, *a description of what is comes mixed with aspirations of a world to be,* and this varies over time and space. There is contingency, ambiguity, and finitude in everything human and historical, so the possibility of failure is always present. The fact that human projects always combine what is with aspirations of a world that could be does not mean that freedom, justice, and peace will prevail.

The economic and political dimensions of life were the focus of previous chapters. As the debate about and the process of globalization demonstrate, other facets of life are also important. Some of these are age-old, like culture and community, while others represent newer developments, like the organizations of civil society. Such factors *de-center economic reason, and politicize issues and situations,* thus questioning conventional statist understanding of politics, as well as the liberal separation of political spheres of the representation of interests from social spheres of the formation of interests.

Many readings of the global context have reinforced the view that we are heading toward a life-threatening future and that, despite all the promises about prosperity and freedom of choice, globalization has unleashed greater instability, despair, and poverty than it has produced in terms of positive accomplishments, for instance, in the areas of the diffusion of technological innovation or communications.

Whether in the form of resistance to the extensive "re-engineering" of the economy, of politics, or of organizational life, people from different countries have tried to halt or reshape the forces of globalization, to exploit its possibilities, or to counter its oppressive dimensions. Cultural resistance and civil society activism have been at the forefront of many of these movements.

Thus, the various elements of the existing social context should be studied and discussed from the viewpoint of (a) how far they are threatened or strengthened by the global flows of capital, information, goods, and power, and (b) what signs of reaction/renewal can be found in the global context that point toward changes in the framework, bringing it closer to ecumenical commitment, as expressed in such ideas as freedom and equality for all, sustainability and care for life, responsibility and solidarity, dialogue and respect for the other.

In the following pages we will try to balance our assessment of globalization in relation to society and culture, taking both aspects as guiding principles.

Relevance of Frameworks for the Good Life/Society

Some clarification is in order about the way in which the notion of framework relates to both context and social ethics. Frameworks may be expressed as "givens," that is, as lasting forms or structures whose life-supporting functions cannot be overlooked, modified, or attacked with impunity by human historical projects, such as present-day economic globalization.

Theological and philosophical traditions offer ideas of frameworks for the preservation and extension of (the good) life. Chapter 4 has dealt with them at length; we are not going to retrace those steps. Two important points are: (a) these images of the good society (the *civitas terrena*), natural law, orders of creation, the uses of the Law, mandates, can be read or interpreted as attempts to think of the conditions in which life can be sustained and freedom expanded; (b) that we are called to be co-participants in God's work as Sustainer of God's creation, and this involves not only the environment and its living creatures but also the structures of human society. In view of the tasks attributed to humankind in God's creation (Gen. 1:28; 2:15; 9:1-11) and to Christians in their role as collaborators with Jesus in the work of reconciling the world to God (2 Cor. 5:18-20), these structures and their specific functions and ends are both a necessity and a responsibility. In the context of globalization, when a particular kind of social change and a particular view of human agency and institution-building prevail, which deeply unsettle traditional forms of life or hard-won accomplishments of modernity (particularly those referring to social rights and state regulation of the economy), ethical concerns about the ecumenical response to these challenges evoke these ideas of divine patterns for the nurturing of the good life on the planet.

Until the advent of modernity, most if not all cultures valued permanence over variation and solidity over fluidity. The way things were was seen as pre-established by God's providence and not to be tampered with. History was viewed as part of nature and was lived with an attitude of acceptance, awe, and resignation before God. Change was seen as an element of disorder and, ultimately, thought of as evil or sinful. These "givens" were thought to be found everywhere, under roughly the same form and content. At their best, they would adapt to particular contexts while seeking to retain their essential traits. At their worst, they were ideas that were forced onto other contexts and used as standards against which to judge them. Thus, for example, ideas of natural God-given inequalities among human beings were used to justify slavery; economic and political oppression was often sanctioned in God's name, and the idea that the existing order was according to God's design was used to block attempts to change it.

A contrasting attitude toward the frameworks is found in ecumenical circles, particularly in the West. This attitude reflects a sympathetic reception of modernity and its historicizing approach to order, authority, and tradition. This view stresses both a diachronic process of God's dealings with humanity and creation and active participation and responsibility of humans in the construction of social structures for the good life.

This view is more at home with conflict and contingency in history and adopts a critical attitude toward the achievements of the past and present and does not attempt to legitimate them in the name of God.

To postulate an unchanging nature of the structures that sustain life and society amounts to forgetting their historic roots, their concrete setting in certain contexts, their modes of reproduction and dissemination to different societies (often through oppressive means), and their contingency. Nonetheless, there must be a basis for criticism of present-day forms of life and social organization that often benefit the few and jeopardize the very reproduction of life on the planet, at the service of growth, accumulation, and indiscriminate consumption. If globalization must be judged for its devastating effects in many parts of the world, and even for its achievements, some horizon, some idea of an ideal society, is required. In the traditions that inform ecumenical thought, an important feature of that horizon is provided by the attempts to spell out the divine provisions for life in abundance on earth.

God's commandments or mandates, to use familiar theological descriptions of the framework, are biblically expressed in terms that stress God's presence in human history (incarnation) and the need for human response and active participation. We are inhabitants of traditions and communities, in which there are many voices who have visions of how human society should reflect or respond to God's will. Our response to the challenges of the times should be illuminated by an attentive engagement with these voices from the past. They bequeath to us a longing for community, peace, justice, and salvation that has not been satisfied by any human social construction. We can only do this from where we stand, thus we cannot help reinterpreting and even subverting our legacy. This is the best way of being faithful to its call.

Our participation in God's work of reconciliation in the social realm impinges on every aspect of the framework of life, including the aspects of contingency and ambiguity. The framework is always short of fully accomplishing hopes for justice, peace, freedom, sustainability; it always limits the aspirations of full communion and full enjoyment of life; it often starts as a liberating experience and then turns away from liberation.

The best way the framework can provide just, participatory, and free forms of life for all is by affirming the *plurality and mutual relationship and engagement* of the different institutions and practices it comprehends in a way that was foreseen, but not fully developed, by Bonhoeffer's doctrine of the mandates: *with, for, and against each other.*[1] His view warrants the conclusion that the elements of the framework (mandates) should be kept in their mutual conditioning and that historical circumstances may give prominence to certain aspects of them, rather than portraying them in a unified way.

Thus, (a) the affirmation of mutual legitimacy and differential possibilities for "partnerships," "alliances," *with each other;* (b) development of cultures of responsibility and solidarity in each one of them directed at the improvement of the others, *for each other;* and (c) the resistance and even open defiance against those structures which trespass or violate their "mandate" by claiming idolatrous allegiance and/or by causing unmotivated and unnecessary suffering, *against each other,* comprise three relationship rules that simultaneously link and keep at a distance the elements of the framework as understood in a given historical context. A dynamics of grace, love of neighbor, prophetic awareness, and courage to take stands, and a double structure of responsibility (namely, readiness to respond to the call of the other — God, fellow human beings, or nature — and accountability for one's acts and for the destiny of others) informs a possible articulation of the framework in which variation, conflict, and agreement are not at odds with, but supplement, each other.

Relevance and responsibility are important criteria in our attempts to follow our theological heritage. We need a hermeneutical and "contextual" methodological procedure for the articulation between the concrete historical challenges and needs of today and the normative and more abstract work of the past.[2] The issue is: confronted with a growing and often not easily converging plurality of moral voices today, how "thick" can/should such a conception of the framework of society be?

A pressing question today is to what extent "the market" has become a master model for social organization and a basis for the modernization narrative (cast in terms of a struggle for efficiency and efficacy through competition, and focused on results, as opposed to development ideals and social welfare through legal constraint and focused on rights and procedures). It seems as though the growth, competition, and efficiency drives

1. Dietrich Bonhoeffer, *Ethics,* ed. Clifford J. Green, trans. R. Krauss, C. C. West and D. Stott, Dietrich Bonhoeffer Works, Vol. 6 (Minneapolis: Fortress Press, 2005), 388, 393-94.

2. Frits de Lange, "'With each other, for each other, against each other': Bonhoeffer's Theory of Mandates as a Theological Contribution to Socio-Ethical Pluralism," http://home.hetnet.nl/~frits.lange/dbmandat.htm (1997).

of current market practices aim at thrusting all social life into the whirl-pool of global capitalism, which leaves little room for alternative scenarios.

But how closed is this system? And in what sense would an encompassing view of a timeless framework for the good society represent a real alternative to "bad" globalization? Is it not legitimate that from different quarters — as yet ill-articulated or unconvincing — broad pictures of a new world attempt to offer alternatives and should be given time to mature or seek space to contest the hegemonic views? Given their fragmentation, can we expect a coherent or persuasive alternative from these reactions against the effects of globalization?

How can we make sense of these multiple pictures and bring them together? This is a demanding ecumenical task of translation, articulation, and recognition. Is there a (common) framework from which, within our moment in time, we can figure out necessary structures for human life, providing freedom and equality for all, and in balance with nature? The framework is one of the elements through which the ecumenical movement can help religious and nonreligious agents find in their own traditions, resources to discern their way forward together (or at least their co-existence in relative peace). It involves finding ethical principles and valued forms of life that we consider to be essential for the reconstruction of a just and fulfilling social life.

In this light, the framework can be seen as a gift, both in the sense of something offered to the other and in the sense of something received from the other. It stands for our awareness of being part of a long-standing effort to interpret the tension between the transcendent and historical sources of order and the organization of difference and multiplicity. We recognize that we are part of traditions — within and outside the Christian church — that conceived and articulated a response to God's good will for God's creation. Relinquishing domineering truth-claims or the will to power within our traditions, we are compelled to offer, by means of reflexive discourse and action, interpretations of our traditions, in solidarity with those who are suffering the harsh effects of this recent wave of globalization. This hermeneutical practice could help bring together those groups advocating change in the present moment, in view of "another world" where work, decent living standards, recognition of differences, and humane values of solidarity prevail over greed, violence, the cold rationality of (self-)interest and efficiency, and the subordination of virtually all dimensions of life to the encroachment of market logic. From a

Christian perspective, this is akin to an affirmation of the possibility of communion amid differences found in New Testament narratives of the early church (cf. John 4; Acts 2; 1 Cor. 12–14; Rom. 12–13; Col. 3:10-17).

The Framework of Society in a Global and Plural World: Culture, Identity, and Civil Society

We live in a plural world. The fact of plurality and its various dimensions provokes many kinds of response. Plurality is the result of centuries of efforts to keep various forms of life alive — through adaptation, negotiation, resistance, subversion, and reinterpretation — in response to wars, colonialism, environmental catastrophes, the uprooting of ethnic groups or local communities/cultures, and gender domination.

Affirming plurality as an integral part of the framework of society amounts to an act of resistance, even of confession: individualism, self-interest, competition, efficiency, accumulation, the commodification of every aspect of life cannot be accepted as the only — let alone the best — framework for sustaining a future for all human beings, especially the billions of poor, disadvantaged, and discriminated people that make up the large majority in our world.

After the terrifying experiences of the last century — wars, totalitarianism, authoritarian regimes, the environmental crisis, ethnic cleansing, growing poverty together with economic development and technological change — an instinctive appreciation of plurality has spread to most parts of the world. In some cases, plurality means noninterference. Some forms of resistance to globalization take this form, which can be either passive ("not-in-my-backyard" politics) or active (defiance of majority rule, xenophobic or racist movements or conflicts). In other cases, particularly through civil society movements and networks, plurality has come to be part of the idea of a democratic society.

Social life is organized through interrelated dimensions and institutions, which form spheres with their own logic. People move across these spheres and experience their freedom in not being entirely within the grasp of any one of them. The spheres of social life (culture, economy, labor, politics, everyday interaction, etc.) provide references, identity, and belonging, as well as exercising control, surveillance, or oppression. Thus no single principle or ethic governs these spheres in a uniform way, and no sphere represents the answer to all aspirations or the solace against all problems or dangers. At present, this much can be said to protest the claims that the market is the overall principle organizing social practice in every sphere.

Culture and Community Life

Cultures have been dramatically affected throughout history by political and economic domination, invasions, wars, and internal conflicts. What is new with globalization is the pervasiveness of market-driven processes and values and the global dissemination of Western consumerism and mass culture as models of the good life. Though rhetoric has insisted on freedom and choice as part of the package, most societies have felt compelled to adopt or accept externally imposed "adjustments" in their economies and polities, which have increased personal and collective vulnerability and loss.

Changes in labor practices have led to growing unemployment; flexibility of labor rights has accompanied legal adjustments to attract foreign investments and keep or increase profit margins of companies. Millions have found themselves alienated from the contexts where they earn their living. Loss of jobs and future perspectives for young generations, closure of companies, obsolescence of economic activities due to the massive influx of imported goods, the growing incompatibility between labor expertise and the new educational requirements of technology — these are some of the consequences that have led to the dismantlement of entire cultural networks.

Faced with the demands of the new economic and political order, everyday routines, traditions, and social relations have been deeply affected. Diminishing opportunities, long-term unemployment, and deteriorating living standards have also contributed to the escalation of tensions between communities and social groups, who have had to compete with each other for fewer resources and sometimes even physical space. The threats to national, regional, and local identity, or the perception that cultural traditions have become unstable, uncertain, and incapable of facing up to the new challenges posed by the global flows, have prompted defensive or reactive responses where intolerance, rivalries old and new, and racial or cultural prejudice have multiplied and increased social conflicts or tensions.

Friction within and among nations, the fragmentation of national identities, and the rise of (ethnic, religious, urban) violence has become part of our everyday experience. The fast-paced rhythm of economic and organizational life has disrupted the ethos of many communities and created a sense of instability and vulnerability that have proven hard to cope with.

On the other hand, the remarkable ability to adapt has allowed capital and market values to redefine social ethical commitments. Ideas of social responsibility become personal choices. Welfare programs either are drastically reduced in favor of calls for self-help or attach strings to them in the form of costs or qualifying conditions. Citizens are taught to relate to the state as consumers of public goods. Poverty and unemployment come to be seen as signs of incompetence, laziness, dependence. Growing urban violence, teenage pregnancy, broken families, and drug addiction are attributed to weakened family values or tolerance toward deviance or crime.

Culture, as a set of practices, attitudes, and values that give meaning to the complexity of the world, undergoes significant change. Globalization introduces a permanent tension between the local and particular and the non-local and general. Global economic dynamics, which largely surpass the nation states' ability to regulate them, are presented as inevitable, as is the need to "open" borders and remove economic barriers.

Many cultures in our world do not have the means — symbolic or political — to resist and counter the force of global culture and economic expansion. Cultural symbols, myths, and rituals have provided meaning and predictability to life. They have helped shape the flow of natural and social events by constructing reasons for developing community ties, explaining differences, sorting out problems, facing challenges, addressing conflicts, resisting evil. Culture also carries patterns of behavior, rules for interaction, techniques for securing survival or expanding influence/dominion. But cultures develop these symbols and rituals according to particular histories. Difference is the rule in culture, not uniformity. Linguistic, dressing, eating and drinking, moral, political, economic, religious codes vary in endless ways.

Globalization has intensified a process of redefinition of culture according to market values and practices that started as long ago as the late 19th century. More and more areas of social life have come under the logic of the market. Commodification, competition, and privatization have increasingly marked cultural practices as much as any other social relations. Western consumer culture has spread toward southern and non-Western societies through the development of cultural industries, which provide information, entertainment, and aesthetic experiences for a mass public. Non-Western cultures have also come closer to the gaze of Western people.[3]

Culture is also a site of power relations. Within and between communities and nations, culture is not the reign of equality, communion, and tolerance as is sometimes claimed. Community and culture can be places where unfair and arbitrary relations develop, which are sanctioned by the authority of tradition, religion, nationalism, or possession of a territory. They do not remain untouched by global flows; some of them are reinforced, others are weakened in many ways (for instance, through the appeal of media messages, or human rights cross-national activism). Culture can also be a means of resistance to globalization, an affirmation of local identities and projects against the powerful interests of corporations, banks, and other nations. Even when invaded by foreign cultural symbols and goods, local cultures find ways to rearticulate themselves and explore the margins left for self-assertion or the possibilities of using the market for their own benefit.[4]

Through globalization's pressures, people have grown more aware of and sensitive toward their differences and often feel the need to protect them at all costs. In some cases, this happens through discovering, under the national identity, a patchwork of other forms of identity (ethnic, regional, religious, gender) that were historically waived in oppressive ways and now claim recognition.

Cultures do not all face the same pressures and do not develop the same strategies for coping with the world external to them. Some of them

3. Cf. Yim Sung-Bihn, "Reflections on Accelerated Cultural Globalization," in Ninan Koshy, ed., *Globalization: The Imperial Thrust of Modernity* (Mumbai: Vikas Adhyayan Kendra and Bossey: The Ecumenical Institute, 2002); Mike Featherstone, ed., *Global Culture: Nationalism, Globalization and Modernity* (London, New Delhi, and Melbourne: Sage, 1990); Arjun Appadurai, "Disjuncture and Difference in the Global Cultural Economy," in Frank J. Lechner and John Boli, eds., *The Globalization Reader*, 2nd ed. (Oxford and Malden, MA: Blackwell Publishing, 2004), 100-108.

4. Cf. Stuart Hall, "Thinking the Diaspora: Home-thoughts from Abroad," *Small Axe* 6 (September 1999): 1-18; Manuel Castells, *The Power of Identity*, Vol. 2 of *The Information Age: Economy, Society and Culture* (Oxford and Malden, MA: Blackwell Publishing, 1997); Néstor Garcia Canclini, *Consumidores e cidadaos. Conjlitos multiculturais da globalizeçã* (Rio de Janeiro: UFRJ, 1995).

JOANILDO BURITY

have survived through *relative* isolation from others. These are less able to
cope with sudden, intrusive displacements to their forms of life. Others
have long gone through processes of *hybridization,* which means that their
very identities are already marked by the other (through intermittent con-
tacts, colonization, immigration, political asylum, exile, tourism, the media). Cultures have for a long time experienced different forms of
interpenetration. There is hardly any human group in the world that is
fully homogeneous and pristine in its cultural identity. Hybridization involves the appropriation and reworking of new cultural elements by the
oppressed or the weak, sometimes turning some of their unfulfilled promises on their heads and reconstituting the necessary framework(s) to sustain life, human dignity, and hope.[5]

If mass culture disrupts and sometimes destroys local ethnic or regional cultures, there are manifold forms of resistance that are expressed
through the performing arts, handicrafts, folk festivals, and claims to em-
powering cultural policies. If cultural domination has prevailed through
policies of assimilation or forced the abandonment of historic traditions by
immigrant groups, there has been in some places a renewed emphasis on reaffirming these (fragments of) differences. Sensitivity toward culture is also
at the root of recent bloody conflicts in parts of Europe, Asia, and Africa. In
all this, the challenge of fostering pluralism as a positive attitude of respect
for difference, as well as the value of plurality, emerges as a burning global
need. This creates new opportunities for ecumenical discourse and action.

Identity

The impact of globalization on society and culture has contributed to a
reemergence of the issue of identity. If for no other reason, globalization
brings the other — and all of its "strange" manners and demands — to
one's doorstep, to the screen of one's TV, to the common spaces where difference is met and experienced. Simultaneity, a sense of nearness of people
and situations (particularly by means of the media), may give the impression that we are surrounded by, or part of, much larger communities, some

5. Cf. Stuart Hall, "The Multi-cultural Question," in Barnor Hesse, ed., *Un/settled
Multiculturalisms* (London: Zed Books, 2000); Homi K. Bhabha, *The Location of Culture*
(London and New York: Routledge, 1995); Néstor Garcia Canclini, op. cit.

148

of which leave strong impressions on or prompt reactions from us. In different parts of the world we hear stories of how such virtual or real encounters have made us more aware of, or sensitive to, the ways we speak, dress, eat, treat others, live out our sexuality, and deal with the authority of tradition or social institutions.

Claiming one's identity has become a protective device against the "invasion" of migrants, technical and economic innovation, political and cultural change. It has also been used as a weapon of the weak to assert their independence, their pride, their rights to welfare or to participation.

But identity adds to the confusion the new context introduces, for in its name, age-old practices of segregation, intolerance, and violence have also been perpetrated against persons and groups who are blamed for situations others are experiencing, or who have certain features in their way of living, their social position, their ethnic origin, or their claims *vis-à-vis* society at large that are considered unacceptable. Religious violence, ethnic cleansing, conflicts between nationals and immigrants or locals and migrants within nations, and active forms of discrimination and exclusion are among some of the things that mark identity with ambiguity.[6]

Identity is everywhere, contesting and contested. Through values, culture, self-interest, historical trajectories, political narratives of the common good, or nomadic views of being true to one's freedom or destiny, identity seems a starting point from which to withdraw, join, or resist the stream. It is a polemical, even threatening, experience.[7]

6. Cf. Craig Calhoun, ed., *Social Theory and the Politics of Identity* (Oxford and Malden, MA: Blackwell Publishing, 1994); Alain Touraine, *Can We Live Together? Equality and Difference,* trans. David Macey (Stanford: Stanford University Press, 2000); William E. Connolly, *Why I Am Not a Secularist* (Minneapolis: University of Minnesota Press, 1999); idem, *The Ethos of Pluralization* (Minneapolis: University of Minnesota Press, 1999).

7. Cf. Stuart Hall, "The Local and the Global: Globalization and Ethnicity," in Anthony D. King, ed., *Culture, Globalization and the World-system: Contemporary Conditions for the Representation of Identity* (Binghampton, NY: Macmillan/Department of Art and Art History, State University of New York, 1991), 19-39; idem, "Old and New Identities, Old and New Ethnicities," in Anthony D. King, ed., op. cit., 41-68; Mike Featherstone, *Undoing Culture: Globalization, Postmodernity and Identity* (London, New Delhi, Melbourne: Sage, 1995); Craig Calhoun, ed., *Social Theory and the Politics of Identity* (Oxford and Malden, MA: Blackwell Publishing, 1994); Ernesto Laclau, *Emancipation(s)* (London: Verso, 1996); Joanildo A. Burity, "Identidade e Cidadania: A Cultura Civica no Contexto de uma Nova Relação entre Sociedade Civil, Individuos e Estado," *Cadernos de Estudos Sociais* 15, No. 2 (July-December 1999).

Even when it is experienced as a comforting, protective device against despair, anxiety, and exclusion, identity is involved in contestation. It protests difference against others, freedom from others, fear of others. It seeks solace from the threats of innovation, dislocation, diverging views or lifestyles, political enemies. It fights opponents, invents conflicts and injuries, draws boundaries, and imagines or resists the destruction of traditions, common cultures, cherished values. Identity reacts against economic degradation and marginalization. Identity mobilizes past and present to secure its credentials, rights, or privileges, to vindicate its reasons for being or acting the way it is/does.

It is not possible to join together all expressions of identity claims under a "rainbow coalition" against globalization, though there is a logical and a strategic connection that can be put to the service of "progressive" change. This means that, while not all identity claims and self-definitions can be accepted, neither should such claims be automatically characterized as reactionary expressions of backwardness and false consciousness.

Because identity is often about (a) disputes over conflicting value systems in search of hegemony or public recognition; (b) the possibilities opened up by the dissemination of social struggles from "central" societies into "peripheral" ones; (c) the reformulation, in particular ways, of universal demands for inclusion and participation; or, more recently, (d) the impact of the global on local situations, it would not be too far-fetched to portray the issue as *political*.[8] So, in the argument that follows, I reflect on identity and globalization, framed by the political elements of their mutual relationship.

Castells, the Spanish sociologist, locates expressions of collective identity clearly on the side of *reactions* against globalization. These reactions can be either proactive or simply reactionary, but they represent a claim to singularity and an attempt to hold control of people's lives in local environments as against the arrogant diagnosis and packages from inter-

8. Cf. David Held and Anthony McGrew, *Prós e contras da globalizeção* (Rio de Janeiro: Jorge Zahar, 2001); Joanildo Burity, "Globalizaçã e Identidade: desafios do multiculturalismo," in Vânia de Vasconcelos, José Antônio Spinelli, and Pedro Vicente Costa Sobrinho, *As Ciências Sociais: desafios do milênio* (Natal: Edufrn, 2000); Carl Schmitt, *On the Concept of the Political* (Chicago: University of Chicago Press, 1996); Ernesto Laclau, *New Reflections on the Revolution of Our Time* (London: Verso, 1990); idem, *Emancipation(s);* Chantal Mouffe, *The Return of the Political* (London: Verso, 1996); Jacques Rancière, *Disagreement — Politics and Philosophy* (Minneapolis: University of Minnesota Press, 1998).

national organizations, or from the floating cosmopolitanism of global executives, journalists, tourists, or intellectuals. He says:

> In such a world of uncontrolled, confusing change, people tend to regroup around primary identities: religious, ethnic, territorial, national. In a world of global flows of wealth, power, and images, the search for identity, collective or individual, ascribed or constructed, becomes the fundamental source of social meaning. This is not a new trend, since identity, and particularly religious and ethnic identity, have been at the roots of meaning since the dawn of human history. Yet identity is becoming the main, and sometimes the only, source of meaning in a historical period characterized by a widespread destructuring of organizations, delegitimation of institutions, fading away of major social movements, and ephemeral cultural expressions.[9]

On the other hand, Castells insists that "the process of techno-economic globalization shaping our world is being challenged, and will eventually be transformed, from a multiplicity of sources, according to different cultures, histories, and geographies."[10] For that purpose, identity can be a driving force, although not always a positive one. Thus, the feeling of being alienated by global developments may lead to the exclusion of the excluders, through refusal of complexity and globality in favor of communitarian, localistic closure.[11] The incapacity of national states (particularly their elites in power) to deal with their citizens' problems in a way that does not require them to surrender before the external pressures of global markets, especially the financial ones, leaves many of those citizens with the feeling that "the nation" should be defended against "the state" and globalization.

Castells also believes in the possibility of "progressive" change, since identity is, in itself, neither progressive or regressive.[12] Though there are "legitimizing" identities, there are also "resistance" and "project" identities. For him, only concrete contexts will indicate "how, and by whom, different types of identities are constructed, and with what outcomes."[13] The

9. Manuel Castells, *The Rise of the Network Society,* Vol. 1 of *The Information Age: Economy, Society and Culture* (Oxford and Malden, MA: Blackwell Publishing, 1996), 3.
10. Manuel Castells, *The Power of Identity,* 3.
11. Manuel Castells, *The Rise of the Network Society,* 25.
12. Manuel Castells, *The Power of Identity,* 8.
13. Ibid., 10.

only direct clue he gives us here is that in the network society the space for legitimizing identities shrinks together with civil societies, and the main site of contestation becomes the construction of defensive identities around communal principles. It is as a prolongation of such communal resistance that the new subjects of project identities (bearers of alternative projects of society) can emerge.[14]

Civil Society

Culture, identity, and community life have been experienced in new ways in recent decades through the spread of ideas on the relevance of civil society as a rallying point and a strategic resource to face the arbitrary power of money and the state. In many parts of the world the existence of forms of associated life, autonomous from the political system, has checked political violence, social inequalities, or the more destructive aspects of global change. They are local groups and associations providing public services or welfare, promoting cultural traditions, and raising awareness to issues covering gender, the environment, family, age groups, ethnic or linguistic minorities, poverty, etc.; as well as more formal organizations dealing with civil, political, and social rights or professional interests and demands nationwide or internationally. Networks of such organizations have increasingly become a reliable source of advocacy and mobilization for social protection, political freedom, and cultural defense. It is almost inconceivable today to address public policy or international issues without immediately being confronted with the existence of civil society actors resisting, proposing, or negotiating demands with representatives of the state and the market.

Even though there is ambiguity in civil society, this form of social action is both politically and ethically indispensable to furthering the demands and needs of the socially underprivileged, the materially poor, and the culturally disenfranchised. Also, civil society discourse has strongly emphasized respect for plurality, difference, and the value of cultural practices and values, for the achievement and sustainability of peace, social equality, and political justice. Both global and national powers (governments, organizations, and companies) have had to make room for such

14. Ibid., 11.

views, and civil society groups are acknowledged as partly responsible for a growing sensitivity toward cultural pluralism. Issues of environmental equilibrium, gender relations, ethnic or racial discrimination, and active citizen participation in policy arenas owe much of their current purchase to the efforts of a myriad of civil society groups, operating locally or cross-nationally, in advocacy, formation, or providing services for excluded sectors of the population.

Today there is a renewed emphasis on civil society as a symbol of efficiency, solidarity, and unbiased public interest. People, organized in civil associations and networks of groups, are given the role of monitoring and even actively engaging some of the distributive and mediating functions hitherto performed by the state. The realization that the politics of equality under socialism had stifled the autonomy of civil society, and the effects the crisis of socialism had on the western left, led to a rediscovery of power as a bottom-up construction, balancing state control over society.

There is also a more conservative reading of civil society, in tune with the policies of neo-liberalism and the "third way." Thus there is an invitation for civil society to take on responsibilities and for individuals to take "control of their own destiny," without relying on the goodwill of bureaucrats and the "illusions" of distributive policies of the state. International policies of most multilateral bodies (the IMF, World Bank, and some UN agencies), and the international cooperation toward poor and "emerging" countries, have conditioned investments or funds on the adoption of a pro-active participation of civil society, mainly channeled through non-governmental organizations (NGOs). The diagnosis of the ingrained corruption, bureaucratization, and inefficiency of state action led these institutions to prescribe direct relationships with civil society organizations, particularly in the areas of social policy and environmental protection.

Enhanced participation in civil society has increased the involvement of people in public management through a number of emerging arrangements such as forums, committees, public hearings, consultations, etc., in both developed and "emerging" countries. This is in addition to civil society's more "expressive," utopian role in broadening the scope of the political beyond institutional politics. The constitution of networks of organizations and movements, made increasingly significant by the big United Nations gatherings and conferences on human rights, population, environmental issues, social development, women's issues, and so on, has been unprecedented both locally and globally. There is certainly more engagement now with issues in faraway places and involving more people and networks. The possibilities of mobilizing transnational public opinion on local and global issues are envisaged more than ever and are becoming at least partially successful.

From the beginning, the discourse on human rights was in tune with the language and repertoire of actions associated with civil society. It was in line with the tension between a natural conception of individual rights and their recognition and enforcement by the state. It insisted on accountability of the state in protecting and promoting those rights. It called for and fostered participation by those directly affected or interested in the issues. This can cut across social classes and cultural divisions, as well as political persuasions, forming the basis for broad-based coalitions for the defense of human rights. The dissemination of human rights discourse in recent decades also coincides with and follows the paths opened up by the spread of global markets and the growing centrality of real-time media communication worldwide.

A question to be raised in this connection is whether civil society is capable of coping with the demands that result from the processes of structural adjustment and the downsizing of the state. There is a dilemma here. On the one hand, as partnerships and deliberative arrangements are multiplied, civil society may get so enmeshed in governmental policies that it runs the risk of being co-opted by the logic of legitimating governmental action and in the process lose its relative autonomy. On the other hand, by taking up tasks that demand a system of resource allocation and adjudication of conflicts, in the face of powerful social and political forces, civil society can contribute to further undermining the capacity of the state to enforce its rights and responsibilities.

From a different perspective, civil society has become the site for multiple experiments with productive arrangements based on solidarity, cooperation, and fair trade relations. Many of these are small-scale and hardly able to compete with the overwhelming force of the market. But perhaps that is not their aim. Rather, they seem to have a prophetic, symbolic character, pointing to the possibility of another form of organizing the provision of material needs according to alternative values. "Solidarity economy," "concerted economy," "social economy" have emerged as names for the new trends. They correspond at a political level to calls for a new social contract that combines democratic institutions with a culture of solidarity, reciprocity, responsibility, pluralism, environmental sustainability, and active participation.

It is debatable whether the reduction of the control of national states on both economic activity and political decisions has led or will lead to the emergence of a *global civil society.* Nevertheless, there are a number of indicators that signal the social bases of such a potential community. They are represented by the transnational networks of Christian churches, other world religions, and ecumenical agencies; the environmental movement; the human rights movement; multilateral aid agencies; large non-governmental organizations operating in liaison with smaller, locally based ones; big cultural events, through which campaigns are mobilized and disseminated; international conferences on various global issues, such as those recently promoted by the UN; cyber-communities of opinion, creed, or political activism, spontaneously developed or induced by specific organizations. The growing interconnection and exchanges among these agents have given the sense of a virtual body with real consequences in political affairs. The World Social Forum and the initiatives that have followed it have been a clear indication of moving beyond the vague and disconnected image of a global public opinion toward concerted forms of action on a longer-term basis (cf. World Social Forum).

The most serious drawback of consolidating global civil society initiatives is with regard to enforcement. Though intergovernmental organizations have a direct interest in mobilizing such forces, since they are strategically important for enhancing their influence on national political decisions, it is apparent that such key actors as the UN have lost much of their capacity to mediate conflicts or to force governments to comply with decisions or recommendations taken in international consultations.

Ethics and the Framework(s) of Society

In drawing some conclusions from the preceding analysis, we should not proceed by stating principles and rules to be applied to situations. In religion, ethics, politics, philosophy, one is *simultaneously* confronted with descriptive and normative elements. So *ethics cannot be simply about the "ought" but also about the "is."* Because both are always involved, an assessment of globalization proceeds with reference to both dimensions of reasoning. This was done in the previous sections. Now we need to resume the at-times implicit thread and spell out some consequences of the analysis for social ethics.

Two crucial issues must be tackled as we move to the assessment of the impact of globalization on the frameworks of human and natural life. The first has to do with how we "receive" the situation we are in; the second, how we respond to it.

Let us take the first issue. We know that too many people have not had any say in the developments leading to the central role of capital and information/communications technology, in making it possible for capitalism to extend its grip over the whole world. We also know that there are aspects of our contemporary reality that have introduced positive changes and opened up new possibilities for the realization of certain projects and dreams of a just, sustainable, peaceful, and participatory social order.

The problem arises when the structures and relations set off by the evolution of capitalism in the past decades (coinciding with what came to be identified as globalization) acquire a self-referential capacity that aspires both to indefinite dominance over all areas of life — living and non-living — and to shut out any competing alternatives as unreasonable, inefficient, and impossible. This can emerge either in the form of actively positing such a view (as the preachers of globalization do), or in the form of social and ethical analysis that portray the situation as closed-off (as many analysts and commentators of globalization do). In biblical terms, such a position can be identified as *idolatrous* (claiming unreserved allegiance for that which is finite and contingent) or *oppressive* (ignoring the harm and pain caused to those who are excluded or who resist the established order). In our terms, it is also idealistic, because, against the evidence, it confuses one interpretation for the whole of reality.

The argument in this chapter is that the human experience of the world is marked by plurality in a constitutive way, and any attempt to reduce such plurality to homogeneity does harm to social and natural existence. This is why, for all its alleged or demonstrated efficiency, the market cannot be accepted as the major or only principle organizing the whole of human life. Plurality of forms of life — expressed in cultures, social and political organizations, economic systems that reflect particular situations developed for historical reasons — coupled with plurality of meanings attached to those forms, are values in themselves.

Globalization hinges on the tension between differentiation and homogenization, but it has also been legitimated in a way that projects particular ideological views onto all societies on earth. This jeopardizes hard-won achievements of the past two centuries, in which the economic drive of capitalism was progressively controlled by forms of social and political organization and regulation. These sought to increase the consideration and participation of those from below, to secure priority for the general or public interest, particularly through the consolidation of mechanisms of legal control of private interests, through conflict resolution and rights affirmation, and through procedures for representing the diversity of views and forms of life in society into policy-making processes. In raising private interests above public needs and rights, the workings of economic globalization have unleashed considerable unease, uncertainty, and instability, especially in poor and "emerging" countries and among the more vulnerable sectors of society everywhere. The positive accomplishments made possible by the new rules of the game have been obscured by the negative repercussions.

We reach now the second crucial issue: what has been the response to the impact of globalization? The prevailing position until the late-1990s was of celebrative "proselytizing" and resigned non-conformity. Those benefiting from the changes described in the last few chapters both hailed the new times and sought to implement a package of policies irrespective of local contexts. Those against the changes but powerless to halt them tended to accept at face value the *description* of reality given by the hegemonic powers and thus overstate its ineluctability. However, it was from these quarters that (a) some open defiance started to occur, usually involving exemplary action by small radical groups, and only slowly getting larger support, particularly from intellectuals and civil society cross-national and local networks; (b) under the impact that these acts of defiance and resistance had on public opinion some voices within the hegemonic forces started to call attention to the need for compromise and re-fashioning. The demonstrations at Seattle, Genoa, or the World Social Forum, for example, were matched by key advisors and actors stepping down in criticism of, say, the Washington Consensus, or UN Summit meetings and the Davos Economic Forum revising some positions on globalization and world poverty.

Breakthroughs happen where there is recognition that economic practices and decisions have deep and immediate effects on the livelihood of millions and may disorganize fragile social ties and safety nets that help people cope with unexpected or unfair circumstances, by mobilizing values of solidarity, reciprocity, respect for others, and participation in decisions that will affect their lives. Such recognition has led to the awareness that the market system cannot govern entirely the "social contract" that binds people as a community, where all have an equal right to participate and have access to the material and symbolic resources available in each society. The crude celebration of profit, competition, and efficiency can be countered by alternative ethical considerations giving priority to the public interest, solidarity, and responsibility. New forms of economic activity and organization; new political mechanisms for coping with cultural differences, plurality of views, and forms of life; and new experiences in autonomous problem-solving at the level of civil society come more clearly into the picture.

The kind of resistance that leads to a constructive alternative agenda has been largely rooted in culture, identity, and civil society politics that affirm democratic participation, pluralism, and solidarity with the excluded, despite their limits and ambiguities as argued above.

Responding to globalization, finally, is more than merely reacting to it. *It is taking responsibility for acting even where there are no clear precedents or rules to follow. It is to take steps in fear and hope, fully acknowledging that there are challenges raised by our present context that cannot be faced by simply reaffirming models from our traditions, our scriptural bases, without an exercise in translation, reinterpretation, and creation of new meanings and principles (hopeful realism).* Responsibility is needed for the elements of the framework, which are not given once and for all, and which can be threatened and destroyed beyond retrieval. Responsibility is needed to reconstruct those dimensions of the framework we recognize as already under attack or being undermined. Responsibility takes place in the context of not having enough certainties or evidences to guide us. So it involves making choices and taking actions beyond the established rules, common knowledge, or enough gathered information about the events that require those choices or actions.

This is where practical agreements can be reached between church groups and ecumenical non-ecclesial actions, under the broad view of working together with all groups and traditions striving for forms of human habitation in the world that affirm and sustain life, peace, justice, and the gift of faith.

Whether this will take the form of "thick" confession or covenant, or "thinner" networks/articulations around particular sensitive, contingent areas must be worked out in contexts. Perhaps neither can be cast off. But it is essential that we resist two temptations: (1) that of mounting a wholesale rejection of globalization in the name of "the community," an image of society as a homogeneous, unchanging group, defined by face-to-face forms of interaction, sharing or having to share a single or a substantive set of values and practices; and (2) that of surrendering to a proliferation of fragmented responses, which resist the totalizing drive of the first reaction, but are similarly unable to dialogue, entrenching themselves in their own particularities. Contemporary societies are not only plural and hybrid in their composition; they also require keeping that plurality alive so that we can avoid more harm to people and the environment, by trying to force them into a community that can only be experienced in small contexts. We need to affirm broad, encompassing values coming not only from morality and religion but also from politics. There will be no lasting future for the framework(s) of society without the reinvention of democracy and citizenship through "social contracts" or "covenants" that articulate the different spheres of social life without merging them in one single space. In political jargon, we need hegemonic projects that are able to gather different demands into alternative scenarios for a just social life.

The framework then can provide imagery for a new moment in history that is respectful toward the heritage of the past, the call coming from all those who suffered and paid the price for a dream of an *oikoumene,* which brings people together without forcing them to submit to others. But the framework must also be an open, enabling picture of that unrealizable dream. It can point to it while always warning against the assumption that we have already reached it. The *oikoumene* is an expression of the messianic character of our faith. It is *nurtured by hope,* derived from the persisting human drive toward forming and selecting frameworks in history to organize survival and thriving, and from the response to God's call to repentance, communion, and service (hopeful realism). These frameworks must be constructed between memory and faith, hope and love. The processional nature of such a hopeful anticipation of the *oikoumene* is expressed through the symbol of "the way" — open future, pilgrimage, disestablishment, longing for the kingdom to come, openness to grace, forgiveness of others' faults. In striving for the good life, the best ecumenical response in line with the argument developed here is: *there is a plurality of views of the good life, and none of them is*

159

good for all places at all times. But there are many ways in which partial overlaps, some of them "thick", some others "thin," can be responsibly worked out, to provide life in freedom and equality for all, while giving due attention to the different ways of interpreting and experiencing the good life, on the way.

PART III

Broadening the Ecumenical Covenant: Following Paths of Hopeful Realism

In Part I of this book we considered the current situation of the *oikoumene* — the whole inhabited world. We paid particular attention to the many challenges that ecumenical social ethics faces today, especially in the light of the process of globalization. As in past historical crises, so today, churches and ecumenical associations within the modern ecumenical movement understand that in order to be faithful to God and to follow the ways that God opens, they need to be involved in constructing frames of reference for social action. Here, we refer to the social, economic, and political institutions that are geared to improving the life of all people and that seek justice and peace.

In Part II we examined some current challenges and opportunities that lead us to be faithful to God's design. We considered the varied contexts where churches and ecumenical associations are called to act. Ecumenical social ethics endeavors to be a testimony to the faith that spurs us into action. Above all, it is to act so that the meaning of social action witnesses to the faith and encourages communities of believers to get involved in their varied situations. In order to be perceived as a testimony of faith, the construction of frames of reference for economic, political, and social life need to follow a meaningful way.

In Part III we see that the orientations to be followed have not been, and are not always, the same. Therefore, when we look at getting involved in social thought and action we realize that the covenants that keep us together in the ecumenical movement may, in the course of history, change.

In this section then, we reflect on the relevance of covenanting among communities of different faiths, particularly those of the Abrahamic tradition. We observe that one of the expressions of the process of globalization is the emergence of multicultural and religiously plural societies; we affirm that the ecumenical movement must recognize "the Other/s." Chapter 8 makes clear the need for new covenants be constructed. Facing the dominant social contract of our time, that is, "the market," which demands competition, and in order to engage with "the Other," a new type of ecumenical covenant is needed that calls for trust, solidarity, and mutual responsibility.

Such a construction has to be undertaken in a period of great tension. Ecumenical social ethics cannot be characterized as "irenic." It is to be practiced on the way, while finding directions through the paths of conflicting ideals. Chapter 9 suggests that what matters is to accept the challenge to widen the ecumenical movement; to give it a more inclusive character; to avoid the temptations of idealism while trying to be faithful to the presence of God in the reality of the *oikoumene;* searching to follow the movement of the Spirit through the complex situations of a common history. It is an ethics that tries to go *beyond idealism.* It is manifest through the practice of what we call *hopeful realism.*

CHAPTER 8

Covenanting for a Renewing of Our Minds: A Way Together for the Abrahamic Faiths

Lewis S. Mudge

Throughout the preceding chapters, we have been seeking a way forward in ecumenical social ethics, and, with that, a way forward for the ecumenical movement itself. Heidi Hadsell's chapter has brilliantly described the difficulties we face. I think we must say today that neither the intellectual resources nor the institutional base exists now for a purely Christian global ethical project. The churches, even if they were united in a triumphant ecumenical movement — which they are not — do not have the means (or, I think, the will) to do such a thing alone. They are too fragmented both within themselves and among themselves.[1] And they are even less prepared for what I think is the next needed step: a dialogue — at least among the "religions of the book" — seeking a covenantal basis for a just and flourishing human life on this planet.

Yet that is the project I now think lies ahead of us. Why so? Much has changed in the four years since this dialogue on accelerated processes of economic globalization began. These processes still accelerate and they still do their damage to the human spirit and especially to the poor. But some of these poor have now found a new champion: radical Islam. That changes a great deal. We are less engaged with revolutionary socialist

1. I have in mind not only the perennial differences over ministry, sacraments, theological outlook, and the like, but also deep divisions concerning the nature of human sexuality and the appropriateness of ordaining sexually active gay and lesbian persons, even those in loving and stable relationships. The last-named issue has had the effect of pushing nearly all other questions of social witness off the agenda, especially in North America.

projects and more with the ambitions of the more radical sectors of another world religion. We also observe an acceleration of religiously motivated violence from all three Abrahamic faiths. Global competition for economic or political advantage, combined with resentment from those left behind, has instigated at least some of this violence. Persons of faith have been persuaded that they have religious reasons for becoming foot soldiers (and sometimes commanders) in this competition. Issues of economic globalization have become intertwined with the geopolitical roles played by sometimes militant groups within Judaism, Christianity, and Islam.

This chapter cannot possibly disentangle all of this. Its purpose is to ask only one question. Can the "religions of the book" find ways to bear moral witness together against economic and political aggrandizement in their sometimes violent forms, rather than allowing so many of their members to be recruited unthinkingly into the fray? I will propose a "way" in which these covenantal traditions can covenant together in a "parallel hermeneutics" of the public world designed to foster global frameworks of human life-together in which the "minds" of our societies can be redirected toward paths of peace.

Global Economic Competition and Religious Violence

Bob Goudzwaard has given us an elegant and persuasive overview of modernity's march toward globalization and of the latter's character as an ideology with the Mephistophelean power to fascinate us into selling our souls. That needs no repetition here. But economic and political competitors at the world level do more than economic analysis can reveal. They also co-opt religious communities, especially the more conservative ones, as largely unwitting collaborators in their rival projects. And, as the evening news can tell us, this collaboration can and does escalate into religiously exacerbated violence, as often does the religious opposition to such globalization. I want to take the further step of briefly exploring this phenomenon of globalization and its meaning for the religious communities that find themselves so used.

But not all agree that the connection between globalization and religious violence is as I have just described it. The most prominent proponent of a contrary view is no doubt the redoubtable *New York Times* diplomatic and foreign correspondent Thomas Friedman.[2] Friedman has long argued that economic globalization, including outsourcing by American corporations, moves people out of religiously traditioned situations in which they are prone to be intolerant of other faiths, and into a different, presumably more peaceful, world of hi-tech corporate employment. His parade example is the cluster of computer programming, data-entry, and phone answering companies around Bangalore, India. Here, several hundred thousand technically educated young people make what by Indian standards are very good wages that, among other things, turn them into brand-conscious consumers of Western goods. Families in which the elder generation paints traditional images of the Hindu gods now have children who employ their artistic genes to do cartoon animation for triple or quadruple their parents' salaries.

Does such modernization, the direct result of globalization, actually tend to reduce interreligious violence? It may. It is said, for example, that the factor that headed off the outbreak of possibly nuclear war between India and Pakistan — Hindus versus Muslims more or less — was an urgent message from the Indian business community to Prime Minister Vajpayee that war would be bad for business. Americans and Europeans would pull their investments out of India. The high-tech park around Bangalore would close down. Foreign exchange reserves would wither. And so forth. Friedman has been known to comment as well that Palestinians and Israelis would cease their mutual violence if they became convinced that, with peace, there would be money to be made.

Friedman urges religious traditions themselves to modernize their

2. Thomas L. Friedman's comments on Bangalore have appeared in numerous *New York Times* Op-Ed Page columns and televised reports. For his views on the Middle East see *From Beirut to Jerusalem* (New York: Farrar, Straus and Giroux, 1989) and *The Lexus and the Olive Tree* (New York: Farrar, Straus and Giroux, 2000). Most recently Friedman has published *The World Is Flat: A Brief History of the Twenty-First Century* (New York: Farrar, Straus and Giroux, 2005). Here he extends his admiring treatment of economic globalization, arguing that the last impediments to galloping globalization have disappeared as newly empowered middle classes in India and China discover their stake in the global economy and energetic entrepreneurism puts them on an essentially level (i.e., "flat") playing field with Western nations. These developments, inevitable and unstoppable, leave weaker players permanently behind. The final 100 pages of Friedman's book offer a fascinating account of the political and economic roots of global Islamism. Friedman, of course, has his critics, notably Clifford Geertz and John Gray. See Gray's review, "The World Is Round," in the *New York Review of Books* 52, no. 13 (August 11, 2005).

self-understandings so as to live harmoniously in this new world of values. One way he hopes they will do so is to modernize education to include mathematical, technological, and business-oriented studies instead of religious education of the sort that teaches hatred of other faiths. In this respect India has done far more than, say, Saudi Arabia. But Friedman has no apparent idea of what it might mean for religious traditions to come to terms with this sort of modernity, apart from submission to the sort of privatization and marginalization we have seen in the West. If it is of the essence of a religious tradition to claim hegemony over all aspects of life, as for example in the Islamic notion of Shariah law, such modernization would be no small adjustment.

Granting the accuracy of Friedman's description of young technocrats in Bangalore, the problem remains that this sort of globalization-driven modernization does not, and almost surely cannot, include anywhere near enough of the world's poor. The jobs in question are with American corporations and vulnerable to the fortunes of those corporations. Little use is made of skills and resources native to the Indian subcontinent and sustainable within that context. In Bangalore approximately 250,000 persons are employed out of an Indian population of nearly a billion. Within a few hundred yards of the Bangalore headquarters of the Dell Corporation lie the festering streets of the very poor that have changed little over the years. If Friedman does not believe that a combination of envy and resentment among these people can make for new kinds of civil instability he is, I believe, mistaken. Economic progress needs to be indigenously based — that is, it must arise out of the sustainable resources and the culture of the people — to make the difference Friedman wants. Executives of trans-national corporations have still not learned how to foster that kind of economic activity.

Why not? First, the economics of globalization involves an ideology that cannot easily grasp the values of the poor. Our studies of globalizing economics have left me with one overwhelming impression: that there is a single-mindedness in such activities that devalues, if it does not blot out, all other notions of purpose in human life. Purely economic evaluations of globalization may miss this point, so it is worth pursuing briefly. The French scholar Pierre Bourdieu[3] stresses that we are dealing not merely

3. Pierre Bourdieu (1930-2002) was a professor of the College de France and the author of books such as *The Field of Cultural Production, Homo Academicus, Invitation to Reflexive Sociology, Language and Symbolic Power,* and *The Logic of Practice.*

with an economic agenda but with a "totalizing" ideological position. He has given us a term for this perspective: "neoliberalism."[4] Bourdieu sees the market as having become so dominant a model as to be largely beyond question. This is the case not only for the power elites that benefit from its assumptions but for many of those injured by those assumptions as well. Here is the "truth" that Western elites now hold "to be self-evident," as if it were pure rationality in practice. So pervasive has this logic become in our time that criticism of it begins to be seen as irrational, as lying outside the boundaries of plausible discourse. We are told that "there is no alternative."

This logic is one of cost-benefit analyses that sometimes make use of "rational choice theory." Here self-interest and profit maximization are assumed to be the only really rational (as opposed to unrealistically idealistic) human motivations. What we have here is in effect a new and greatly narrowed kind of social contract, refined to the point at which it is thought capable — through the application of complex formulas — of predicting human actions and reactions. The Chicago economist Gary Becker indeed won the Nobel Prize in Economics for a book extending such calculations to the understanding of all human behavior.[5]

As Jürgen Habermas has shown, such reasoning "colonizes" the life-world in ways that are often systematically and cleverly hidden. This ideology has the means, largely through capture of the media, of making itself

4. The term "neoliberalism" in this sense was until recently virtually unheard of in North America and, if uttered here, was likely to be misunderstood as some sort of new Rawlsianism. The minute one travels to Western Europe, or to Latin America, however, one hears the term being used, as Bourdieu does, to mean the dominance of the "market" model for all human interaction.

5. See Gary Becker, *The Economic Approach to Human Behavior* (Chicago: University of Chicago Press, 1976). A useful brief discussion of Becker can be found in Larry Rasmussen, *Moral Fragments and Moral Community* (Minneapolis: Fortress Press, 1993), 49f. As Rasmussen says, Becker is "arguing against Adam Smith's refusal to extend the logic of self-interest into noneconomic territory, together with Smith's corollary conviction that different spheres require different moralities.... In this scheme individuals are all 'utility maximizers' who operate from a relatively stable set of personal preferences.... Quite apart from markets, then, there is a mental process of market behavior and logic that supplies all the guidance needed for moral and other considerations necessary to the thousands of decisions we make." One may add, however, that some forms of rational choice theory, particularly in the work of John Nash, stress the advantage-maximizing properties of market cooperation. This does not, however, reduce the primacy of self-interest in the equation. Cooperation here is not altruism. It is a self-interest strategy in itself.

seem quite simply true, thereby forcing the progressive disappearance of "autonomous universes of cultural production." Independent publishers and filmmakers, independent media outlets, and other cultural institutions are forced to make their way with ever-diminishing public support. The "neoliberal" ideology, as Bourdieu sees it, eventually takes over all that lies in its way, but does so in an imperceptible manner, "like continental drift." Paul Treanor, a Bourdieu interpreter, has summed all this up in three short aphorisms:

- Act in conformity with market forces.
- Within this limit, act also to maximize the opportunity for others to conform to the market forces generated by your action.
- Hold no other goals.[6]

This seems to betoken a terrible diminishment of the possibilities of the human spirit. Hold no other goals? The commercialization of all values? No wonder such a mentality is blind to the consequences these commercial activities have for most of the poor of the earth. No wonder the poor feel sidelined, marginalized, and resentful. But, and this is my second point, this very fact has handed the globalizers and their political protectors a weapon they probably did not expect to have, but which they certainly know how to use. That weapon is religiously motivated violence against the demonized opponents of given power-interests. The rage of the people is thus directed away from those who actually oppress them toward their oppressors' adversaries. What is really a matter of economic justice at home is turned into a religious crusade against the religious or cultural other far away.

Examples are very numerous, and certainly complex. Terrorism by radical Islamists is rooted in economic injustice, and the sense of humiliation that goes with it, exacerbated by religious grievances. Oil-rich Saudi Arabian royalty and other Muslim elites can condone such activity if they sense that it can weaken their Western competitors without destroying markets for their oil. The Jihad is allowed to go on, and Saudi schools are allowed to teach hatred of the West on religious grounds, just so long as

6. This trenchant summary is the work of Paul Treanor in his article "Neoliberalism: Origins, Theory, Definition," on the web at http://web.inter.nl.net/users/Paul Treanor/neoliberalism.html.

these activities are thought to confer competitive advantages in the real game, which is political and economic.

The corresponding phenomenon in the West is hardly symmetrical, but it offers some interesting similarities. The present United States administration is interested in projecting American economic power around the globe and is willing to protect its markets and oil supplies by military means. Those who actually profit from these tactics form a very small elite of the super-rich. But the many poorly informed persons who support these policies politically, and particularly the young men and women who bear the brunt of battle, are encouraged to believe that they are on a great religious or moral crusade. George W. Bush himself is allowed to (and certainly does most earnestly) believe this, while many of his advisors probably do not.

The conflict between Israelis and Palestinians is a point where these Eastern and Western problematics meet. Israel is seen by Arabs as an outpost of American power and European culture bent on taking over Palestinian land. The Palestinians see the Israeli presence as a military and economic occupation. But both sides are willing to exploit the convictions of some of their people in order to portray the conflict as one between good and evil seen in religious terms. The training of Palestinian suicide bombers is a case in point. Muslim young men and women are allowed to believe that they detonate themselves for righteousness' sake when the real point is ending the Israeli occupation and gaining control of an economic asset, the land of Palestine. But, on the other side, consider the placement of very conservative Jewish families in some of the furthest-out West Bank settlements. These are people who believe that the biblical accounts of the gift of land to Abraham and his descendants remain politically valid today, and who are willing to fight for that original territory. While the real issue is the clash over land between two economic and cultural worlds, those inclined to do so are encouraged to believe in religious crusades. (That word in this place, I know, is ironic.) This game, of course, is dangerous. The Palestinian authority may not be able to stop its religiously motivated (or other) terrorists even if it wishes to do so. If Ariel Sharon were to wish to withdraw the settlements, the religious settlers could, and might well, use their weapons to fight him.

But this is not all. African nations, particularly ones already divided between Islamic majorities in the north and Christian majorities in the south, are possible future battlefields as well. The danger is that both Islamic and Christian politicians will use the people of these respective faiths as foot soldiers in conflicts billed, once again, as religious struggles, when the actual issues have to do with political and economic power. On the Islamic side, Africans are recruited into broader Islamic agendas, including those devoted to Jihad. On the Christian side one finds increasingly conservative churches whose people simultaneously succumb to advertising that leads them to covet Western consumer goods and can be led to see themselves militantly on the side of religious truth in a struggle against religious falsehood. A series of violent struggles between these forces for control of African nations and territories has already begun, and could well spread.

In all three cases, the Jewish, the Christian, and the Islamic, the religious traditions in question are being exploited and distorted for purposes that are, as Bourdieu suggests, expertly hidden from the foot soldiers involved. The question, then, is why these faiths are so vulnerable to such misuse.

Some of the vulnerability comes from internal features of the Abrahamic traditions. Mark Juergensmeyer has written of their moralistic tendency to polarize light and darkness, virtue and evil, which in turn is derived from dualisms encouraged by their respective creation narratives. He speaks of cosmic battles joined on the playing fields of human history through images of struggle and transformation. Religion becomes fused with violent expressions of social aspiration and nationalism. All this is exacerbated by the renewed role that religion plays in many lands at the heart of ideologies of public order.[7]

René Girard, still more complexly, writes of a primordial state of "mimetic" violence pitting all against all that eventually becomes religiously transformed by the collective sacrifice of a scapegoat. This sacrifice halts violence for a while; ritual repetition of the act suffices to absorb belligerent impulses. But soon enough an inner need arises to substitute new, actual, victims for the ritualized original victim. Others — those of different ethnicity or different faith — then answer to this need. Original violence then repeats itself, this time with the religious legitimation it has acquired along the way.[8]

---

7. See Mark Juergensmeyer, *Terror in the Mind of God: The Global Rise of Religious Violence* (Berkeley: University of California Press, 2000).

8. See René Girard, *Things Hidden Since the Foundation of the World* (Stanford: Stanford University Press, 1987).

Quite apart from such theories, it is plain that groups that feel marginalized and humiliated can be vulnerable to believing themselves invited, on almost any beguiling terms, into anything represented as a world-historical crusade or campaign to protect home values against foreign values, good against evil. Such involvement confers on the co-opted ones an instant sense of importance or significance that is otherwise denied them by the sophisticated powers that be. Religious leaders, motivated by their own desires for personal importance and proximity to power, often give full cooperation to this co-optative process. Such vulnerability to being used, combined with the tendency to intensify otherwise secular struggles, makes religion one of the most dangerous forces in the world today.

What is needed, then, is not the mere "modernization," that is, neutralization of religion by privatization and marginalization, that Friedman's proposals seem to imply. The tendency today is, if anything, the opposite. Religions East and West are becoming, if anything, more intrinsic to the different civilizations of humankind rather than less so. Certainly they are increasingly at the heart of many competing national ideologies. Hence they must take on a new sort of responsibility for determining what they are to be in the public world. The Abrahamic faiths in particular need to become far more critically aware of the roles they are often being asked to play. They need to find in their own traditions, and not merely in the blandishments of modernity, the resources not only for resisting exploitation but for making positive contributions to human well-being. And, above all, they need now to do so together.

A Way Forward Together for the Abrahamic Faiths and Their Allies

Leading off this anthology, Julio de Santa Ana introduced the idea of "frameworks" of common life making for justice and well-being in particular historical-cultural "situations." It is striking how "un-revolutionary" Santa Ana's proposition sounds. We have come some distance from the heyday of liberation theology (of which much more could be said) even as we hold on to many of that theology's basic insights. In no way do we repudiate Paulo Freire, or forget "the preferential option for the poor." But the world longs for stability and peace. We doubt that any one party, any one movement, truly has hold of the human future. So we are less partisan than we were a generation ago. Rather we reach out to others in search of a "framework" for human life generally, a renewal of our minds toward a mentality that can at least enable us to live together.

That is easier said than done. It is striking how coherent today are the forces making for globalization, and how incoherent are the energies of resistance to it. The economic expansion of the West employs violence and provokes violence in return. One can at least understand such a process. It all makes a kind of diabolical sense. But those who want no part in this equation, who think that human beings should live in alternative frameworks of understanding altogether, have no common creed or strategy. Not only are religious communities divided over these issues. The secular resistance forces, most of them various nongovernmental organizations, differ enormously among themselves as regards both means and goals. One longs to discern some spiritual unity in all this activity. The resisters need somehow to be gathered to a single task.

To this end, we have taken up the ancient Christian figure of the Way, this time interpreting it as a path along which to walk side by side with those who share a similar vision, even if they do so on different grounds. To what extent, for example, might the Abrahamic faiths make common cause with certain secular organizations — those that resist both globalization and the violent manifestations it both employs and provokes — thereby lending them a more coherent sense of life in the Spirit?[9] To what extent might the Abrahamic faiths, consistently with the full integrity of each, act together to do this? The rest of this chapter argues for a way of thinking about such a project. It employs the category of covenanting common to these faiths, and seeks to connect this in various ways with the notion of social contract underlying the frameworks or institutions of human life.

---

9. We should note that the "religions of the Book" and secular groups of "good will" are precisely those that the Vatican II documents *Gaudium et Spes* and *Lumen Gentium* mention as being potentially within the realm of salvation. Jürgen Moltmann makes this point with even greater emphasis in *The Church in the Power of the Spirit*. But in these and other sources the notion of shared involvement of these groups in what Moltmann calls "God's dealings with the human race" remains largely theoretical, rather than programmatic.

A Covenantal Coalition of Resisters

For these faiths and secular agencies actually to make promises to each other and to the oppressed of the world not only to resist totalizing ideologies but also to work together to renew humanity's value-frameworks would be a stunning step forward in our common journey through history. The world desperately needs something like this, but is ill-prepared even to conceive of it at the present time.

Trying to think out such a possibility, I reintroduce the ancient notion of "covenanting." I do this in full knowledge that this term has different meanings for Jews, Christians, and Muslims, that it has a variable resonance in secular circles, and that the arguments for it to be set out here employ intellectual categories very largely of Western origin. Furthermore, one cannot but be aware of the enormous internal complexity of each of the faiths concerned. Each has numerous theological trends, traditions and subtraditions, culturally specific expressions and organizational features. To speak of a pact of resistance to ideological totalization among the Abrahamic faiths and their potential secular partners is to raise the question: What Jews? What Christians? What Muslims? What secular partners? Who would answer this call? And what ideational and sociological profile might such respondents represent? What schools of thought, allegiances, and interests within these respective faiths might eventually be represented, and with what results?

Ideally, one would want the argument of this chapter to be made, at the very least, by well-informed persons representing each of the faiths concerned. Who might they be? A useful starting point might be to speak of "traditioned cosmopolitans," meaning by this people who are well formed in, and informed by, their religious traditions, people for whom these traditions are part of their identities, and yet who are also full participants in, adaptable, well-connected, citizens of the contemporary world. Such a combination of relationships and qualities is not unknown by any means. But it is very important that those who take part are not mere generalizers and assimilators who are willing to water their traditions down. The impetus to a covenanting project of resistance to totalization and of a reframing of life-together needs to come from within the deep integrity — the fullness — of each faith tradition that plays a role in this discourse.

Narratives with covenantal implications for the entire human race are interwoven throughout the complexly interrelated scriptures of Judaism, Christianity, and Islam. Many different scriptural passages might lend themselves to such a search for covenantal coherence. My initial suggestion would be the story of the gift of children to Abraham and Sarah, children in whom they rejoice but for whom they must be responsible for the very continuation of the covenantal gift. There are partly parallel Qur'anic and other Islamic traditional materials, where, of course, the descent from Abraham is through Hagar and Ishmael.

These traditions in particular give a certain interfaith coherence to this material. Abraham himself is neither Jewish nor Christian nor Muslim. He is prior to these distinctions. The Abrahamic covenant is thus a foundation for all three faiths, even if differently understood in each case. The fulcrum passage is Genesis 12:1-3:

> Now the Lord said to Abram, "Go from your country and your kindred and your father's house to the land I will show you, and I will make of you a great nation, and I will bless you and make your name great, so that you will be a blessing . . . and by you all the families of the earth will bless themselves."[10]

This text has Abraham summoned from the routines familiar to a Bedouin chieftain to a new sort of trust, a new sort of solidarity, a new sort of responsibility. Abraham believingly undertakes a role in the fulfillment of God's promise of a universal blessing for humankind. This undertaking is "reckoned unto him as righteousness" (Gen. 15:6).[11] There are significant

10. I have omitted the words "I will bless those who bless you, and those who curse you I will curse" not only because I find them difficult but because there is evidence that the Hebrew redactors of Genesis found them so, too. The summons to Abram is recalled on four other occasions in the Book of Genesis, and in all four of these passages the words in question are left out.

11. There is, of course, a second Abrahamic text — relevant to these concerns — to be considered. The famous passage, Genesis 22:1-19, concerning "the binding of Isaac" (known to Jews as the Akedah) must be read concurrently with Genesis 12:1-3 because the "binding" passage represents itself as an account of the test of faithfulness to which God puts Abraham regarding his worthiness to be the instrument of the divine promise to "all the families of the earth." It is also a passage fundamental to understanding what could be meant by an "Abrahamic" or "covenantal" coalition, for at its conclusion God renews the covenant promise of blessing to Israel and the nations in Genesis 12:1-3.

Commentary on Genesis 22:1-19 has been endless over the centuries, no doubt because this passage seems to represent a moral conundrum: God commanding Abraham to

echos in the New Testament, and later in the Qur'an. As for the former, see Peter's sermon in Acts 3, and the argument of Galatians 3, where Paul recalls the promise to Abraham as the basis of his own ministry to the gentiles and his understanding of salvation by grace alone received in faith. As for the latter, see numerous Qur'anic references to Abraham and his righteous obedience, for example Sura 37:108, in which Abraham is promised his reward for his submission to Allah, before he has done any righteous work.[12]

No doubt the foreseen blessing to "all the families of the earth" is understood differently in Judaism, Christianity, Islam, and the prospective

---

sacrifice his only son Isaac, who is, so to speak, the genetic bridge toward fulfillment of God's promise of future blessing, only at the last moment to provide a ram to be sacrificed instead. Any attempt to unravel all this in a few sentences would be the height of presumption. Is the divine command only part of a dream? In what sense is this a true test of faithful obedience?

12. The Abraham stories, considering the fullness with which they are told in Jewish and Christian Scriptures, are only partly present in the Qur'an. The Qur'anic dependence on these stories is unmistakable, but many of the original details are not repeated, some are changed, and some are elaborately embroidered. Some of the original Abraham material seems to be present "by reference." That is, certain Qur'anic passages only make full sense if the reader knows the original stories supplied only in part in the Qur'anic text. Yet it is probably true to say that Muslims are not interested — as Jews and Christians are — in arguing their spiritual descent from the Hebrew Book of Genesis. The Qur'an knows Genesis and uses it, but provides its own account of the origins of the Abrahamic covenant.

Sura 6:74-89 describes Abraham remonstrating with his father Azar for idolatrously "associating" other gods with the One True God. Abraham refuses to worship the heavenly divinities worshiped by his father. Neither star, nor moon, nor sun is worthy of such worship. They all rise and set. "I am through," Abraham says to his people, "with those you associate with God" (6:78). Abraham believes in the true God, not in beings associated with him. All this is within God's knowledge. Allah here gives Abraham an argument he can use. Allah exalts Abraham, Isaac, Jacob, Moses, Aaron, Jesus, and many others, favoring them above all other people, showing them the right path and expecting faithfulness in return. These are the people to whom Allah gave the Book, the Law, the prophethood. If they reject these things, Allah will give them to a people who will not deny them. God guides those among his creatures whom he will. It is vain to associate other divinities with him.

This "covenant of Allah," broadly understood as just outlined, is mentioned many times in the Qur'an. This covenant offers Allah's favor and protection in return for "submission" (the meaning of the word Islam). Submission includes the duty to spread the faith. Covenants (in the plural) are thought to have been concluded with a whole series of prophets, Abraham among them (Sura 2:124), who submitted to the responsibility of keeping and propagating the faith. The Qur'an then refers to communal forms of covenanting among those who have accepted the covenant of Allah.

partner communities. But can some version of resistance to totalization and renewal of the common mind be seen as characteristic of the "Abraham community" in whatever form it may have existed? There is a school of scripture interpretation that sees early, pre-Jewish, Israel precisely as a community of covenantal resistance to the imperial life-assumptions of the ancient Near Eastern empires — Sumeria, Babylon, Egypt. This community is seen as simultaneously engaged in creating a new frame of reference for life that, later redacted and crystallized, underlies Torah, Gospel, and Qur'an alike.[13]

Even so, the problem of appropriating all this for today is complex. One thing we learn from others who have previously tried something like this is that a serious dialogue among serious persons on this subject can quickly generate conflict rather than harmony. The most significant conflict-hazard lies not in differences of interpretation as such but in the ways these differences can be interpreted and exploited for political purposes. Apart from the simplistic idealism that just ignores the rocks along the path, the most prominent hazard of late has been the misuse of the stories of Abraham and his descendants to justify different modern interpretations of God's gift of the land of Palestine, whether to Jews or to Muslim Arabs or to both.[14] Christians and Jews, whatever political views they may

13. See Henri Frankfort, *Before Philosophy: The Intellectual Adventure of Ancient Man* (Baltimore: Penguin Books, 1974), and George Mendenhall, *The Tenth Generation: The Origins of the Biblical Tradition* (Baltimore: Johns Hopkins University Press, 1973). Of course it is clear that we know of "early Israel," if such an entity ever existed in history, only through texts redacted in the later period of the Israelite kings, priests, and prophets by persons with commitments variously reflecting the theopolitics of their own times and situations. How, then, distinguish early Israelite material from subsequently framed narratives that either tell the patriarchal stories or subsequently interpret them for their own ulterior purposes? My point is not that we can make such a distinction with any confidence today, but rather that the Abrahamic narratives in principle do not belong to any one set of redactors or interpreters. In principle what underlies these narratives belongs to all and passes judgment upon all. Whatever redaction may have taken place was likely for the purpose of accommodating the narratives to a royal ideology, and therefore unlikely to have introduced these critical features.

14. The notion that Islam is descended from Abraham and Hagar by way of Ishmael is not present in the Hebrew Bible as such (written long before Islam began to exist) but is rather an interpretation of these texts. For Muslims, they lead back to Abraham (Hagar, interestingly, is not mentioned in the Qur'an) and a claim to Abrahamic territory. Some Jews and Christians see the descent through Hagar and Ishmael as giving Muslims at best a tainted or secondary relationship with Abraham, an honorable status perhaps, but without any scripturally based claim to territory.

entertain, will do well to avoid this mode of argumentation. All three faiths have authentic, if different, connections with the Abrahamic covenant. The manner of their descent from the Patriarch "according to the flesh" is not the issue. Islam honors Abraham as one who behaved righteously, as one who "submitted" to God. Jews and Christians will be wise to do the same.

Practicing Parallel Hermeneutics

Our task is to find a hermeneutic of all three versions of the Abrahamic tradition that not only takes account of such hazards and others like them, but also aims at resistance to totalization and the reconstruction of frameworks for abundant life. I propose that we come at this task by pursuing a practice of "parallel hermeneutics." By this I mean that Jews, Christians, Muslims — together with the "secular" partners in struggle whose solidarity we solicit — should all continue to interpret their sources, their historic traditions of shared life, with the fullest independence and integrity, but now begin to do so walking next to one another along on a common path. This would not be for the purpose of devising a doctrinal or symbolic merger, or for seeking to construct a "common belief system." We are too attitudinally postmodern to want to do any of that. But along this path we can ask whether the notion of a covenant of resistance to totalization, and of a renewal of our minds for a more just social framework, can be seen as supported, however variously, by the Abrahamic traditions from which we come. As we ask this question in our own various ways, we ask it in the knowledge that others alongside us are asking it in their ways too. Hence we pursue hermeneutics in a "parallel" relationship with one another.

A program of "parallel hermeneutics" recognizes that within each tradition of life and faith there is what William Schweiker calls "hermeneutical realism"[15] at work. I take this to mean that symbolism located within a certain identity-determining context lends authority to moral assumptions and precepts for those who inhabit it. Finding one's identity within a given community lends a quality of self-evidence or apparent apodicticity to that community's expectations. That quality of specific,

15. William Schweiker, "Religious Convictions and the Intellectual's Responsibility," in *Criterion* (Autumn 2003): 5.

contextual, moral awareness needs to be carefully preserved. It is precious in an age such as ours.

And yet, we are now unprecedentedly living in a common social space-time, a world of currently competing and overlapping identities. As William Schweiker again has written, our world is one in which "cultures or civilizations act back upon themselves with respect to information coming from other cultures and civilizations."[16] Schweiker calls upon the word "reflexivity" to describe this global phenomenon of continuous mutual adjustment of religions and cultures to one another. We are able to observe and reflect critically upon the ways we respond to the roles of others in contexts we find significant. We can critically appropriate the meanings we find in their presence. We must try to make those reflections as inwardly searching and as outwardly constructive as possible. In short, however different from each other we may be, we bear hermeneutical responsibilities toward one another: to hear accurately and to reply fairly. We are responsible also for the practical consequences of our interpretative work in the worlds we share. All these are reasons for using the word "parallel."

Religiously uncommitted interpreters of common human experience, such as secular NGOs, also need to participate in this parallel hermeneutical process. Many of them reflect former or ancestral religious commitments in their work. They can tell us much about the journey of such ideas through the forms and expressions common in the public world. "Social contract" thinking, for example, often embodies ideas of religious origin. The paths such ideas have taken "outside" religious communities can be very instructive to those who are now trying to make sense of them "inside." Awareness of the many "worldly" transcriptions of covenantal narratives can help religiously committed communities to position themselves more imaginatively in society. They can try to discern where their own narratives are, or are not, resonant with what can be heard meaningfully at any given time in the public world.

Most important of all, such worldly resonances can also function as bridges among the different religious traditions. We can see, in a commonly shared world, the consequences of what we do and believe. We can see what has been made of our covenantal traditions by thinkers and actors who know these traditions but stand personally apart from active participation in them.

16. Ibid., 13.

One such person was the Jewish philosopher Hannah Arendt, who left us an account of the Abraham narrative that invites parallel-hermeneutical treatment. Her treatment focuses upon what she calls "the power of stabilization inherent in the faculty of making promises." Of this, she writes,

> [W]e may see its discoverer in Abraham, the man from Ur, whose whole story, as the Bible tells it, shows such a passionate drive toward making covenants that it is as though he departed from his country for no other reason than to try out the power of mutual promise in the wilderness of the world, until God himself made a covenant with him.[17]

I confess that I do not find the matter put exactly this way in Genesis. Theological critics will say that Arendt's restatement of the Abrahamic tradition simply leaves God's prior initiative out of the picture, thereby fundamentally distorting the message. Or perhaps we may infer that God's covenantal intention is indeed theologically prior, but that Abraham — or anyone — must live into its earthly meanings, and the moral conundrums associated with their finitude and incompleteness, before the promise behind, and ahead of, human promise-keeping can be fully articulated as God's. Is this what Arendt is telling us? I think her interpretation of Abraham is open to such a construal, even if she does not make it explicit.

Whether or not Arendt would have agreed with this view of her intent, it is important methodologically to see what she is doing. She is translating the Abrahamic covenant narrative from confessional terms available only to believers into philosophical language accessible to all. She has in effect anticipated a characteristic idea of Paul Ricoeur: that philosophy begins when we provisionally adopt "the motivations and intentions of the believing soul," but then proceeds as that provisionally adopted symbolic language "gives rise to thought."[18] Ricoeur argues that all philosophical reflection rests in this way upon some original "gift" of sense provided by "the fullness of language": narrative, parable, metaphor.

In the case of Abraham, both the original covenantal language and

17. Hannah Arendt, *The Human Condition* (Chicago: University of Chicago Press, 1978), 219.
18. Paul Ricoeur, *The Symbolism of Evil*, trans. Emerson Buchanan (Boston: Beacon Press, 1967), 19.

its philosophical yield have to do with the basis of human society as such, the "blessing" of "all the families of the earth" (Gen. 12:3). The possibility of "stability" in Arendt's terms (read moral-social framework) in "the wilderness of the world" (read the present human situation) lies in an ability, understood theologically as a covenantal gift, to make and keep promises to one another. This ability to make and keep promises is for Arendt the basis for all human social institutions. It is the payoff in secular terms of what the scriptures understand in religious terms. It is thus understandable both to persons committed to it in terms of their faith-traditions and to persons without such commitments.

As I have already claimed, this secularizing, open-to-anyone, translation of covenanting as social promise-keeping has a potential bridging function among the Abrahamic faiths. Whatever their differences, and they are many, these faiths live in the same social world and have to deal with the same conundrums of human interrelationships. They are seeing their own covenanting traditions, secularly transformed, being acted out in the world around them. Promise-keeping, something they know well, turns out to be fundamental to the stability of all social institutions.[19]

The Givens and the Gift

But now the argument takes a further step. The institutions made possible by various patterns of promise-keeping are experienced by us as social givens. Each of us is born into a world in which such givens are already present. Each of us is initiated through processes of formation into the promise-keeping behavior needed to maintain these givens. But the given structures, just as they are, are never good for all time. As circumstances change, the established frameworks become inadequate for defining and maintaining "the good society." But covenantal relationships, once in place, are hard to change. We typically resist altering the patterns of promise-keeping we have become used to, even when they cease to serve

19. I use the word "institutions" in the two senses described by Robert Bellah: institutions as organized structures (e.g., the Roman Catholic Church, or the British Parliament, or the United Nations), and institutions as established patterns of behavior (e.g., marriage, or churchgoing, or shopping, or apartheid). Institutions in the first sense typically provide frameworks for the support of institutions in the second sense. See Bellah et al., *The Good Society* (New York: Alfred A. Knopf, 1991).

their social function. Patterns of promise-keeping confined to a certain social class or race in which others are considered outside the covenant (for example in the social institution of apartheid) will not suffice when others deserve and demand justice. Marital promise-keeping confined to heterosexual relationships will not do when homosexual persons deserve and demand the right to make such promises too.

Arendt is well aware of these ways in which the given patterns of promise-keeping become too narrow and exclusive. She also knows human nature. Keeping promises sometimes requires more of us than we can deliver. In short, the human making of covenant promises is not sufficient of itself. There are moments when one needs loyalty to a promise to humankind that lies beyond the patterns of promises behind our accepted social habits, if these covenanted givens are to be challenged and changed in order to do justice in new situations. Hannah Arendt acknowledges this point mainly in her separate discussion of "natality," the new thing. But it belongs in her discussion of promise-keeping.

In short, human beings are not the only promise-keepers in the covenantal encounter. Arendt mentions the covenant God finally makes with Abraham. But she leaves the impression that this divinely initiated covenant is a kind of reward for effective work, or a decision to put Abraham on the payroll to continue doing something he does well. But much more is involved. Abraham, the exemplary promise-keeper where family and tribe are concerned, is summoned to risk entering into relationships beyond routine, beyond the evidence. The Abrahamic faiths need to say that, in taking this risk, Abraham becomes founder of a new kind of covenantal society based not only on his promise-keeping but on God's.

This interpretation of human promise-keeping as needing to be taken up into some form of divine promise-keeping is obviously relevant to the notion of a covenant of resistance among religious communities, and their secular allies, to the totalizing givens of current political and economic life. We are asked to undertake covenantal, promise-making, relations to one another beyond our usual tribal routines, thereby challenging the too-limited patterns of promise-keeping that undergird our unjust social givens. And that is possible only if we believe fervently that the givens of our world are both grounded and challenged by a promise to humankind that is God's gift. Human promise-keeping, for its very salvation, has to be taken up and included in the promises of blessing inherent in God's purposes for the human race.

LEWIS S. MUDGE

Covenantal Modes of Worldly Interaction

I now want to amplify this dialectic between the givens and the gift. I will do so by illustrating it in the case of three clearly covenantal qualities of human interaction. It is plain that we can learn a great deal from studying the passage of religious ideas we thought we owned through "the wilderness of the world." That is why today's interpreters of common human experience — especially the historians, the sociologists, and the political philosophers — need to be in our dialogue. With their help we need to look at the worldly passage of several of the most important social concepts — in addition to those Arendt treats — derived from narratives of covenanting. The next paragraphs of this chapter try to do this.

I have chosen three such social-narrative concepts: (1) fostering conditions of trust, (2) acting in solidarity, and (3) taking responsibility. There are no doubt many others that would serve our purposes. I choose these three because they have the particular quality of belonging both to faith traditions and to the public world, although not necessarily with the same meanings in each case. These are expressions for patterns of human conduct in relationships. Note their verbal-noun (gerund) forms: not just "trust," but "fostering conditions of trust"; not just "solidarity," but "acting in solidarity"; not just "responsibility," but "taking responsibility."

Such expressions also have significant inter-cultural valence, picking up meanings from virtually every context (novel, poem, culture, period of history) in which they appear. I will argue further that each of these expressions points to a different pattern of human promise-keeping. Each is maintained in its true (or redeemed) nature only through actions that make sense only as expressions of faith in a Promise beyond the promises human being can make on their own. In doing this I will argue that our given frameworks of life, our institutions both organizational and behavioral, can only fulfill true human needs when they evince interrelational qualities of action such as these. I will therefore argue that trusting one another, living in solidarity, and taking responsibility can become qualitative criteria for judging the validity of directional orientations for joint social action and the specific social proposals that flow from them.

Finally, each of the action-expressions here profiled, along their different historical paths, move through three broad stages of development. First, one can trace in them the influences of religious covenantal narratives. These origins show up in different ways. Sometimes they are simply transmitted through the general cultures in which they arise. Sometimes there are specific ties to scriptural narrative models.

Second, one can note a deterioration in the social potency of these ideas as they move further away from their religiously covenantal connections. One sees a corresponding decline in the quality of social relationships and the colonization of society by absolutist ideologies of the market and the state. The meanings of our social concepts, such as they are, become routinized and thereby confined within standardized role expectations.

Third, all such covenantal social ideas are capable of revival by persons and communities willing to take the risks of embodying them beyond routine. One risks the project of trusting strangers, one risks new kinds of solidarity, one risks taking on responsibilities that others will not assume. Clearly one has to ask what deeper confidence is at work when people, in such ways, risk their own futures for the human future.

Tempting as it would have been to do so, however, I have not tried to impose this grid in any rigid way on the brief histories of ideas that follow. No crypto-Hegelian intention is present here. These accounts are quite different, as befits the different histories of our three socio-covenantal notions. But I think nevertheless that one can discern the pattern just laid out in each of these narratives, even as it emerges historically in very diverse ways.

Fostering Conditions of Trust

The factor of trust in human relationships underlies the very possibility of cohesive civil society. But evidence for an atrophy of trust in Western cultures, if not in others as well, is too obvious to need much reiteration. An ample sociological literature testifies to this insight, not to speak of numerous studies of this subject in political and economic theory. Among more recent writers, both Robert Putnam[20] and Francis Fukuyama,[21] in their different ways, find trust to be an indispensable ingredient in the "so-

20. Robert Putnam, *Making Democracy Work: Civic Traditions in Modern Italy* (Princeton: Princeton University Press, 1993).

21. Francis Fukuyama, *Trust: Social Virtues and the Creation of Prosperity* (New York: The Free Press, 1995).

cial capital" needed to make contemporary societies work. Putnam finds a strong factor of trust (especially in the political realm) in the stable, relatively law-abiding, communities of northern, as opposed to southern, Italy. Fukuyama studies the positive economic consequences of trust as social solidarity, or practice of the "art of association," in certain countries such as Germany and Japan, as opposed to the United States with its looser social structures. Add to these two penetrating studies by Adam Seligman,[22] the first identifying trust as the key ingredient within a broader treatment of civil society and the second focusing entirely on "the problem of trust" as such.

The works mentioned supply rich empirical data and illuminating conceptual analysis. But they offer little of a constructive nature. Seligman, in particular, after two volumes of philosophical effort to give trust a secular rational basis, seems close to despair. He believes that without trust we lose "the very terms of rationality," a catastrophe that could land us in a "more brutal and Hobbesian" world.[23]

The notion of "trust" is notoriously hard to define. What trust "is" depends on the conditions, shared assumptions, and institutions — in short the "givens" — that make it possible. These vary enormously from time to time and from place to place: infant and responsive parent; investor and responsible accountant; pacts of all kinds that are expected to be kept. Indeed "trust" becomes tangible only in act. An act of trust makes sense only if someone else — over whom I have no control — can be counted on to respond as I expect.

My reasons for entertaining such an expectation may be of various kinds: past experience, knowledge of the person concerned, traditions of the organization of which we both serve, cultural assumptions about the nature of human integrity, or even calculation of how the other person will see his or her interest in the matter concerned. Whatever my reasoning, my action is an instance of trusting behavior.

22. Adam Seligman, *The Idea of Civil Society* (New York: The Free Press, 1992) and *The Problem of Trust* (Princeton: Princeton University Press, 1997).

23. Seligman, *Trust*, 175. He writes, "we may well query if the loss or transformation of trust as a mechanism of social interaction (public and private both) is not part of a broader transformation which will see a transformation of the very terms of rationality, perhaps in the direction of a *wiederbezauberte* world. Whether, as I suspect, an enchanted world is also a more brutal and Hobbesian one is an empirical question, the answer to which may not be long in coming."

All this indicates why I speak of "conditions (circumstances, narratives, dispositions) of trust" rather than "trust" alone. In our world, such conditions may or may not exist. But at least we are able to talk about what they are, or could be, in any given case. Analysis of "conditions" takes our study beyond dictionary definitions of a word into the historical and social circumstances of the sorts of expectant actions I have described.

Characteristic early-modern notions of the conditions of trust tie them closely to social contract doctrines. Several of these, in turn, draw on Christian versions of the covenant tradition. In the work of John Locke, for example, the social bond is moored in a providential (remarkably Calvinistic) narrative of each individual's accountability lived out under God's watchful benevolence. In Locke's view, the worldly reasoning that constitutes society arises from a "law of nature" (strikingly different from Rousseau's later vision of the "noble savage") in which individual persons — pictured as already property-holders — stand responsibly before God and voluntarily take leave of their "natural" state to form a commonwealth reflecting the fundamental principles of a primordially God-given order or framework. If persons could be trusted, it was because all — the trusters and the trusted alike — were assumed to stand accountably in such relationships. Rights, privileges, freedom, equality, a complex set of social "givens," all follow. Human affairs and the reason that governs them are thus validated in implicitly covenantal terms.

But by the late 18th century, Scottish Enlightenment thinkers such as Adam Ferguson and Adam Smith began to avoid references to the Deity in their theories of society, and to couch these theories increasingly in economic terms. The individual was thought to be constituted in his or her individuality through the very act of exchange with others. Yet the world of exchange still functions within relations of "moral affections" and "natural sympathy." Interpersonal bonds surround and mitigate the raw operations of rational self-interest. The world is still seen in a general way as ruled by divine providence, but such factors less and less enter into social explanations.

But soon we begin to see an outright disengagement of this trusting moral sense from any direct theological linkage.[24] The thinker who undermined the former fragile syntheses was David Hume. Hume separated interest-based exchange relations from grounding in any other type of re-

24. Adam Seligman, *The Idea of Civil Society*, 30.

lationship. He argued, in effect, that society-engendering agreements to work together are simply based on the desire for efficient resource use. Here, as I have already argued, are the foundations for a new social world of rationally adjudicated, jostling, individual interests.

We have today in effect generalized Hume's notion into a conception of individuals as morally autonomous actors whose activities, whatever they may be, alone constitute the marketplace, the political realm, and a multitude of accompanying institutions. The problem of social coherence then becomes one of grasping the conditions of trust among such agents. We may have confidence that such institutions work. But, under such conditions, trust is only confidence in the predictability of one another's "reciprocal behavior," because the economic or political rationality of such behavior is in principle transparent.

But such a conception of society and of our reasons to be confident in its workings suffices only up to a point. As modernity advances, institutions themselves begin to become differentiated and insecure. Social roles come to be more fluid. As individuals come to play multiple roles in different aspects of their lives, an element of risk begins to enter the picture. At a certain point one cannot count on mere institutional expectations in taking actions that anticipate predictable responses. Increasingly, we mean by the word "trust" an inner disposition to risk initiatives that confidence in institutions as such cannot justify: the honesty of a business partner, the decency of a contractor. Trust, as opposed to mere institutional confidence, begins to be focused on a notion of the intrinsic integrity — the trust-worthiness — of the enlightened and principled individual.[25] Social institutions increasingly depend on people being willing to take such risks: risks that cannot themselves be institutionalized.

Inevitably, and especially as postmodernity dawns, this turns out to ask too much of us. We find diminishing agreement concerning the nature and content of the moral personhood on which institutions depend. The neighbor cannot be comprehended today within any set of putatively universal concepts. The neighbor is now genuinely Other: unfathomable in his or her freedom. We may gradually cease to produce the kind of individuals who trust and are trustworthy because of who they are, and begin to

---

25. See Luhmann, "Familiarity, Confidence, Trust: Problems and Perspectives," in *Trust: Making and Breaking of Cooperative Relations,* ed. Diego Gambetta (Oxford: Basil Blackwell, 1988), 102.

produce persons having largely group-based identities with very little sense of individuality, persons with no disposition to trust individuals of other groups at all, and indeed see, not the personal risk of trusting in dealing with others, but rather the danger these others pose because they are members of another group not to be trusted at all. Society today is becoming a sphere of systemic ethnic or religious distrust of others. These others are seen to pose potential dangers just because their inner lives and motives are anything but transparent.

So we proceed to limit the dangers posed by such opaque otherness by subjecting public behavior to a plethora of rules and regulations in many arenas of life: for the stock market, for academic behavior, and even for relationships between the sexes. Regulation enhances what sociologists call "system confidence." But this is not the same thing as trust. As people look for ways to get around the rules, we are burdened with endless questions of interpretation. What, exactly, constitutes securities fraud, plagiarism, or "date rape"? It may, and often does, take thousands of pages of legislation to answer such questions.

Rational choice theory then comes to the rescue. It develops in directions designed to help economic and political players turn the rules to their advantage. Human interactions become understood in terms of game-theory. Social thinking becomes the calculus of how a relentless pursuit of private interests, even in highly regulated environments, will lead ourselves and our competitors to behave.

Such a situation is ultimately unstable because it leads either to tyranny by those who win the power game or to an anarchy of competing interests.[26] Either way, genuine human potential in the form of social capital is substantially diminished. There is no "invisible hand" at work here. Our present economic nexus will not even be sustainable unless there are new associational relationships capable of moderating purely economic forces. In the end, an absence of trust, however defined, between persons, institu-

---

26. I have in mind Kenneth Arrow's insight that there is an essential inconsistency in public reasoning unless all are of one mind, which means submission to the will of a "dictator." See Kenneth Arrow, *Social Choice and Individual Values* (Cowles Commission for Research in Economics, Monograph No. 12, 1951). I infer then that a world reduced to "rational choice" principles will be either an inconclusive competition among "preferences," or some interest will corner the market and be able largely to determine the direction of common life. I am indebted for the Arrow reference to Dr. Austin Hoggatt, professor emeritus in the Haas School of Business at the University of California, Berkeley.

tions, and social groups means that instead of building relationships based on mutual confidence we constantly have to use our wits to defend ourselves against competitors who will take advantage of us if they can. This absorbs attention and energy to the point that society cannot be openly democratic and cannot proceed to build truly participatory institutions.

There is another possibility, however. It is the one we are pursuing here: a redeployment of covenantal visions living in conscious parallelism with one another in the global public sphere. Such a development could help restore the conditions of trust that the good society needs for its existence. That would indeed be a "gift" to humankind.

But how might that happen? A fuller explanation needs to wait for the final section of this chapter. But this much may be said. Now that we live (in Schweiker's sense) in a "reflexive" world, the threatening Other is no longer a purely blank cipher. He or she may be working at the next desk, gossiping at the same watercooler. A parallel hermeneutics of traditions becomes increasingly feasible. That can include many topics, but finally it needs to become a mutual inquiry into what it is in our respective traditioned self-understandings that makes us trustworthy. And that question, I will argue, comes down to this one: What, in the context of the promises for which we live, has been entrusted to us?

That is, as we have seen, the Abrahamic question. It is answered differently in the different faiths. But what I believe to have been entrusted to me, that is, to keep faith with the most fundamental Promise in my life, is the basis of my own trustworthiness. And in a truly parallel relationship, I expect that this is true of the Other person as well. Hence trusting becomes a form of expectation that promises will be kept because the Promise in which we believe entrusts that responsibility to us. A parallel hermeneutics of promise-keeping, in some form, is then a primary condition of trust in our time, especially as that hermeneutic, step by step, fosters the formation of trust-based frameworks or institutions.

Acting in Solidarity

But there is another publicly accessible conceptual derivative of covenanting or promise-keeping. We may call it "acting in solidarity." This term has meanings that overlap with some just discussed. It, too, has scriptural connections, but also a complex secular pedigree. And its contemporary usage is likewise highly context-dependent. All this makes it potentially useful in stitching together a sphere of discourse in which the "religions of the book," with their secular partners, can meet in a shared project of resisting ideological totalization.

The *Oxford English Dictionary* defines "solidarity" as "the fact or quality, on the part of communities, etc., of being perfectly united or at one in some respect, especially in interests, sympathies, or aspirations." The word came into the English language as recently as the 19th century from the French term *solidarité,* whose history has left its mark on contemporary usages.

That the general idea of "living in solidarity" has biblical connections is quite clear. The evidence is everywhere. I point to the covenant renewal ceremony in Joshua 24 as an example. The message in this and related passages is that the tribes of Israel are being drawn from relative isolation into an amphyctionic solidarity around the worship of YHWH, a solidarity over against the political and metaphysical totalizations of the ancient Near Eastern empires. Of course the word "solidarity" itself is much too recent to appear in the Bible. It is rather a term we use to grasp and communicate a social reality that the Bible describes.

A different line of development occurs in classical Latin. The use, for example, of the term *solidum* in ancient Rome is very suggestive. I am in a state of *solidum* with a person if I agree to guarantee his or her repayment of a loan. I bind my own integrity to that of that other person. I stand alongside that other person in such a way as to protect him or her from the debt collectors should he or she default. I promise to come if necessary to that person's assistance, and that person now has an obligation to me to see that that necessity does not arise. These facts create a very concrete relationship between us.[27] Based on this pedigree, the noun "solidarity" may be thought to refer to such a state of affairs given collective meaning. We stand alongside one another in a manner that involves our own integrity and an expectation of integrity from our comrades, over against an alien, potentially totalizing, power.

The French usages that underlie, and continue after, the adoption of the term into English *may* go back to the revolutionaries of the late 1780s. But certainly the term is in use among the revolutionaries of 1848 and of the Paris Commune of 1870-71. Such usages in every case express a solidar-

---

27. I owe this classical example to conversation with Julio de Santa Ana.

ity of resistance to entrenched power. It quickly spreads to European anarchists or radical socialists of all kinds whose objectives were to bring down established orders in the name of new social principles, often defined only as other than the present ones.[28] Solidarity in this sense referred to the binding together of militant groups with common identities and common causes.[29]

But by the late 19th century in France solidarity has also come to refer to a decidedly unrevolutionary political theory of society. It has become a form of social contract doctrine in which people recognize their personal and collective dependence on one another in a network of taken-for-granted social support. Here solidarity is a social "given," not subject to question. Common social identity now becomes the primary value, as well as being a collective form of wealth (one form of what we today would call "social capital") that is in everyone's interest to uphold and preserve.

Society, with its fabric of solidarity, is considered in effect to have been always there, yet always subject to negotiation through which it gradually evolves. Societies organized on this principle provide what amounts to a collectively funded insurance (like the Latin *solidum*) against the consequences that may befall individuals. There is a known level of risk that this will happen, and solidaristic societies take that into account. In this form of solidaristic doctrine society is not founded on the basis of some principle external to it — say "natural law." Society is just there, a "given," the context into which one is born. It therefore legitimates itself. It is in each person's interest to live by it and uphold it.

In the 20th and 21st centuries, as communications improve and societies become more mobile, we see a somewhat new phenomenon. A sense of community against a common adversary or around a common cause

28. A rudimentary Internet search under the headings "solidarity" and "revolutionary solidarity" gives this impression very strongly. These terms seem almost to have been taken over by groups, mostly very small, that call themselves "anarchist" or use language to that effect. The sense of unequal struggle against tyrannical regimes sets these groups looking for allies that can be trusted.

29. Such an awareness of common cause and possibility continued into the 20th century. It lay behind the independent trade union federation among Polish shipyard workers — formed in September 1980, and taking "Solidarity" as its name — under the leadership of Lech Walesa and supported by the Roman Catholic Church. Forced underground for a time by government repression, "Solidarity" grew in power until it achieved recognition in 1989 as a party eligible to compete in the Polish general elections. This led to a "Solidarity"-led coalition government in 1990.

can be combined with important differences on other points. Thus coalitions develop among otherwise highly diverse groups that come together where their interests or aspirations intersect. Many Americans who otherwise have little in common unite in solidarity to "defeat George Bush." A common enemy, let us say the State of Israel as seen by different Palestinian terrorist brigades, can invoke the sense of solidarity among those who share that position whatever other analyses-of-situation and purposes these persons and groups may entertain. Solidarity in the face of a common enemy can also transcend sharp differences of opinion as regards ideology and tactics.

We also see situations in which little sense of solidarity exists at all, where by rights there ought to be at least some such awareness. This is often because the connections between different objectives and causes are ignored in favor of "single issue" politics. People work on environmental matters through the question of air pollution but not of water rights. The issue of torture becomes disconnected from the wider question of state-sponsored violence. Solidarity, if the word is to be used at all, becomes focused on smaller and smaller groups of the very like-minded. And even when larger coalitions are formed they are generally based on evanescent and short-lived agreements. The experience of participation is often more strategic, and even calculating, than it is solidary. There may be no more than a temporary realization of commonality among persons of diverse identities, momentarily bound together by their similar reactions to striking public events or causes. Experience of this sort is hard to connect with commonly held philosophical doctrines.[30]

And it is notable in our day, especially in the West, that groups of persons who, objectively seen, do have common interests and common adversaries, let us say in the economic realm, often cannot grasp that commonality because the ideology of individual economic calculation and striving blocks the awareness of it. Such strivers feel no sense of solidarity with others in the same boat when by all rights they should. If I may be shamelessly partisan for a moment, it seems clear that southern "poor

30. The decline in contemporary thought of Marxist philosophy as a coherent and current system may have something to do with this. The thought of Karl Marx is of course as inherently coherent as it ever was. What I mean is that we seldom today take it on board as a whole. Certain Marxist ideas, e.g., his theory of ideology with its implications for the sociology of knowledge, are alive today at least in intellectual circles. Other Marxist ideas, e.g., "the dictatorship of the proletariat," are not.

whites" in America who vote Republican do so against their own economic and political best interests: interests that successful political propaganda and their own misperceptions have prevented them from seeing.

It seems fair to say, then, that the notion of solidarity has lost much of its capacity to hold together the many ways persons organize their resistance to totalizing forces in the world. For there to be coherent communities of solidarity today, different narratives of resistance to totalization need to intersect in something other than philosophical analyses or strategic expedients. Perhaps this can happen in the interaction of covenantal communities such as the "religions of the book" whose narratives contain sources out of which the notion of solidarity originally arises, and which may yet transform its meaning in the contemporary world. The religions of the book, meeting around their parallel interpretations of the public world, may find ways of linking today's forces of resistance to totalization in solidarities that reanimate and embody their underlying covenantal traditions. They would then be translating the "gift" of God's promise-keeping to them as distinct peoples into a common "gift" to humankind. They would be seeking to articulate concretely God's prevenient will to solidarity with the human race.[31]

Such a notion, I believe, lies behind the phrase "covenantal solidarity," used today to refer to a form of solidarity with a "vertical" as well as "horizontal" dimension. This notion has many implications. One is that one group, emulating God's reaching out, reaches out to another to identify with the other group's cause, to stand with them, to share their suffering. The idea of a "preferential option for the poor," adopted in 1968 by the Second General Conference of Latin American Bishops at Medellin, Colombia, is a declaration of this form of solidarity.

Here something quite new is at work. The term "solidarity" is increasingly used now in this new perspective to express the idea of one community's total support of, and self-implication in, the burdens and aspirations of another. One community invests its grace-given capacity for promise-keeping in an act of identification with the other in need. This "investment" is not an act of calculation but an act of communion. The return on it, as for the act of trust, is not subject to calculation. Through my

31. I am aware that the notion of "God's will to solidarity with the human race" is Christian in origin, even if it is not an "orthodox" or traditional formulation. Is there any echo in Judaism or Islam?

community of faith I invest my being and hope in the being and hope of another community. I imaginatively stand in that other's place. I associate my story of hope for fulfillment with that other community's different story of hope for fulfillment. I enter that other community's Abrahamic story. But this can also mean letting the other stand in for me. It means letting the struggling ones represent me also in their struggle.

Such solidarity often involves a move toward a place materially weaker but spiritually stronger than one's own. The gift is not merely given; it turns out to move more strongly in return. To be in solidarity is to receive a gift, to receive the Promise once again through the Other. To be in covenantal solidarity is to gather around, and share the blessings of, those in whose struggles the God of Abraham is perceived to be keeping promises in the world.

Taking Responsibility

In the sense in which it now generally used — in such expressions as "the responsibilities of office," "I take responsibility for this," and so forth — the noun "responsibility" in English has almost as short a history as does "solidarity." It is, as H. Richard Niebuhr says, a "relatively late-born child . . . in the family of words in which duty, law, virtue, goodness, and morality are its much older siblings."[32] Perhaps, then, we should by rights attempt the impossible task of sketching the history of each of these words. But "responsibility" did mean something in its own right before it picked up its current broad range of significations. It meant "relatedness" or "correspondence": notions suggesting elements of various kinds — including persons — interacting harmoniously together.[33] And such harmonious interaction, for human beings, requires some sort of purposeful promise-keeping.[34]

32. H. Richard Niebuhr, *The Responsible Self* (New York: Harper and Row, 1963), 47.

33. H. Richard Niebuhr quotes an earlier usage from the *Oxford English Dictionary:* "The mouth large, but not responsible to so large a body" (1698).

34. No longer are we thinking of "responsible society" in terms of the perspectives of 1948-1968. At that time these words reflected a great deal of confidence in the leadership and ethos of the Western nations — and particularly those of the North Atlantic community — for fostering a peaceful, prosperous, post–World War II world. But it appears that the meanings of "responsibility" in this connection were very largely taken for granted. Perhaps the

Walter Brueggemann, in his essay, "Law as Response to Thou," makes clear the scriptural link. He writes:

> Abraham and his family after him are a responding community that takes responsibility for a world. . . . [T]his first utterance in Genesis 12, is defined by the demand of YHWH that Israel be a vehicle and an instrument for assuring the well-being, security, joy, and dignity of all nations. . . . Israel has responsibility for the health of the world. It is a responsibility, given in the same breath, given in this initial utterance of generosity.[35]

Still today, the Abrahamic faiths and their secular partners know themselves called to "take responsibility" for addressing humanity's burdens. What might such generous responsibility-taking come to mean? The possible contemporary meanings of responsibility-taking are just as context-dependent as are the vocabularies of trust and solidarity. Different cultures see it in different ways. The Japanese, I am told, equate it with "taking blame" for mistakes or for things that have gone wrong, seeing little that is positive in the idea. I, reflecting my own culture, see "responsibility" as the indispensable accompaniment of "rights." But there is something more important, even, than that. One may see "taking responsibility" as the threshold of ethical consciousness as such: meaning that I pay evaluative attention to what I and others do. Hence Niebuhr's list of nearly synonymous virtues. For me to "take responsibility" means that I acknowledge, and in fact undertake, a personal obligation to be engaged with others in handling every significant matter with the fullness of my personal integrity.[36]

official status of "responsible society" as a theme made much organized ecumenical exegesis of the term seem unnecessary. That is why, in what follows, I have so much recourse to secular philosophers, among whom there is today something of a renaissance in "responsibility" studies. In any case, if the term "responsible society" is used today it has significantly different overtones.

35. Walter Brueggemann, "Law as Response to Thou," in *Taking Responsibility: Comparative Perspectives*, ed. Winston Davis (Charlottesville: University of Virginia Press, 2001), 91. Italics in the original.

36. Two books among many deserve to be singled out as basic to defining "responsibility" within a Christian context: H. Richard Niebuhr's *The Responsible Self* (New York: Harper and Row, 1963), and William Schweiker's *Responsibility and Christian Ethics* (Cambridge: Cambridge University Press, 1995). I have learned much from each, but my argument is largely independent of these sources.

But for purposes of this discussion I want to focus on only one dimension of such engagement, and to make only one distinction among all the distinctions that could be made: that between routine responsibility in the established structures I have referred to as the "givens" (with their ideologies, whether blinkered or otherwise) and "taking responsibility" to meet new needs for which there are few if any precedents to guide us. It seems clear that the resistance movements I have been describing, and the individuals animating them, "take" responsibility beyond routine in matters for which they "have" little or no accountability in the ordinary course of events. In this latter sort of situation, I will argue, responsibility-taking is a humanly unaccountable "gift," both in the sense of being a gift to society and a gracious gift at work in those who have the courage to answer such a call from beyond themselves.

The distinction between "given" responsibilities and taking responsibility beyond routine comes out in different ways in the work of contemporary thinkers. Hans Jonas is not speaking of entrepreneurial totalization as such but of the fateful capacities it places in our hands. In *The Imperative of Responsibility*[37] he argues that the coming of modern technology (never the strong point in liberation analysis), including nuclear technology, has utterly changed the fundamental premises of moral argument. Where before it was assumed that the nature of human beings, with their capacities and possibilities, was largely determined in a static set of circumstances or "givens," and hence that human responsibility was quite narrowly circumscribed, these simple premises no longer hold. With the development of radically new human capacities through the industrial and communications revolutions the nature of human action as such has changed. And this change calls for a different kind of ethics.

It is not just that we have new subject-matter for moral rumination. Rather, as Jonas says, "the qualitatively novel nature of certain of our actions has opened up a whole new dimension of ethical relevance for which there is no precedent in the standards and canons of traditional ethics."[38] There are now questions facing us for which "nobody is responsible," in the sense that nobody has these things directly in their job descriptions. Ethics is now forced to look beyond the direct, immediate dealings be-

37. Hans Jonas, *The Imperative of Responsibility* (Chicago: University of Chicago Press, 1984).
38. Ibid., 1.

tween people and consider actions that have an unprecedented reach into the future. A new sort of moral responsibility, with no less than humanity's fate for its concern, must, in Jonas's view, be moved to center stage.

A more recent work moves in the same direction. In his symposium titled *Taking Responsibility: Comparative Perspectives*,[39] Winston Davis makes a crucial distinction between two kinds or levels of responsibility that seem congruent with what we are saying here. The first he calls simple responsibility, meaning the sum total of our conventional, settled, duties. At this level responsible people are dependable, reliable, trustworthy, and prudent. They are content with the givens of their situation. But there is another level: responsibility that is complex or reflexive. This is responsibility corresponding more to what Jonas is calling for: responsibility in novel or unprecedented circumstances such as those faced by the human race today. This sort of responsibility is an (almost Abrahamic) "move forward into the unknown" in which we seek, but may not find, guiding principles that make any sense in advance. Yet we know that the human race is threatened by its own injustices, its own despoiling of the environment, and much else, and we must take responsibility for fashioning responses to such threats, including taking responsibility for the possibility that we may be mistaken. This is something quite different from bearing routine sorts of responsibility in stable, known, circumstances.

Other philosophers are now chiming in. Jacques Derrida, for example, declares that "there is no responsibility without a dissident and inventive rupture with respect to tradition, authority, orthodoxy, rule, or doctrine."[40] Comparably, Thomas Keenan says that "the only responsibility worthy of the name comes with the removal of grounds, the withdrawal of the rules or the knowledge on which we might rely. . . . It is when we do not know exactly what we should do . . . and when we have nowhere else to turn . . . that we encounter something like responsibility."[41]

One honors the intention of such radical philosophical statements. But one also sees the dangers of living by them too exclusively. There are

39. Winston Davis, ed., *Taking Responsibility: Comparative Perspectives* (Charlottesville: University Press of Virginia, 2002).

40. Jacques Derrida, *The Gift of Death* (Chicago: University of Chicago Press, 1995), 27, as quoted in Davis, ed., *Taking Responsibility*, 282.

41. Thomas Keenan, *Fables of Responsibility: Aberrations and Predicaments in Ethics and Politics* (Stanford, CA: Stanford University Press, 1997), 1-2, quoted in Davis, *Taking Responsibility*, 282.

hints here of solitary presumption — particularly in the last-mentioned quotation with its seeming claim to existential courage — that runs the risk of spiritual distortion. But Derrida clearly intends something else. Responsibility means breaking away from spiritual mysteries, from a "fervor for fusion" that counsels retreat from this world. In a manner doing justice to which is clearly beyond the scope of this chapter, Derrida considers how responsibility can be seen as a gift that projects me into the world.[42] Yet taking responsibility, even in the midst of radical uncertainty, may easily become an expression of pride, or just plain dogged obsession with an idea. One brings off the revolution and then one becomes a tyrant. The responsible ones can become certain that their vision is superior to all others and zealously defend the power they have achieved.

Indeed the suicide bomber, by his or her own lights, almost perfectly fits the profile just sketched. A certain interpretation of a religious tradition, fueled by desperation and the belief that in this way one can participate in a world-historical grand narrative called Jihad, adds up to violent death for innocent people. Christians and Jews have not been exempt from Jihad-like responsibility-taking either. Think of the Crusades, or of Ariel Sharon's current strategies for protecting the integrity and security of the State of Israel.

Once again we see the deterioration and confusion of meanings in an originally covenantal idea. Not all responsibility-taking is salutary for the human community. Our responsibility-takers can be like true prophets, or they can be like false ones. We have offered a description of the role, but not yet a criterion for judging how authentically it is played out. Everything depends on the kind of sense made by the narrative that shapes the action. And by "sense" here I mean primarily the kind of immediate or ultimate promise the narrative contains. Taking responsibility means being responsible to some kind of promise, and this in three senses. One must be responsible to the promise implied in one's own life as a conscious actor (integrity in identity). One must be responsible to the promises to Others implied in one's actions (solidarity in relationships). And one must be responsible to the ultimate ends of the human community implied by one's

42. On page 31 of *Gift*, Derrida makes this same point with reference to the thought of the Czech philosopher Jan Patocka, his interlocutor throughout a chapter titled "Secrets of European Responsibility." "Patocka," we read, "speaks of a supreme being, of God as one who, holding me from within and within his gaze, defines everything regarding me, and so rouses me to responsibility."

philosophical or religious tradition (the dimension of faith). Absent these dimensions of promise-keeping, taking responsibility can become false prophecy. With these dimensions, responsibility-taking has in it an element of the transcendent that can only be described in the vocabulary of the gift.

The presence of this sense of giftedness — this sense that the responsibility we take is not in the end merely our own doing — is a matter of testimony rather than of argument. Finding one's life defined in terms of responsibility to promises in oneself, to others, and to an ultimate end is not the result of reasoning but of discovering, seemingly unaccountably, that it is so. I believe that this is what Calvin meant by making public responsibility a fruit of sanctification, in turn a work of the Spirit. It is sheer gift to certain people, not something to be explained conceptually.

The citizens (some Calvinist, some not) of the village of Le Chambon-sur-Lignon in southern France who took responsibility for rescuing Jews from the Gestapo between 1942 and 1945, when asked why they put themselves in such danger, could only reply that this needed no explanation. Is this not what one does? Well, no. It is not what most people do. It is a remarkable gift, seemingly given only to some. The word used in the village for these gifted neighbors was apt: "les résponsables."[43]

What Can Religious Communities Offer?

I have discussed three publicly accessible notions, that is, ideas that people can understand on the evening news, whose meanings in our consciousness have been influenced by covenantal traditions. But, passing through "the wilderness of the world," such perspectives on human interaction have become weakened, confused, and corrupted. The social conditions under which such notions maintained meanings close to the scriptural originals have shifted and changed. They are no longer available in their original covenantal, promise-keeping, meanings as orientations for reframing human life.

My claim is that a practice of parallel hermeneutics of such publicly accessible ideas and actions in the light of the traditions of the Book can

43. On the village of Le Chambon sur Lignon and what happened there see Philip Hallie, *Lest Innocent Blood Be Shed* (New York: Harper and Row, 1979).

do much to reconnect such understandings with their covenantal origins: to restore the conditions of trust, to reanimate life in solidarity, and to empower the taking of responsibility. The accounts I have already given of each of these ideas show how this has been so, and could continue to be. Taken once again into covenantal narratives, these qualities of human relationship can be freshly seen as needing to be gifted by a still more ultimate promise.

The religions of the book need to bring the fullness of their scriptural self-understandings to bear on making this happen. This will mean reframing covenantal understandings away from we/they, or inside/outside dichotomies toward offering them as gifts to the human community as such. Not all Jews, Christians, and Muslims today are likely to be tuned in to such a task. But some have been and still are. The Jewish philosopher Emmanuel Lévinas was one who was tuned in. He made the whole of his scriptural and Talmudic heritage available to human beings looking for the foundations of their relationships to Others.

There is no space here to go into the details of this example. Only to say that Lévinas offered not only a fascinating philosophical description of the grounds for trusting, solidarity, and responsible human relationships[44] (establishing "ethics" as "first philosophy") but also a form of access, a doorway open to anyone, to the first of our traditions of the Book. Lévinas indeed wrote in such a way as to permit us to term the relationships he describes as "covenantal" obligations.[45] Through his work, such an understanding of life is available on permanent loan to anyone who will make the effort to master it.

Furthermore, Lévinas did all this in a way astonishingly apposite to our project of resistance to dominating powers. His work constitutes a massive repudiation of the claimed givenness of economic and political structures, and their "totalizing" founding narratives, generating what he called "ontology," the philosophical justification of a uniform view of the world in fact maintained by means of power. Lévinas wished to break through all this to the lineaments of actual human relationship through which we have glimpses of the "traces" left by "infinity." In relation to the

44. See, for example, Merold Westphal, "Emmanuel Lévinas and the Logic of Solidarity," in the *Graduate Faculty Philosophy Journal,* published by the New School of Social Research, vol. 20, no. 2; vol. 21, no. 1.

45. See, for example, the chapter titled "The Pact" in Séan Hand, ed., *The Lévinas Reader* (Oxford: Blackwell, 1989), 211ff.

"Other," I discover in myself absolute obligations of trust, solidarity, and responsibility (all three terms seem appropriate): obligations that grow more insistent and comprehensive as they are acted out.[46]

I am not sure that Muslims and Christians can offer comparable writings: works that offer such profound entrée into their own covenantal narratives for others who desire to work in parallel with them. Perhaps for Christians Paul Ricoeur is one who does this. And it is only my ignorance that prevents me from naming an Islamic philosopher whose thought offers similar opportunities. Parallel hermeneutics would surely involve staging encounters and interactions among the works of scholars who work not only for in-groups but seek to share the riches of their traditions with the human race.

The works of such writers constitute a form of mutually proffered "moral hospitality,"[47] an opportunity to share the essential "moves" of another's tradition of faith: to share these moves in neutral terms open to anyone, without the need to become a "believer" within that tradition, or a member of that ethnic group. This exposition implies that, when traditioned communities meet to pursue agreements over practical issues, it is possible for representatives of each imaginatively to "get inside" the thought of the other, and indeed for each tradition to make moves that invite such reciprocal understanding.

I see such interaction, conducted in relation to the experiences and

46. It is significant to compare the thought of Lévinas to that of Ricoeur in *Oneself as Another*. Running through the latter's argument is a notion of the moral self as constituted in the face of the "other" who says, in effect, "Do not kill me, do not steal from me." Without this "other" we are not "ourselves." In constructing such a position it is inevitable that Ricoeur would be in conversation with Lévinas. This is indeed the case in the final chapters of *Oneself as Another*. In his books *Totality and Infinity* and *Otherwise than Being* Lévinas is known for having made a case for "ethics as first philosophy" and for arguing that we gain our moral being only in response to the "face" of the other, whose mere presence makes apparently unlimited claims upon us. Indeed, in the call of the other we encounter a kind of transcendence. Ricoeur's critique is that, for Lévinas, there is no place within my interiority for such an ethical response. Rather, there is already an alterity within ourselves that grounds the possibility of "solicitude." The claim of the other does not evacuate our selfhood. If that were the case there would be no basis for a relationship. Rather the claim of the other appeals to a strength that is the self's capacity for appropriation and integration.

47. See Lewis S. Mudge, "Moral Hospitality for Public Reasoners," in *Rethinking the Beloved Community: Ecclesiology, Hermeneutics, Social Theory* (Lanham, MD: University Press of America and Geneva/WCC Publications, 2001), 275ff.

categories of the public world, as a further stage of the practice of parallel hermeneutics. The hermeneutical processes of the Abrahamic and other faiths, always maintaining their own identities and forms of integrity, encounter one another and their secular partners in the democratically constituted spheres of action needed to generate and maintain just frameworks for common life: frameworks that can resist the ideologies and consequences of economic and political totalization.

Covenant, Social Contract, and the Contracts of Everyday Life

The elements in diverse religious traditions most regulative of the character of the agreements people can justly enter alongside others are no doubt those concerning the very meanings of promise-keeping in the cultures concerned.[48] If an agreement is largely built on reciprocal cultural commitments engaging values such as these, deeply articulated within the sacred stories of the parties to the understanding, we may well call it a "covenant." If, on the other hand, the agreement only represents those reciprocal interests defined within the agreement itself enforced by sanctions defined in some existing legal tradition, it may be termed a "contract." Most "thin" agreements between "thick" traditions of life (I am here adopting terminology introduced by the anthropologist Clifford Geertz)[49] have elements of each in varying proportions and combinations. If, for example, respect for public law is a value represented in each contending group's internal traditions, there will likely be both covenantal (Durkheim's "precontractual"?) and properly contractual aspects to any agreement between them. Somewhere in this process lies the effective social contract: the fundamental way we commonly imagine the meaning of our interactions.

It may help to compare and contrast what I am urging here with the proposals of contemporary social contract theorists, such as John Rawls and Jürgen Habermas.[50] These thinkers work by proposing alternative secular social models: models for the way we should relate to one another

---

48. Much valuable information on the way different cultures understand the notions of responsibility and obligation can be found in Davis, *Taking Responsibility.*

49. See Clifford Geertz, *The Interpretation of Cultures* (New York: Basic Books, 1973).

50. See John Rawls, *A Theory of Justice* (Cambridge, MA: Harvard University Press, 1971), and Jürgen Habermas, *Theory of Communicative Action* (Boston: Beacon Press, 1984).

rather than simply models of the way we actually do relate. In such models-for, the actual meeting of religious traditions for addressing public issues occupies a secondary place. Rawls sees such encounter as reflecting only a rather sedentary "overlap" of "reasonable comprehensive doctrines" in support of an independently conceived theory of justice as fairness. Habermas does something analogous with his notion of a "discourse ethic" enacting the philosopher's ideas of the basic characteristics of "communicative rationality" and the "ideal speech situation." Within such independently derived but culturally shared understandings of the nature of moral discourse, different groups are invited continuously to adjudicate their various interests.

My notion of "parallel hermeneutics" as a ground for our interactions resembles both these theories in certain respects, but differs from them as well. My parallel-hermeneutical description of the meeting of religious traditions in the public world aims to be independent of any theory of society reached under conditions of idealized rationality in the scholar's study (i.e., all interests represented behind Rawls's "veil of ignorance" by morally perfected versions of themselves). Instead of a passive, rather blurry, "overlap" of traditions judged "reasonable" if they support the philosopher's theory, I want to see independent, tradition-based, interpretations of the public world going on in a manner actively responsible to one another. I want to see actual covenanting, followed by contracting, among value-laden communities as a source of public values. I think of a very down-to-earth political process in which many different cultures try to reach ways of living together that untidily embody practical compromises that can grow into just social relationships.

A helpful model of such relating among value-laden communities can be found in the writings of another political philosopher, Michael Walzer, above all in the small volume *Thick and Thin*.[51] Walzer's vision sees "maximal" moral identities, precisely such as those of religious or other specific cultural groups, as primary in the constituting of the larger society. Holders of "thick" moral codes interact with one another so as to produce "thin" agreements for specific circumstances representing society as a whole. These "thin" public agreements constitute the building blocks of more covenantal, more just, social contracts in the public world fostered

51. Michael Walzer, *Thick and Thin: Moral Argument at Home and Abroad* (Notre Dame: University of Notre Dame Press, 1994).

by the kind of interactions among "thick" traditions that I have described as "parallel hermeneutics." There is no appeal here in Walzer to common "liberal" theory (e.g., that of Rawls or Habermas) of what "the" social contract ought to be like. Rather, Walzer describes a process of dialogue by which one group appeals to the experiences or sympathies of the other, thereby building a solidarity of responsible trust between them. As Mark Douglas has written, "So understood, one group's appeal to another group's moral sense is not an act of derivation, but one of imagination."[52]

Here is the value of the mutual moral imagination fostered by parallel hermeneutics. How do we imagine such acts of imagination taking place? In a considerable variety of ways, depending on circumstances. Certain metaphors for such a process are helpful. One may think of Abrahamic traditions and secular initiatives discovering, or pursuing, a certain "resonance" between their visions of life and public policies: a recognition that, however unfamiliar may be the public languages in use, they are tuned to nearby wave-lengths.

To hear such resonances we need discernment of the ways covenantal impulses have worked themselves out in the complexities of social history: as described for example in our paragraphs on fostering trust, living in solidarity, and taking responsibility. These verbal expressions, we remember, are ways of denominating certain kinds and qualities of human interaction that express what religious covenants are about: by restating them so far as possible in terms of common human experience. These restatements may function to bridge the gap between Abrahamic covenantal traditions by articulating the quality of relationships they together hope to foster in the

---

52. Words of Mark Douglas from *Thinking Again about the Reformed Tradition and Public Life,* drafted by Mark Douglas, Lewis Mudge, and James Watkins on behalf of the Consultation on Public Leadership group representing Presbyterian Church-Related Seminaries, October 10, 2001, published in *Theological Education* 40, no. 1 (2004): 169ff. This report suggests that Walzer's position has some interesting implications. I follow Douglas in drawing out two of them. First, if Walzer is understood to mean that thin moral propositions are persuasive — and therefore useful — only because they arise out of thick ones, "it follows that only those accounts that are sufficiently thick to cope with the moral complexity of the world — that is to say, quite thick accounts indeed — can give birth to helpful thin accounts." The thick moral accounts supplied by specific cultural groups thus deserve a place in public discourse: at least in discourse about the thin agreements based imaginatively upon them. "[I]t follows," Douglas continues, "that the range of arguments that may be admitted into public conversation is considerably larger than the classic liberal tradition has allowed" (p. 184).

world of public institutions. They refer to qualities of human interaction in society in which the keepers of the Abrahamic traditions may be able to recognize a certain degree of congruence with their own experiences of moral formation, thus generating public spaces in which the traditions can meet.

In this perspective, the social contract has evolved from being a hypothetical construct by political philosophers to explain society's very existence (as it is in Locke or Rousseau, Rawls or Habermas) to become a set of imaginatively shared assumptions about the ways we live together, the ways we are "minded" to relate to one another. Being "so minded," we then are able to enter into specific legislative agreements that regulate the contracts we enter into in everyday life. Insights such as these prod us to revise our effective social contract so that the now dominant totalizing ideological trends are no longer supported, no longer taken for granted.

One could then ask of a proposed piece of legislation (1) whether it is offered in such a way as to engender conditions of trust, (2) whether it is conceived in solidarity with the interests of those least able to defend themselves, and (3) whether it represents a stance of responsibility for the future of the community in question, and ultimately of the human race. Such questions could make possible certain directional decisions, certain common agreements about the character of possible next steps. These could, again in turn, help guide specific actions: drafting a particular piece of legislation, supporting a particular initiative, voting for a particular bill. Such particular actions in themselves would be regarded by Walzer as "thin," focused on very specific matters, specific small steps along the way toward the goal of an intercovenantal society.

Presumably a succession of many such at-first-minimal steps gradually produces a public political tradition. This in time grows "thick" in its own right, generating institutions, laws, customs, public culture, all the products of parallel actions authorized by the many more maximal cultures of their origin. In Walzer's terms, thickness interacts with thickness (tribe meets tribe) and works out limited practical agreements which both express mutual obligations and expectations and face common threats. Such pacts in turn help generate the social capital needed to deal politically with questions related to the future of humanity as such, not just the survival of particular groups in competition with one another.[53]

53. Is Walzer, like Lévinas, here offering us insights from his own Jewish tradition in a

Perhaps there is need to make an agreement over land-use, water rights, inter-group marriage, or some other vital interest. The resulting arrangement — perhaps a treaty or legal precedent — will be very specific (Walzer will call it "thin") in comparison with the cultures on either side of the agreement. But it will need to draw, at least indirectly, on those factors in the cultures of the parties concerned that offer promise that the terms are understood and that the bargain will be kept. Each side finds in the other sufficient grounds for expecting support of the common agreement. Each discovers elements within its own culture that offer analogies for comprehending the terms of the treaty and reasons for observing it. Each ideally finds parables of its own "truth" in the other's songs and stories. Covenant-breaking is then seen by both to violate who they are, to undermine their very identities.

I suggest that such elements of social contract, in their original "thin" forms, function subsequently as "armatures" on which thicker cultural flesh may form. The analogy from sculpture seems to me apt: you build up the human shape in layers upon the thin, minimal framework. If you live for a while with a "thin" agreement you begin to supplement it with other sorts of relationships. At the very least, the agreement needs to be commonly interpreted, founding a shared legal culture, grounded in a shared moral "framework." Confidence raised by trust-building, solidaristic, and responsible behavior at one point spawns confidence at other points.

Indeed, I believe that this is most often the way a common culture begins to emerge out of cultural pluralism. Around each formal or informal pact, a new common culture extending to other matters arises. To the extent that the core agreement fosters some form of life-together, analogous stories may come to be shared. The fact that a dominating culture is likely itself the product of many previous accords between disparate groups does not change the basic equation. If new groups are encouraged to join, there is still the need for covenantal acts of mutual imagination. But then, of course, disparities of power need to be recognized and taken into account. Each group needs to find its own reasons for taking the risky responsibility of reaching out to establish such rela-

---

neutral philosophical form, thereby inviting us to accept that tradition's "moral hospitality" without incurring specific religious commitments? One might conjecture so. Walzer is now at work on a multivolume edition of the political and social wisdom of Judaism that will offer readers — Jewish and non-Jewish, religious and nonreligious — access to this store of wisdom.

tionships in the culture of the other (at least as manifest in the negotiation if not through deeper knowledge), for confidence that the agreement is fair and will be kept.[54]

Confidence in the Power of the Promise

What reason have we for supposing that the sorts of things I have just described can happen, or that they can be sustained for long enough to make a difference? Let us in closing go back to Hannah Arendt. For her the needed energy lies in what she calls the "miracle" of "natality," the birth of the child who makes all things new, signifying the human capacity to bring the unprecedented thing into being. "The new," she writes, "always happens against the overwhelming odds of statistical laws and their probability."[55] But it happens.

Why should we believe this? Because, Arendt says, we believe that "with the creation of man, the principle of beginning came into the world itself, which, of course, is only another way of saying that the principle of freedom was created when man was created, but not before." This implies a design, inherent in the process of the universe, that leads to the emergence of self-reflecting, "historical" actors capable of trust, solidarity, and responsibility. We human beings are self-conscious agents operating in the context of the evolutionary unfolding of all things. We are given the task, within that evolutionary unfolding, to make the meaning of the process itself articulate: to put words to it, to act it out. We are called to keep promises with regard to the future of the human community, and therefore of all life as we know it.

But does it work out that way? Promise-keeping involves wrestling with the very truths about us that other scriptural narratives describe so well. In Arendt's terms, these are the "darkness of the human heart," and "the basic unreliability of men who never can guarantee today who they will be tomorrow, and . . . the impossibility of foretelling the consequences of an act within a community of equals where everybody has the same ca-

---

54. Narratives constitutive of long-established and dominant communities (the Horatio Alger myth, for example) will often valorize certain sorts of economic behavior, which may or may not be in the interest of the weaker parties.

55. Arendt, *Human Condition*, 158.

pacity to act."[56] Other secular writers agree. André Gide is reported to have said, "all things human, given time, go badly." Isaiah Berlin wrote a book around the metaphor of "the crooked timber of humanity."[57] Today, "rational choice theory," as the logical-mathematical instrument of totalization, can be seen precisely as an attempt to rationalize, and thus to foreclose, the uncertainties of human behavior that go with freedom. Promising in freedom, Arendt said, is "the only alternative to a mastery which relies on domination of oneself and rule over others."[58] This is a mastery that relies on reducing both others and oneself to calculating machines playing games designed to get the best of one another. How are we to escape from such domination and open ourselves to the power of the promise?

For one thing, in Arendt's view, the keeping of promises is humanly impossible without forgiveness. "Without being forgiven," she writes, "released from the consequences of what we have done, our capacity to act would, as it were, be confined to one single deed from which we could never recover."[59] But, in the end, we cannot forgive ourselves, nor can we receive transforming forgiveness from other poor sinners. Here Arendt reaches out toward the Christian tradition for the model she needs. The notion of "forgiveness" in ordinary secular language owes everything to its original use in religious language, going back, in fact, to the words and actions of Jesus. She writes:

> The discoverer of the role of forgiveness in human affairs was Jesus of Nazareth. The fact that he made this discovery in a religious context and articulated it in religious language is no reason to take it any less seriously in a strictly secular sense.[60]

I have argued, indeed, that the passage of originally religious ideas through secular contexts like Arendt's can teach us a great deal about the intrinsic power of those ideas. But the heart of this essay lies in the notion of discerning the worldly echos of formerly religious covenanting traditions in order to reconnect them creatively with their origins among those who,

56. Ibid., 219.
57. Isaiah Berlin, *The Crooked Timber of Humanity: Chapters in the History of Ideas*, ed. Henry Hardy (New York: Knopf, 1991).
58. Arendt, *Human Condition*, 220.
59. Ibid., 215.
60. Ibid., 214f.

like Abraham, "believed God" (Gen. 15:6). For the truth concerning Arendt's "secular" insights about the persistence of sin and the need for forgiveness is that human societies cannot go forward on their own for long without falling into catastrophic self-contradiction. She sees the depth of the problem without offering any reason to believe that human beings in their own power can solve it.

Needed is a renewal of our minds in a fresh frame of reference altogether. The "givens" of history and society need to be transformed by the presence of the Gift. The Jesus who teaches us about forgiveness is also the One who said "It is the Father's good pleasure to give you the Kingdom" (Luke 12:32). What does that mean? And how does it happen in a world of many faiths?

CHAPTER 9

Following the Way through
the Paths of the World

Julio de Santa Ana

On the Way with Hope

This book has emphasized that we must not lose touch with the real facts of life. It is not claimed that its proposals can overcome the contradictions of the world or that the present historical situation is darkly desperate. As people who believe that God became incarnate in the person of Jesus Christ and that the Holy Spirit is acting through the concrete situations of real human beings, it is essential that we not fall into the trap of different forms of idealism. That is, actions must be rooted in reality, without illusions, and without concessions to what is incompatible with faith. At the same time, moved by the same faith, the source of courage to be and to act, believers must be on "the way" with hope, a hope that in covenanting with others, trusting one another, acting in solidarity with the underprivileged, and mutually taking responsibility, persons can build those conditions for life, peace, and justice that lead away from hopelessness and despair.[1]

It is at times difficult to discern the difference between hope and illusion. The history of the peoples of the world, churches, religious communities, and even some ecumenical ventures shows that believers have been deceived by what appeared to be possible, but in real life turned out to be

1. A helpful discussion of issues concerning hope is found in Miroslav Volf and William Katerberg, eds., *The Future of Hope: Christian Tradition amid Modernity and Postmodernity* (Grand Rapids: Wm. B. Eerdmans, 2004).

illusory. Religious belief endeavors, in one way or another, to envision a better world that can become part of our life either by divine transcendent action or by the combination of divine providence and human effort. Religious belief sometimes takes historic events and trends for what they are not. When theologians isolate an issue from the existential conditions of people in order to consider it abstractly, idealism prevails. They fail to perceive that theology has to deal with the unavoidable contradictions of life. When this happens even hope is taken away, losing its concreteness and existential reality. Nietzsche severely criticized those who were caught in the confusion between hope and illusion. In such cases, "hope" becomes a beautiful idea without solid substance. It is not concrete. It helps to console people who are not ready to face the hard facts of existence.[2]

The Bible has another message: that hope is always related to the concreteness of a believer's life. In the New Testament, hope is possible for the faithful because of the resurrection of Jesus who put death to death. Biblical faith affirms the possibility of confronting the forces of evil without fear because death will never be totally imposed upon life. Believers cannot accept death as a definitive fact imposed upon the whole of life, for as Paul wrote, "Christ in you, the hope of glory" (Col. 1:27). Paul Ricoeur, following this same line of thought, argued that it is fraudulent when human beings accept the holism of death with fatalistic resignation.[3] The Bible shows that even in the most dramatic moments of an individual's life, there is always the possibility of doing something. If it is not by oneself, it is by the action of "the Other(s)."

Hope is related to faith and love: to faith, because without the courage to be that is brought by faith (Heb. 11), hope would not be possible; to love, because in biblical terms, hope is an expression of trust, above all in God, but also of confidence in others. Rudolf Bultmann has pointed out that when fixed on God, hope embraces expectations that are not grounded solely on calculations made only after a careful consideration of objective and concrete realities.[4] To fulfill hope demands more than considerations developed through analysis of the material facts of life.

2. Friedrich Nietzsche, *Human, All Too Human: A Book for Free Spirits,* trans. R. D. Hollingdale (Cambridge and New York: Cambridge University Press, 1996; orig. pub. 1878).

3. Paul Ricoeur, *The Conflicts of Interpretation,* trans. D. Ihde (Evanston: Northwestern University Press, 1974).

4. Rudolf Bultmann, "Elpis [hope]," in Gerhard Kittel and Gerhard Friedrich, eds., *Theological Dictionary of the New Testament,* vol. 2 (Grand Rapids: Wm. B. Eerdmans), 529-35.

One can be committed to fulfill hope when he or she waits patiently, believing against hope, as Abraham did (Rom. 4:18-22). Hope is made manifest by patient endurance; a serious consideration of life shows that agony and suffering cannot be avoided. Paul wrote that "suffering produces endurance, and endurance produces character, and *character produces hope,* and hope does not disappoint us, because God's love has been poured into our hearts through the Holy Spirit that has been given to us" (Rom. 5:3-5, emphasis added). Because we live in "hope against hope," humans can engage with others in the construction of new frames for life. To do so without triumphalism, but with a sober and humble commitment to follow the way of those who lived by faith, love, and hope, is what is meant by insisting that the attitude to assume is a *hopeful realism.* We must not fall into the trap of believing that we can eradicate evil, but we can commit ourselves to working to overcome some of its manifestations. Again Paul: "Do not be overcome by evil, but overcome evil with good" (Rom. 12:21).

This is our journey as human beings. The Bible, especially the Old Testament, is a kind of "log book" of humankind's journey. The saga starts with Abra(ha)m, who was called to leave Ur of the Chaldees to go on a journey to a country that God wanted to show him (Gen. 12:1-3). With Abra(ha)m and Sara(i) began the story of God with his blessed and chosen people. It is a new beginning, after the experience of failure, expulsion, and punishment recorded in the first chapters of the Hebrew Scriptures (Gen. 9). All nations are to benefit from the blessing of Abraham; the blessing applies to all peoples of the earth. The crucial moment came when Abraham decided to be faithful and demonstrated the courage to go on unknown paths.

The framework of the way is rooted in that story of a nomadic people, constantly on the move, living in a permanent tension between trust and despair — moving to Egypt because of hunger; experiencing a miraculous exodus from slavery through Yahweh's strong hand; expressing doubt during the "long way" across the desert; establishing the covenant at Sinai "on the way" (Exod. 24); breaking the covenant by worshiping the golden calf; going into exile in Babylonia after 587 BCE, etc. The story of the people of God requires an acknowledgment that *there is no way,* while at the same time seeing that *new ways are open* through the paths of the world.

It is also a story of injustice and the suppression of the poor by rich

JULIO DE SANTA ANA

landowners during times of economic prosperity after 931 BCE, in the kingdom of the North. The prophet Amos raised his voice to the powerful, foretelling "the day of judgment." He complained bitterly about the rich and powerful breaking God's law by "trampling the head of the poor" (Amos 2:6ff.). The only way for the Israelites to rescue themselves from this situation was to return to God. And "re-turn" meant changing direction, taking heed of God's word to find the way back to Yahweh: "Seek me and live" (Amos 5:4). Seeking implies being in motion, not resting in false security, but searching for God in every way.

In both the Old and New Testaments, "the way" is a symbol of human life. In almost all the religions of the world the image of "the way" appears, the journey and pilgrimage to God. The life path or the lifestyle of humanity can be good or bad; the decisive issue is whether humanity is on this path with God or without God, as is shown beginning with the story of Abraham's trust and carrying on to the death of Jesus of Nazareth ("My Father, if it is possible, let this cup pass from me; yet not what I want but what you want" [Matt. 26:39]). In the Gospels the path followed by Jesus can be traced from Galilee to Jerusalem. While on the way, living an itinerant existence, he taught and bore witness to the kingdom of God. With his crucifixion and resurrection his mission among men and women was fulfilled. In retrospect, the Gospels report his life as a path of suffering in a manner that seems to be predetermined (Mark 10:32-34). From early Easter morning, his way of life became the hope of Christians.

The Psalms make clear that it is better to progress on one's path with God than without God (Ps. 23; 25; 121; 139). "He leads me in right paths for his name's sake" (Ps. 23:3). "You know when I sit down and when I rise up; you discern my thoughts from far away" (Ps. 139:2). To trust in God means to be moved by the hope that a full life is possible, for oneself and for others. "He will not let your foot be moved. He who keeps Israel will neither slumber nor sleep" (Ps. 121:3).

The image of the way in both the biblical and the early Christian traditions is a metaphor that presupposes a sinful existence characterized by unacceptable behavior. The challenge that God puts is to abandon the sinful way and to discover his path. What matters is to be instructed to follow his way of justice, righteousness, and truth (Ps. 23:3; 25:4, 8-9; 139:23ff.).

212

New Dimensions in Contemporary Ethical Awareness

Throughout this book it has been stated that economic globalization is to be perceived mainly as the integration of world markets. However, globalization cannot be reduced merely to its economic dimension. Resistance to some of the trends linked to globalization — the transformation of labor, a culture of mass consumption, degradation of the natural environment, globally concentrated power — is seen at local and regional levels of society. The ecumenical movement is called to take all these dimensions into account; they must not be ignored. They involve the historic process of the *oikoumene* — the whole inhabited earth.

These trends in world history introduce tensions for the ecumenical awareness of churches and religious communities. The changes, while producing benefits for some, also create pain and suffering for many and cause unbearable contradictions for vast sectors of humankind.

In such situations people often feel the need to distance themselves from what has become intolerable. This is, in the first instance, an act of *conscious realism*. To continue to live in such conditions would be to betray their own being. Faith and courage are needed for such decisions. This was the experience of many Europeans during the 19th and early 20th centuries when mass migration, mainly to the Americas, became commonplace. Nowadays, many African, South and Central American, and Asian peoples are ready to run dangerous risks and dramatic dangers because they can no longer accept the prevailing socioeconomic and/or political conditions in their countries. To continue to accept such conditions would be to deny themselves, something that would be a source of shame. These migratory trends, accentuated since the 1950s, are a powerful factor in today's creation of multicultural societies and pluralistic religious situations.

However, people often do not accept this call to greater freedom. To move forward, to break with the prevailing situation, is a genuinely new beginning that requires a "renewal of the mind" (cf. Rom. 12:1-2). This becomes an expression of courage — *the courage to be* — and thus an expression of faith, hope, and realism, *hopeful realism*. The ethical experience, then, is not only about the will (or the formation of a good will); rather, it is above all a *process of conscious reflection involving an interaction between thought and action, between faith, hope, and love in tension with the actual condition of people's lives.* It involves the various dimensions of oneself, not only with like-minded people but also with those who are "the Other."

"The Other" is part of the objective environment where we live. The Other may be from a different people. The Other may also be the natural environment, which often seems to be a stranger, although we cannot exist apart from it. When the Other erupts within the space where we are, it cannot be put aside. As Emmanuel Lévinas wrote, "We arc captive of the other."[5] Like it or not, we cannot move without taking him or her into account. Furthermore, we discover — or rediscover — our subjectivity in our relationship with the Other, the foreigner who without being invited penetrates the circle of our existence and challenges us to modify our way of being.

In one of his writings, Paul Ricoeur tried to clarify the complicated relationship that we may develop with the Other. He or she can be a *socius* (comrade, associate) or a neighbor.[6] In either case, the Other becomes a person. Maybe he or she is a member of those associations where we participate in civil society, or he or she may be a member of the communities where we become closer to one another. It may also happen that the Other suddenly appears unexpectedly on our horizon. Jesus of Nazareth taught this clearly in the parable of the Good Samaritan (Luke 10:25-37) when he showed that to be a neighbor is to become near to the Other. The Other cannot be reduced to an abstract "type." She or he is a living being who calls us to act, often demanding changes in our life. That is, the Other challenges us to move from comfortable existence in order to develop new living relationships together. The Other challenges us to transform our life. When the Other erupts amid us, we are challenged to change our minds; as we wrote above, we are called to conversion *(metanoia)*.

A prevailing way of dealing with others is to persuade them to accept what we think they should be. For example, they must practice their faith as we do; they must adopt our economic and political systems and/or the logic of present globalization; and their culture should evolve to be as modern as ours. If these things happen we follow again the paradigm of action narrated in the story of the Tower of Babel (Gen. 11:1-9). When God saw what people wanted to prove with the construction of the tower, he scattered all those who wanted to impose their own governance, a com-

5. Emmanuel Lévinas, *Totality and Infinity: Essays on Exteriority,* trans. Alphonso Lingis (Pittsburgh: Duquesne University Press, 1969).

6. Paul Ricoeur, *History and Truth,* trans. Charles A. Kelbly (Evanston: Northwestern University Press, 1992).

mon language, and the same way of life *("la pensée unique")*. Another narrative, rather opposite to that of the Tower of Babel, is found in Acts 2. On the day of Pentecost, the message of salvation was heard by all who were in Jerusalem from the diaspora, as it was proclaimed "in the native language of each" (Acts 2:6). Here there is a double challenge for those involved in ecumenical social thought and action: *First, to be ecumenical today moves us to practice a wider ecumenism. Second, it is the most underprivileged and oppressed who need to receive recognition and priority in order to become members of the whole diverse ecumenical community.* To follow this path would be to listen to Paul, who called on the Corinthians to become "ambassadors of reconciliation" (2 Cor. 5:14-20).

As has been said consistently in this volume, this is not idealism. We try to move beyond idealism to a position of *hopeful realism,* closely related to the image of "the way." The challenge is not to develop perfect solutions and responses but rather to become involved in a process that attempts to find ways of acting to ensure a better quality of life for everyone.

At this point the tension between sedentary inactivity and being in motion, getting involved, and joining the movement of faithful people is often experienced. *Hopeful realism* requires — on the existential level — a readiness for departure as with Abraham and a search for a new way of life like the disciples of the early church. Both are fundamental attitudes that allow movement from the local — sedentary existence, everyday security, familiar relationships — to the global: readiness to depart and search for new ways of humanizing societies so that the blessing of all peoples becomes alive in the present. On the existential level, hope is grounded in relationships with the Other and trust in him or her. *Hopeful realism* urges us, very often, to move against the stream, being open to explore other paths in order to create better conditions for a good life with justice and peace. Those who do not want to conform themselves to the mainstream are invited to reorient their journey. But one must always remember that going against the stream often leads to the experience of the cross.

We recall the words of Jesus, "Do to others as you would have them do to you" (Luke 6:31). To act in this way is a witness of grace, a grace that we have received from God but that is not exclusive to Christian communities. These words challenge us to make progress in reconciliation among peoples, nations, and cultures. The acceptance of the Other demands that, up to a certain point, our visions, traditions, and fundamental narratives should be open to interpretations provided by people of other faiths and cultures. In this way the Other enriches our own self and our own faith, while, perhaps, we might also contribute to their cultural and spiritual wealth. Therefore, the Other is neither enemy nor adversary. Such a way of reconciliation puts us in the "post-Babel world." Our actions can no longer be determined by the process of globalization, nor by the border of our church, confession, economic system, country, or particular way of life. The horizon toward which we move is the *oikoumene,* whose evolution treads various paths on which we share a life that we want to become more just, fair, and good for all. Therefore, our horizon is not fixed or forever defined. It is suggested by symbols like the *kingdom of God,* or images that help believers discern metaphorically the meaning of last things, the goal, the *eschaton.*

However, our understanding of the ultimate is not definitive; it changes throughout history. In our time we are called to renew ecumenical thought and action so as not to lose the horizon, trying to avoid any kind of mirage that presents itself as "the end of history."[7] To be open and to accept the reinterpretation of our traditions, symbols, narratives, and values, taking into account the perspective of the Other, calls us to mourn some elements that we may think are fundamental to our identities. These lines of thought have been explored in the preceding chapter, where Lewis Mudge developed the proposal for interaction and dialogue — "parallel hermeneutics." This too calls for a wider ecumenism. As Mudge states, it implies an act of trust, of solidarity, and of taking responsibility together with the other.

Constructing Frameworks So as Not to Lose the Way

In the first chapter of this book some crucial issues that challenge ecumenical social thought and action today were identified: the threat to the natural environment; technology and modernity in the context of the prevailing neo-liberal globalization; the crisis of labor at a time when financial capital leads the process and industrial capital is submitted to the imperatives of financial markets; the growing influence of media on our societies; increasing violence; and the close relationships between these issues and

7. These reflections are indebted to a lecture given by Paul Ricoeur at UNESCO, Paris, April 28, 2004. The framework was the "Entretiens du XXI siècle."

the aspirations of the prevailing powers to rule and establish global dominion. In the second chapter it was made clear that in a global *oikoumene* there are many contexts in which churches, religious communities, and ecumenical associations exist, and that it is no longer possible to talk about "an" ecumenical social ethic because there are many expressions of ecumenical social thought and action.

Chapter 4 gave an overview of the ethical proposals of some important names from the history of Christianity and showed how they formulated guidelines for the construction of frames of reference for Christian action in society. It was also shown that this tradition can already be perceived in the Hebrew Bible. Christian churches, other religious communities, and ecumenical associations are challenged to do something similar in our time.

Of course, the sharp tensions that exist today must be recognized. The vested powers want to impose their views everywhere, *urbi et orbi*. However, we also see that the peoples of the world are learning to overcome their conflicts, changing traditions, reorienting their history, and attempting to resolve some of their common problems by means other than force, violence, and suppression. Philip Potter, former General Secretary of the World Council of Churches, in 1981 perceived this and shared a vision of an ecumenical movement in which a platform is constructed for a dialogue between cultures. But "cultures" are not equal. Unfortunately, at other "ecumenical forums" of our world (for example, the UN), the inequality among cultures is taken as a reason to privilege one or two cultures to the detriment of the others. So, the task indicated by Potter is to construct a ground where diverse and different cultures could be treated with equality.[8] That is, having in mind that the socio-historic point of departure of the ecumenical movement is the diversity of the peoples of the whole inhabited earth, and that another point of departure is theological, faith in a God who desires the reconciliation of all peoples of the world, the ecumenical community is moved by the will of God to seek reconciliation between all the peoples of the *oikoumene*. The point is made in the Epistle to the Ephesians: God, through the action of his faithful servant Jesus Christ, has broken down "the dividing wall," that is, the hostility between humans, thus overcoming the separation that seemed to be institu-

8. See Philip Potter, *Life in All Its Fullness: Reflections on the Central Issues of Today's Ecumenical Agenda* (Geneva: WCC Publications, 1981).

tionalized among the peoples of the world (Eph. 2:11-18). In order to make concrete this will of God, we are called to deepen dialogue and construct frames of reference for action based on trust, solidarity, and responsibility among people of different cultures and religions.

This direction demands that we confront economic, cultural, and political powers, recognizing at the same time that there are groups in the world who struggle to construct alternatives to the prevailing order. Some of these groups represent civil society, others the political realm of our nations. Some also represent religious communities that join forces with others to overcome traditional barriers. They develop trust between one another and emphasize that one of their priorities is solidarity with the victims of neo-liberal globalization. Such groups, explicitly or implicitly, provide validity for the practice of covenants and social contracts that advance people's rights. They refuse to accept the market as the world's prevailing and exclusive social contract.

These initiatives respond to contextual challenges. They aim to construct clear socioeconomic and political signposts that design and erect frameworks for progressive social action. The five realms of life described in the first chapter and mentioned again here need to be transformed by the construction of peace, justice, and better conditions of life. Words, ideas, and symbols can motivate social action, but a major challenge is to become involved in the building of frames of reference that will enable the peoples of the earth to resist those powers that seek to dominate and oppress. Chapters 5, 6, and 7 have shown the direction that ecumenical social thought and action must take without providing precise indications of concrete actions.

On the Way . . .

Some readers of this book may find it strange that we make no proposals for specific actions. As was affirmed in Chapter 2, concrete actions must relate to specific contexts. Our ecumenical commitment acknowledges the diversity of cultures, traditions, and styles of life of the people of the *oikoumene,* but we continue to affirm that our world is "one world" — one world of different peoples in which diversity must be respected. Among these peoples, there are groups who traverse different paths toward a common vision. To progress along these paths, as often stated, implies that we accept, at least at the level of reflection on social ethics, that we must work for the renewal of our minds.

We are called to deal with concrete realities, for the dilemmas that we face are also concrete:

> [A]nd the LORD your God will make you abundantly prosperous in all your undertakings, in the fruit of your body, in the fruit of your livestock, and in the fruit of your soil. For the LORD will again take delight in prospering you, just as he delighted in prospering your ancestors, when you obey the LORD your God by observing his commandments and decrees that are written in this book of the law, because you turn to the LORD your God with all your heart and with all your soul. *Surely, this commandment that I am commanding you today is not too hard for you, nor is it too far away.* It is not in heaven, that you should say, "Who will go up to heaven for us, and get it for us that we may hear it and observe it?" Neither is it beyond the sea, that you should say, "Who will cross to the other side of the sea for us, and get it for us so that we may hear it and observe it?" *No, the word is very near to you; it is in your mouth and in your heart for you to observe. See, I have set before you today life and prosperity, death and adversity.* If you obey the commandments of the LORD your God that I am commanding you today, by loving the Lord your God, walking in his ways, and observing his commandments, decrees, and ordinances, then you shall live and become numerous, and the LORD your God will bless you in the land that you are entering to possess. But if your heart turns away and you do not hear, but are led astray to bow down to other gods and serve them, I declare to you today that you shall perish; you shall not live long in the land that you are crossing the Jordan to enter and possess. I call heaven and earth to witness against you today that I have set before you life and death, blessings and curses. *Choose life so that you and your descendants may live,* loving the LORD your God, obeying him, and holding fast to him; for that means life to you and length of days, so that you may live in the land that the Lord swore to give to your ancestors, to Abraham, to Isaac, and to Jacob. (Deut. 30:9–20, emphasis added)

The way is not one of exclusion; the invitation to choose life and not death is to all. It is an invitation that takes into consideration "the Other." It calls us especially to trust those who are victims of totalizing and colonizing systems. It is a way that invites us to act in solidarity with the underprivileged; it is a way that takes responsibility for its own actions and for the history of the *oikoumene* in which we participate. It is a way for the renewing of our minds and for the renewal of the social thought and action of the ecumenical movement.

Contributors and Participants

Joanildo Burity is Lecturer in Sociology and Political Science and Director of the Fundação Joaquim Nabuco, Recife, Pernambuco, Brazil. He received his Ph.D. in government from Essex University in the United Kingdom. Among his published works is *Identidade e Politica no Campo Religioso,* 1997.

Bob Goudzwaard is Professor Emeritus of Economics and Cultural Philosophy at the Free University of Amsterdam. From 1967-71 he was a member of the National Parliament of the Netherlands. Among his publications is *Capitalism and Progress: A Diagnosis of Western Society,* 1979.

Robin Gurney is a British journalist who has served as Media Secretary of the Methodist Church in the United Kingdom and from 1990-2001 was Secretary for Communications of the Conference of European Churches, Geneva. His first book was published in 1965 in Buenos Aires, *Pasado, Presente y Porvenir.*

Heidi Hadsell is President of Hartford Seminary in Hartford, Connecticut, USA. From 1997 to 2001 she was Director of the Ecumenical Institute at Bossey, Switzerland. Her Ph.D. is from the University of Southern California and her academic specializations include social and environmental ethics as well as issues of globalization.

Ninan Koshy resides in Trivandrum, Kerala, India. He was formerly Director of the Commission of the Churches on International Affairs of the

World Council of Churches. He was also Visiting Fellow in the Human Rights Program at the Harvard Law School. Among his most recent books is *The War on Terror: Reordering the World*, 2003.

Lewis Mudge is Robert Leighton Stuart Professor of Theology, Emeritus, at the San Francisco Theological Seminary and the Graduate Theological Union in Berkeley, California. Among his works are *The Church as Moral Community: Ecclesiology and Ethics in Ecumenical Debate*, 1998, and *Rethinking the Beloved Community: Ecclesiology, Hermeneutics, Social Theory*, 2001.

Leopoldo J. Niilus is a graduate of the Faculty of Law of the University of Buenos Aires. He was, before retirement, General Secretary of "Church and Society in Latin America," Director of the Commission of the Churches on International Affairs of the World Council of Churches, and Advisor for Peace Services to the Lutheran World Federation and the Middle East Council of Churches.

Julio de Santa Ana received his Ph.D. in Religious Sciences from the Faculty of Protestant Theology at the University of Strasbourg in France. He served as Director of the Commission of the Churches on Participation in Development of the World Council of Churches and as a faculty member of the Ecumenical Institute at Bossey from 1994 to 2002. His publications include *El concepto biblico del Trabajo*, 1990, and *Globalization and Sustainability*, 1998.

Additional Participants

Reinerio Arce, Professor of Theology and Rector of the Union Theological Seminary at Matanzas, Cuba.

Sung Bihn Yim, Professor of Christian Ethics at the Theological Seminary of the Presbyterian Church of Korea, Seoul.

Russell Botmann, Professor of Practical Theology and Missiology and Vice-Rector of the University of Stellenbosch, South Africa.

Rob van Drimmelen, General Secretary of the Association of WCC Related Development Associations in Europe, Brussels.

Christian Lepper, pastor of a Reformed parish in France and author of *Deux perceptions du "Kirchenkampf" en Alsace,* 2005.

Martina Schmidt, Secretary for Diakonia and Social Issues of the Federation of Swiss Protestant Churches, Bern.

Faitala Talapusi†, former Professor of Ecumenical Theology and Academic Dean of the Ecumenical Institute at Bossey, Switzerland.